PARA(GRAPH) TROOPER FOR MacARTHUR

by
Joe Snyder

PARA(GRAPH) TROOPER FOR MacARTHUR

From the Horse Cavalry to the USS Missouri

by
Joe Snyder

One ordinary American's experiences in World War II: from a "Blister Bottom" cavalryman at Fort Riley, to exciting times as Press Liaison Officer handling war correspondents in the storied islands of the Southwest Pacific.

Copyright 1997
Printed in the United States

ISBN: 1-890622-14-1

Leathers Publishing
4500 College Blvd.
Leawood, KS 66211
Phone: 1 / 888 / 888-7696

Table of Contents

Foreword

1. Drafted, Horsed Around .... Page 1
2. Stripes to Bars .... Page 12
3. Armored in Arkansas .... Page 23
4. Bats and Navy Sex .... Page 32
5. GHQ Press Section .... Page 42
6. MacArthur, One of a Kind .... Page 55
7. New Guinea Jungle .... Page 67
8. My Life is Spared .... Page 80
9. Invasion of Leyte .... Page 95
10. Bataan Retaken .... Page 114
11. Corregidor Adventure .... Page 131
12. Manila Aftermath .... Page 148
13. Borneo Excitement .... Page 160
14. "Downfall" for Japan .... Page 173
15. USS Missouri Spectacle .... Page 185
16. Nagasaki Inferno .... Page 199
17. Tokyo Duty, Then Home .... Page 210

Foreword

"It is well that war is so terrible, or we should become too fond of it."
— **General Robert E. Lee**

THEY'LL NEVER KNOW IT, but my grandfather and my uncle motivated me to write this account of my experiences in World War II.

Uncle Will was in the Spanish-American war, but all the family ever knew about his participation is that he had a pet monkey. The monkey cut its throat one morning when it attempted to mimic his master's shaving with a straight-edge razor.

Grandpa Franklin was wounded, shell-shocked and gassed in the Battle of the Argonne Forest in France during World War I. We also know he carried a U.S. flag beneath his shirt during that battle. I am proud to have that flag in my possession.

The sad thing is, that's all the family knows about these two citizen soldiers who answered the call to arms in an era when going off to war was truly a heroic and noble act of patriotism. Their willingness to serve, without being hog-tied and dragged to the nearest induction center, demonstrated a loyalty and allegiance to the United States of America that has since seriously eroded.

Volunteers of that era flooded recruitment offices and the mere sight of our flag, or even its casual mention, produced cheers and tears. Those of us who came along later have witnessed a deteriorating level of old-fashioned patriotism and love of country. How serious the deterioration we do not know because it has not been severely tested lately.

Today we have among us a new breed of activists who believe it is their right to desecrate, even burn the flag. It appears our colors hold no special significance to them; it's merely a piece of fabric. Respect for government has all but disappeared, caused in part by a lack of character and integrity of those in high places. Respect for anything or anybody is in short supply.

In more recent wars a few young men actually abandoned America for another country in order to avoid military service. During World War II there were slackers, but the thought of military service caused relatively few to leave "the home of the free and the brave." Rebellion in the face of need by our nation was once considered near-treason.

Perhaps World War II was a more "acceptable" war. There was no discussion or lengthy debate. Pearl Harbor erased all doubt about justifying our entrance into the conflict, both in the Pacific and in Europe. It was easy to hate Tojo and Hitler.

Perhaps the treachery of Pearl Harbor welded the American people together as never before. The nation discarded the theory of isolationism and replaced it with single-minded determination to destroy our enemies.

Congress was not divided by pure politics then. They united behind their president and wholeheartedly supported all of us who would soon be in harm's way. Parents gave up their sons and daughters to the cause with understanding and resolve, but with tears and apprehension.

While thousands volunteered for military service, jamming recruitment stations and draft boards, admittedly some began calculating how they might benefit from staying home and make money from the war. Some sought commissions from politicians so they might detour around the hazards of war and escape the fear and danger of foreign battlefields.

These were the early signs of deterioration of the Spirit of '76 and the decline of patriotism and loyalty that once was part of the American philosophy. Alas, this decline has continued. Today the services are made up largely of career people. I have known only a few young people whose mind-set was directed toward the military. Over the years I have been pleased to assist several in qualifying for entrance into our military academies.

There was something about World War II that was different. The entire nation was involved in the struggle. America had been attacked; its honor blemished. It was easy to work up anger over "the enemy." To refuse to serve one's country under such circumstances carried a far greater social stigma than during subsequent wars.

I did not volunteer for service in the war because I was about to be promoted at *The Kansas City Star*, where I worked, and I was also publishing a small community newspaper. Something had to be done with *The Blue Valley News*. I knew I would be drafted early anyway because I was the right age, single, and had no excuse not to be inducted. I was definitely expendable.

I went into the army a month before Pearl Harbor. I'm sure I must have been a question mark to them: Could I be trained to kill people? Would the army decide I did not have the temperament to make a good soldier? My father, who never served in World War I because of employment in an essential industry, couldn't tell me what war was like.

Well ... let me tell you! I was just what the army wanted. I was a typical young American male who was not particularly harmed by having to serve. In fact, I have always appreciated what the army did for Edyth's little boy, Joe. As a result of my war-time service, I became better equipped to be successful in my occupation of choice, newspaper reporting and publishing.

Because I devoted myself to learning all I could while in service, I actually received my "college education" in the four years I served in World War II. I was excited about the war. To me it was a great adventure, despite being separated from the work I was doing and the people I loved.

Leaving my parents to go overseas, and my wife, Kathy, to whom I was married in April of 1943, was painful. I had not been exposed to much of life's unpleasantness, aside from being poor, having been sheltered from the seamy side of life by my mother. I was shy, trusting, and vulnerable to many of life's pitfalls. Not too many years before entering the army I had been a choir boy at Grace and Holy Trinity Cathedral in Kansas City and a carrier-salesman for the old *Kansas City Journal-Post*.

This, then, is the story of one very ordinary American's experience during World War II. If there ever was a "GI Joe" it was me, both in name and lack of worldly experience, with no special advantages either in appearance or intelligence. I'm sure you've heard it said "the army made a man out of him" or words to that effect. They must have been talking about me.

I am proud of my army service in two wars (I was called back for service during the Korean War) and I have great respect for the army and all it did for me and men like me. If I had had a son, I would have been proud had he chosen a military career. As it is, Kathy and I have two great daughters, Kathy Ann and Cindy, and we're just real happy they didn't choose the military.

I'm dedicating this work to my grandchildren, Douglas and Ryan Fessler and Molly Lawrence, all of whom I dearly love. It is my hope at some point in the future they will want to consult this manuscript so they will know what war was like when grandpa was a young man and falling in love with their grandma. A love, I remind them, that has endured and blossomed for 54 years.

I have made every attempt to be accurate in these accounts, but half a century has taken its toll on my memory. Had I known that one day I would want to detail my time as a soldier in the Southwest Pacific as a member of General Douglas MacArthur's press staff, I would have kept copious notes. How I wish I had.

What I have written is based on my personal experience, observation and opinions on a wide range of events. The details of some happenings or incidents, outside the limits of my personal participation, came from fellow officers, reporters, or from GHQ printed materials of general distribution which were accessible to all headquarters personnel. Many of the photos used were taken by photographers assigned to me.

Trying to recall what occurred on certain dates, and the identity of those correspondents with me on various landings and islands, has been difficult. My intent was to be accurate, and I have been truly surprised at how the memories came charging back into focus, and how details long forgotten suddenly reappeared as I began to put this material into narrative form.

Still, the tapestry of war embraces a wild, confusing whirlwind of action, and I am the first to admit that each individual thread cannot always be guaranteed to be in its proper place without fear of unintended bias or error. It is my hope this account will add a personal touch to your interest in the war and what it all meant to "the boy next door," and the thousands of families involved.

I want to express my sincere thanks and appreciation to Marsha (Houghton) McBee, Karen Rogers and Debbie Carroll, employees of my former newspaper, for their reading and editing of this manuscript in order to eliminate signs of my "poverty of language," and to Darryl and Elizabeth Wilkinson, publishers of my former newspaper, for their kind help. They are all valued friends and I appreciate the assistance they have so generously extended.

Joe Snyder
Gallatin, Mo.
May 1997

Drafted, Horsed Around

Chapter 1

"A story goes that a colonel once asked a junior officer in a famous regiment of cavalry, "What is the purpose of cavalry in war?" The young man replied: "To give tone to what would otherwise be a vulgar brawl."

— **Bernard Brodie**

WOULDN'T YOU KNOW? I had never been on a horse in my life, but a month or so after I was drafted in November 1941, I was at Fort Riley, Kansas, in the saddle on the back of a crusty, obstinate army horse that always knew what he wanted to do even if sometimes I didn't. My mother didn't raise me to be a soldier, but there I was, in boots and breeches, learning to ride, shoot, and use dirty words.

I was working nights on the sports desk at *The Kansas City Star* and (then) *Times* at the time my draft card arrived. Because I had ink in my blood, I was also publishing a small community newspaper, *The Blue Valley News*, on the east side of Kansas City. I thought putting words together and seeing them come off a press, "down in black and white" as they say, was like Christmas and the Fourth of July all in one.

I had purchased a new 1941 Chevrolet five-passenger coupe for $841 and had the cash to pay for it. I had met the gal I wanted to spend my life with, Katherine Lucille Weide, and I wanted to impress her so I bought the car.

It might have helped some, although I believe she had already sort of picked me, too. Kathy had the nicest looking legs and, really, she was the grandest and sweetest girl I had ever met.

I knew the war situation was bad. Many of my friends had already been drafted. I finally received my notice to appear before the draft board and recognized my days as a free and carefree young man were limited. I appeared before the board one evening, and its chairman said I had been "selected" (how I loved that term) to defend our nation. He added:

"Now don't go marching off anywhere we can't find you, boy, because I'm tellin' you right now, after I get done speakin' to ya', you're gonna' be in the service of Uncle Sam."

In a few days, following sentimental good-byes with my parents, Ralph and Edyth Snyder, and my long-sought squeeze, Kathy, I boarded a free bus to Leavenworth, Kansas, for induction. At that time I had no idea to which of the services I would eventually be assigned, and I hadn't given it a lot of thought because I knew my opinion wouldn't be worth much there.

My leaving home was very hard for my mother, who found my going away quite difficult. My father told me some months later she refused to accept the fact I was going off to war and would no longer be under her wing. Dad said she set my place at the table for weeks, just as if I would come walking through the door any minute and sit down for supper.

Her heart really ached. I was her "little Joe" and an only child. I knew she was hurting, along with thousands of other mothers who were saying good-bye to their sons and, sometimes, daughters.

I'll never forget the milling around, the intimidation, and the quick change in my life that occurred at the induction center at Fort Leavenworth. For most of us it was a demoralizing and dehumanizing experience, which was just the way the army planned it — and the army was the service to which I would eventually be assigned.

There we were, standing around with no clothes on, getting medical exams and signing papers, the doctors looking into every little crack and crevice, including a few I didn't know I had. Oh yes, before that we had all taken a shower together. I never got used to bathing with 50 other guys, having their backsides rubbing against mine, or those other things flopping against my hips or midriff. It was disgusting.

The physicals were interesting. I was in a long line when I heard the phrase: "Spread your cheeks," believing the command had something to do with dental work. When it became my turn I was ordered to bend over and discovered the doctors were mainly interested in hemorrhoids. I really never knew what "piles" looked like until a man in front of me bent over.

Of course, there was the "short-arm" exam by the doctor who checked your bladder faucet. Down the line I heard one doctor exclaim: "What the hell you tryin' to do, start a cheese factory? Later on, short-arm inspections were frequent, occurring at all hours of the day and night, in order to detect venereal disease which a few tried to hide.

Of course, they hit our knee caps with little hammers, checked the alignment of the spine, checked for flat feet, asked you to answer certain questions to determine if everything was clicking in your brain — and a dental check. I had never lost a tooth until Fort Leavenworth, but the dentist saw a decayed spot on one of my molars and promptly pulled it instead of filling it.

Another examination caught hernia problems. The doctor thrusts a finger into your scrotum — and then suggests you cough. I despise this procedure with a passion, but each year I pay my doctor good money to repeat it during my annual physical. I think most doctors delight doing this to you.

I had been brought up to respect privacy. The army didn't know what that was and didn't care, at least as far as draftees were concerned. I'll never forget a big, burly staff sergeant coming into the room where we were all standing jaybird naked. He placed his hands on his hips, looking at us like we were aliens from another planet and bellowing: "Hell's bells, they must be scrapin' the bottom of the Goddamned barrel."

The sergeant didn't place any value on our self-esteem. Had I been six feet tall and 200 pounds, instead of five-seven and 125, I'd a punched him in his big pot-belly. But I wasn't and I didn't.

I was interviewed about my military assignment, filled out numerous forms, answered questions, and eventually learned I would be training with the cavalry at Fort Riley, Kansas. I wasn't too unhappy with that. There was a time when I gloried in the legend of General George Custer, whom some considered a flamboyant hero while others labeled him an arrogant fool.

I figured I could be either one. Besides, I thought, the cavalry uniform was the best-looking in the army. I couldn't wait to put on my boots, spurs and breeches and simply stun Kathy and my relatives on my first weekend pass.

The biggest reason I didn't mind going to Fort Riley was that it was close enough that I could continue to see Kathy on a reasonably regular schedule.

One interviewer said I ought to consider the air force because with my newspaper background I might "go far" with the wild blue yonder boys.

I thought to myself: Do I want to be in the air force with all that fresh, clean air, or do I want to ride a horse in the Kansas dust and see Kathy more often? It wasn't even close. I chose Fort Riley and the cavalry where I soon became a "pilot" anyway. While on stable duty, I "piled-it" here and I "piled-it" there. Those horses never knew what constipation was.

Since I had missed the beginning of a 13-week basic cavalry training cycle at Fort Riley, it was decided I would remain at Leavenworth and launch a weekly newspaper for the induction center. It was to be called the *Fort Leavenworth Reception Center News*. I was assigned as editor, given a desk, a typewriter, and a clerk to help out.

I didn't mind doing this because the military history of the west is rooted in Fort Leavenworth, established in 1827 to protect the wagon trains headed west. It is a beautiful post.

In two weeks we had our first edition. It wasn't the best thing I had ever done, but it was presentable, informative, and received praise from my superior there. He was a first lieutenant who in civilian life had been an apple grower. I continued to polish the apple, awaiting my orders for transfer to the Cavalry Replacement Training Center.

The only mistake I made at Leavenworth took place one day on assignment as "duty clerk." There were no flesh and blood buglers available there, so they had the bugle calls on a recording. Trouble was, I played retreat instead of reveille, and the switchboard lit up like a Christmas tree.

The duty officer came running in like gangbusters, and I received a lecture on intelligence, army tradition and stupidity. Since I was leaving soon, I suppose he saw no reason to issue me any brains, or inflict punishment.

On my arrival at Fort Riley I learned, despite the horse cavalry not having a role in modern warfare, the traditionalists were still insisting that World War II could be won on horseback, and if I didn't adopt that philosophy I would be in deep stuff. I adopted the philosophy.

For the next 13 weeks I polished leather, shined brass, shoveled manure, cleaned out stalls, scrubbed latrine floors, walls, urinals and toilet bowls, mopped mess hall floors, used lots of Ben-Gay on my backside, saluted everything that moved, and discovered my horse was the most cantankerous critter God ever supplied the cavalry.

In addition, I had to adapt to barracks life, which included no privacy and going to the toilet with 20 other guys sittin' on the potty making anal sounds like I'd never heard before, and boasting they could "write their name in the snow," or hit a seam in a ten-foot ceiling, while taking a pee.

Over the urinals there were signs: "Stand close, the next man may be barefoot," or "Stand close, these Kansas crabs can jump 10 feet."

People do get witty in the john. Over three of the stools were signs that read: "For venereal disease only." That scared the heck out of me. What guy with gonorrhea or the clap would identify his problem by sitting on those stools?

I developed a sudden and desperate interest in hygiene.

I was introduced to new language, too, including hearing "that" four-letter word at least a thousand times a day to preface everything from breakfast food, to horses, officers, the draft board, government, and the army in general. It involuntarily became part of a recruit's vocabulary, used so casually one hardly realized it had come from one's own mouth at a time of frustration, exhilaration, stress or all three.

During a weekend home, I was eating lunch with my mom and dad. I was vividly describing my new and exciting experiences in horsemanship the previous week, a week that had not gone extremely well, when all of a sudden I heard myself say: "And that f——— horse ..."

My mother dropped her fork and my dad sat there with his mouth open.

Both were pale and in shock. I don't think they had ever heard that ugly word in our house before. They certainly never expected it to come from the mouth of their perfect little son. I was so ashamed and embarrassed; I wished I could have just melted out of their sight.

I could only apologize and try to explain to them it was a word I heard a thousand times a day at Fort Riley, but one I did not intentionally use in front of them, and one I hoped I would never use again. I apologized again and again, but the incident was one all three of us never forgot. I feel sure that day they realized their son was going through "the change."

I was doing KP December 7, 1941, scrubbing the mess hall floors, when I heard over the radio the Japanese had bombed Pearl Harbor. My heart sank, for I knew that I would not be leaving the service anytime soon.

I believe it was the same day when our mess sergeant came by where I was mopping and said:

"Hey, Joe, I see a spot under that table you didn't touch. "I wasn't

By early 1942, I had become a confident and competent cavalry "trooper." Of course, that was my opinion.

offended. I was pleased he knew my name. I felt real good about that until I discovered the sergeants called everybody Joe. Right, GI Joe!

Sergeant Larry Collins was my barracks and training sergeant. He had been in the service several years and came up from Private First Class as mobilization developed. He was strict because he had a lieutenant over him who felt like the weight of the entire war was on his shoulders.

Collins told us early on: "Now there will be some things happen to you here at the CRTC you will not like. Now don't go calling your parents or your distinguished congressman about abuse, because the day will come when you will thank me for the misery I'm gonna' put you through the next 13 weeks. You may find that hard to believe, but you can Goddamn bet on it.

"I'm not your daddy and I'm sure as hell not your mamma, but I'm your sonuvabitchin' drill sergeant who will help you get ready for war. You won't get any sympathy from me and I don't expect any compliments from you. But pay attention to me and you might just survive this Goddamn war."

Lieutenant Wallace Hightower, our troop commander, insisted on going by the book. He gave out demerits, chewed recruits at the drop of a hat, piled on extra duty, and made life as unpleasant as he could. I suppose that was his job.

As it turned out, I became a "trooper" of sorts, hardly at the top of the class, somewhere in between. I discovered I enjoyed riding my horse, "Crackers," and learning to hit a target at a gallop, aiming my pistol over my mount's shoulder, was very exciting. In reality, the horses we rode had been through the cycle of training so many times it was unnecessary to give them a command. They anticipated the routine and knew how to intimidate a recruit as well.

For instance, one day in mounted drill, Lt. Hightower shouted the command:

"Trooper, right about," which was similar to: "To the rear, march," given during dismounted close order drill. For some reason, Crackers refused to cooperate. When the lieutenant yelled, "Trooper, right about, ho...," Crackers deliberately turned around to the left. Man, oh man ... all of a sudden I was disoriented and knew I was in deep trouble.

The lieutenant came charging over to where I was sitting in the saddle, "like a sack of s—" my sergeant said later, totally embarrassed and confused. The lieutenant looked at me like I was one of God's worst mistakes, and roared:

"Trooper, don't you know your left from your right?"

"Yes, sir ... my horse ..."

"You don't know your a— from a hole in the ground, Private Snyder," the lieutenant yelled. "Why don't you just try riding at a trot without the stirrups for about ten minutes and see if that gets your brain working. Will you do that for me, Private Snyder? You do know where the stirrups are, don't you. Private Snyder?"

Greatly embarrassed, I took off at a trot, my feet out of the stirrups. I did my best to reduce the jolt by clamping my thighs against my horse. I had worn heavy underwear since it was a cold January day, but even that did not help the chafing.

Soon blood was seeping through my breeches. The next time Crackers tried to foul me up, I jerked the bit just like the big boys did, and used that four-letter word. It was amazing! Crackers turned around nice and smooth.

The first day we actually mounted our horses to ride out of the corral, nearly everybody thought he had the cinch strap tight but neglected to check to see if his horse had filled his belly with air to keep it loose. The lieutenant gave the command:

"Prepare to mount ... mount!"

About half the troopers landed in the dust. They had barely placed their weight into the stirrups when their saddle slipped from the back of their horse to below its belly. I discovered more experienced riders, even though it was against regulations, snugged the cinch strap and then drove their fist into their mount's belly. The horse would go "ouff" as the air was expelled, and then you could tighten the belt securely.

Lt. Hightower was seriously injured one morning in the corral as we prepared to go to the flats for mounted drill. His horse suddenly bolted, tried to jump the fence, then fell over on the officer. He was still hospitalized when I left basic, and even though he had embarrassed me a few times, I knew I deserved it and I felt no joy in his accident. In fact, I was truly sorry he had been injured.

In the cavalry we not only had KP (kitchen police), which meant working the mess hall, but we also had SP (stable police), which included feeding and cleaning the horses and keeping them in their stalls. Each trooper on duty had four stables with 16 horses in each stable. They were kept in their stalls by a 2 x 6 board which fit into a U-shaped steel bracket.

Those horses weren't dumb. They learned to place their rumps against the board and force it up out of the bracket. It was not uncommon during the night to come into a stable and find at least six horses out of their stalls, fighting, biting and kicking each other in a wild melee. For a guy who had only seen a horse behind a bakery wagon before the war, this was a problem.

If recruits had any spare time, there were always horses to care for; head to tail and in between.

It took some hard work and muscle to restore order, and I usually wound up with some cuts and bruises. I never liked stable duty much because I could never see what I did there was going to hurt the Germans or the Japanese one bit.

I made a serious mistake one day. I fed oats to the horses first, then watered them. All the oats floated right in and right out of 'em. We had two rags to clean critical parts, one for the eyes and one for the rear.

You'd lift up the tail with the dock rag around your finger and, with a spiral motion, clean the horse' rectum. One day I accidentally cleaned the eyes of the horses with a used dock rag and they developed eye infections.

I truly regretted doing that to the animals. I would have preferred ramming it up the lieutenant's rectum.

I held another questionable distinction. I was the only guy in my troop to get chewed, squeezed in the stall, and thrown off his horse in one day. I was thrown off after the lieutenant ordered "Charge!" and our platoon thundered across the Republican Flats west of the post at a full gallop. We reached the Republican River, and my horse abruptly stopped but I didn't, tumbling over his head into the river.

It was very embarrassing and very wet.

Sgt. Collins was a dedicated instructor. His belief was: "If you learn it wrong, you'll do it wrong." He taught us thoroughly about our weapons, how to assemble, disassemble and fire them. We spent hours on our weapons, and woe to the trooper whose weapons were dirty. Even though we were mounted soldiers, we had plenty of dismounted close-order drill because the cavalry considered it basic to achieving discipline.

The theory was that after months of such drilling, learning to obey commands without even thinking or hesitating, that instinct would strengthen unit response time and combat effectiveness. Once I had experienced actual combat, there was little question in my mind that this often boring training was paramount to the saving of lives in battle.

Also vital to maintaining pride and discipline was achieving a mindset that, as cavalry troopers, we could not tolerate anything less than perfection. Even if it were such an insignificant thing as a thread sticking out of a pocket seam, the sergeant might just burn it off with his Zippo. Beds had to be made up tightly enough for a quarter to bounce off the blankets to the barracks floor.

Footlockers had to be arranged just so-so; clothing neatly pressed, our hair short, shoes and boots shined to such an illuminating degree the sergeant could see his face in them. I learned what "spit and polish" meant and, even today, I cannot tolerate unpolished boots or shoes.

Failing these challenges brought demerits, and you could find yourself scraping off the inside of a toilet with a razor blade. Or the punishment for fouling-up might be scrubbing the kitchen floor with a toothbrush, or doing 50 push-ups, even extra guard duty. Most of us quickly learned that preparing for war was serious business, and the quicker we accepted the Army way, the better off we'd be.

We were not really being punished, but acquiring a sense of discipline. It may have seemed like "Mickey Mouse" stuff early on, but we soon realized there was a realistic purpose to everything they threw at us. I began to be a soldier when I ceased being irritated by reprimands but, instead, became embarrassed by them.

We had a celebrity of sorts in our squad. Does the name Ira Grossel mean anything to you? Well, how about Jeff Chandler? Sure, Jeff Chandler, the movie heart-throb. They were the same guy. Ira was a big, strapping six-footer who made a good soldier. He was a standout in our troop, and he was accepted, not because of his reputation, but because of his fine soldiering and "regular guy" attitude.

Ira didn't die glamorously in battle. His death came a few years after he returned home from the war, his fantastic movie career ended during rather routine surgery in a West Coast hospital. What irony!

The 13 weeks at the CRTC went very fast. When my orders arrived, I learned I was being transferred to Camp Funston, located on the east side of Fort Riley. There I joined the Second Cavalry Division, commanded by Major General John J. Millikin. As it turned out, I wasn't an "in the saddle" trooper very long because, within a month, I was transferred to division headquarters.

Before leaving my squadron I had the thrill of participating in a mounted review, with the entire division on horseback, the artillery units dragging caissons, the division's colors and unit guidons flying in the wind at the front of the columns. It was quite a sight to see hundreds of horses in age-old formation.

The scene made me think of the old Irish drinking song, *Garry Owens*, which became the official regimental song of the famous Seventh Cavalry, whose troopers died with Custer in the battle of the Little Big Horn; the Cheyenne, Sioux, and the Apache, who are now only ghosts from the past.

That day I was very proud to be a cavalryman. The "yellowlegs" of old left behind great traditions that many soldiers lived by — and still remember.

The review was officially arranged for the visit of Lieutenant General Ben Lear, commanding the Fifth Army. However, the troopers really put on a show when it was learned that Ann Sheridan, the sexy movie actress, would be on the reviewing stand. Everybody "snapped to" as we rode past this glamorous lady!

I believe that mounted review was the last of division size ever held in the Army, because within a few weeks, the decision was made in Washington to abolish the horses and replace them with tanks. That had to be a demoralizing disappointment for many old-timers.

I hadn't been in the army long, but I understood the anguish of career cavalrymen. I also understood the need for modernization. America wasn't fighting Indians any more, but Nazis and Japanese. I had become attached to horse soldiering; I loved my campaign hat with the yellow cord and tassels, the boots and breeches, but it was obvious the horse had become obsolete for modern-day warfare.

Nostalgia for past achievements, and all the fanciful pride in the glint of sunlight on sabers, the creaking of harness and McClelland saddles, were not enough to delay change or hide the doom of the faithful horse on the field of battle. Monsters of metal, made by man and forged in steel, were the cavalry's undoing. Its ideals, its spirit and traditions, however, will forever remain an exciting chapter in America's rise from the wilderness.

I'm glad I played a minor role in this tradition, even if it was for only a few months. I'll never forget how proud I was of my uniform and the yellow braid of the United States Cavalry!

Stripes to Bars

Chapter 2

"The officer-enlisted man distance helps. This is a painful thing, having to withhold your affection for them, because you know you're going to have to destroy them on occasion. You use them up: they're material. And part of being a good officer is knowing how much of them you can use up and still get the job done."

— **Paul Fussell quoted in *War***

MY NEW JOB was not only trying to please a sergeant, but Lt. Robert C. Stratford, the division public relations officer, who in turn had to please Major General John Millikin, the division commander. I will admit, however, my introduction to the army's public relations effort as an enlisted private was not all that bad.

Bad was what my former trooper-buddies were experiencing in the dirt and manure out in the corrals and the mounted drill fields during advanced cavalry training. When I thought of the cleaning and grooming of all those horses, I quickly grabbed a piece of paper, put it into a typewriter and tried to justify my good fortune.

Historic Fort Riley had been a part of the Junction City community for a long time, since frontier days. The people of that city, most of them anyway, appreciated having a multi-million dollar army payroll next door.

Civilian jobs at the fort numbered in the thousands. No question, the economic impact of around 20,000 soldiers at your doorstep the year 'round kept the cash registers ringing and happy faces on just about everybody.

Everybody that is, except the Junction City Police Department who often had their hands full with drunken, boisterous soldiers creating havoc and disturbing the peace with regularity. In some instances, the city police were aided by Military Police from the post. Their responsibilities included regular rounds of the places where Fort Riley GIs were most likely to congregate, which included brothels and booze joints.

A small hamlet at the east end of the fort's boundary, Ogden was also a favorite hangout for soldiers. It was also a source for pleasures and spirits, that combination leading to frequent altercations and brawls. It remained a constant problem for law enforcement.

One of the jobs of the Public Relations Office (PRO) was to cooperate with the *Junction City Union*, the city's daily newspaper when Fort Riley soldiers created, or were involved in, news both favorable and unfavorable. The public relations office assisted the newspaper staff in identification of those involved, plus details of incidents or accidents that involved military personnel stationed at the fort.

As a private, I had only minimal contact with the newspaper's staff. This responsibility was left to Lieutenant Stratford who, as far as I could determine, had never set foot in a newspaper office prior to his army service. This may not have been his fault. The army often came up with round pegs in square holes. Indeed, some of my superiors might have thought that of me in those early days.

Anyway, I found myself a staff member of *The Fort Riley Guidon*, which served all the units stationed on the reservation. It was not a particularly important assignment, but it was relatively simple and easy and interesting work for me. I loved ink and I loved newspaper presses.

All I had to keep clean there were the typewriters and the top of my desk.

I was still subject, however, to KP and occasional barracks duty, unless I was given an excuse by the lieutenant.

One morning, I was assigned to prepare a half-hour-long program for a local radio station. This was a regular service the station provided the fort and the 2nd Division. For some inexplicable reason, the sergeant who was supposed to have completed the script had not done so. He was on a three-day pass, and since I was the new guy in the office, I inherited his job.

I was told about it at 9:30 a.m., with a 4:30 p.m. deadline. I was not only totally unprepared for such a thing but, let's face it, not even qualified. Fear gripped my very soul. I figured I would foul up royally. I had never written a radio script before, much less one involving commentary directed toward both civilian and army personnel, plus music by the division's band, live! What to do?

I racked my brain for a time, putting it in "emergency" mode, finally deciding to use the old phrase: "For want of a shoe a battle was lost," or words to that effect. I first selected three musical numbers for the band including "The Anvil Chorus" from opera; the familiar "Caissons Go Rolling Along," the old horse-drawn artillery theme song, and wound it up with "Yankee Doodle." You can't go too wrong with "Yankee Doodle."

The musical numbers took nearly half the time allotted, the commercials took several minutes, thank goodness, and I completed the balance of the time with what had to be the lousiest radio script ever produced, containing quotes from prominent people on the war effort, patriotism, war bonds and Mom's apple pie.

I felt terrible about writing such trash and nonsense but, believe it or not, the lieutenant said I did a good job on such short notice.

I was willing to settle for that. Nobody but me will ever remember how bad that piece of work was because the folks who presumably heard it either turned off their radio or quickly forgot it. I was never asked to write another radio script.

The weeks and months rolled by. I knew my skills in the PRO office were improving, and my contributions to the camp newspaper were increasing.

Every chance I got, I would head for Kansas City. I got to know every bump in Highway 24 between Camp Funston and 7200 Baltimore in Kansas City where Kathy was living with her sister, Peggy Alber. Peggy had become more or less a mother to her after Kathy came to Kansas City from Great Bend, Kansas, to find employment.

Peggy had a fireplace in her home, and Kathy I would sit it front of it, look into the flames for answers to our future and talk about the things young people talk about. At that time, with a war going on, our plans for the future were about as uncertain as they could be. I am forever indebted to Peggy for allowing me to see Kathy and indulging us some privacy.

Of course, we smooched, and it was wonderful, but we always managed not to let it go too far. Kathy always had a lot of character and exercised good judgement. I loved her for it then, and I love her for it now, after 54 years of marriage. I try never to let a day go by without telling her so.

I cared for her so much, I was caught trying to leave camp one weekend during a quarantine due to chicken-pox or something. I knew I was restricted to camp, but I just had to see Kathy, and tried sneaking out of camp on a bus. It didn't work and I suffered extra duty and was not given another pass for about a month. That taught me a painful lesson. I never challenged the MPs at the gate again. I obeyed the orders.

By this time it had become obvious the war was going to last quite a while.

There had to be some way I could improve myself within the army. Earlier I had received a promotion to private first class and, finally, I was made a Technician 5, which was equivalent to corporal in the line outfits. Once I had been making $21 a month; now I was up around $62 a month.

I knew several cavalrymen friends who were considering applying for Officer Candidate School. Such schools existed for every branch of the service, and there was a great need in the expanding army for additional junior grade officers. Since the cavalry's OCS school was located at Fort Riley, and I was convinced the cavalry officer's uniform was the sharpest in the entire army, I really wanted to give it a try.

I submitted an application, and within a few weeks I appeared before a board of officers whose job it was to determine, in a span of about 10 minutes, whether I was officer material or not. I was asked a number of questions by various members of the selection board in an effort to determine why I wanted to become a commissioned officer and, of course, if in their judgment my answers assured them I had the necessary qualifications.

The thrust of my answers centered around my conviction that I could contribute more to the army and my country as an officer than remaining in the enlisted ranks. I told them I knew I could develop into a valuable asset to the army as an officer, where opportunities existed for those with leadership abilities, and for those who would not settle for mediocrity.

I may have stretched things a little bit, but I never indicated anything to them I could not back up with determination and ambition.

I made a real effort to appear soldierly and to speak in a confident, commanding voice which wasn't all that easy for a guy who, a relatively few years earlier, had been a boy soprano in the choir at Grace and Holy Trinity Episcopal Church in Kansas City. My uniform was spotless, neatly pressed, and I didn't have a hair out of place. I saluted smartly upon entering and again on my departure.

Nothing happened for several weeks. Then the stuff really hit the fan. The Department of the Army in Washington officially abolished the horse cavalry as an official army branch of service, leaving only a couple of active troops here and there for ceremonial purposes.

With the stroke of a pen, I lost my chance to strut before Kathy in a cavalry officer's uniform. Wow, was I disappointed!

The generals had finally decided to trade the horses for tanks, and overnight the Second Cavalry Division became the Ninth Armored Division. It wasn't long until the cavalry troopers were cleaning boogie wheels on tanks and servicing a variety of other armored vehicles instead of horse flesh and stables.

The familiar yellow and blue patch of the 2nd Cavalry Division would be replaced by the triangular multi-colored patch of the 9th Armored Division. This was a painful experience for the older, career horsemen, but in reality it was a decision long overdue. Yet I felt sympathy for those who would find the change difficult to bear.

Eventually, my orders for OCS came, and after some sentimental moments with Kathy who was now wearing my engagement ring, and visiting my parents, I left by train for Fort Knox, Kentucky. I regretted leaving Fort Riley, and even today when I pass by the reservation, old memories return. I drive past the fort on I-70 with appreciation to the army for the opportunity it provided me at a critical point in my life.

Yes, even the memory of some rowdy moments spent on Breakneck Ridge and in the rim-rock canyons at the camp when we rode like roughnecks are pleasant to recall, even the time I was swept off my horse by a low tree branch. A friendly doctor in the dispensary helped me escape punishment by writing on my report: "In line of duty."

My attitude toward army life changed at OCS at The Armored Center. I knew OCS would challenge me and I really wasn't sure if I could make it there. At the same time, I wanted to succeed because when I became an officer, I would be making a rather handsome salary compared to the $62 a month I made as a corporal. Kathy and I had often talked about getting married.

Maybe, when I became commissioned ...

The OCS had classes of new second lieutenants (shavetails) graduating every two weeks, so that gives you some idea of how badly junior grade officers were needed as mobilization continued. It was the luck of my class to be housed in barracks built during World War I. My classmates and I spent most of a horrible winter in those old ramshackle structures, heated by coal which we had to carry in by the bucket to be dumped into an old pot-bellied heater.

There was no way for everyone to be comfortable; those nearest the heater stayed warm while those in the corners got along the best they could. The ashes from the stove had to be emptied frequently and, of course, each time this was done, despite every precaution, the barracks was filled with dust from the ashes as well as dirt that constantly kept sifting up between the cracks in the old warped floorboards.

This would have been easier to tolerate had it not resulted in demerits, the system for punishing us for infractions of strict rules. Demerits were bad at the Cavalry Replacement Training Center, but they took on a far more serious nature when your future as an officer depended upon your avoiding them.

Two of my classmates discover that OCS instructors do not cover all situations in the field.

The fact we were in old buildings didn't mean a thing. It was our responsibility to keep our floor and walls spotless; clothing, bedding and all other belongings had to be kept clean and dust-free. This was no small task, and all of us had a bit of a disadvantage over other candidates who were in newer barracks. We just worked harder at cleaning up each day and thus minimized our situation.

OSC regulations on footlockers, beds, personal belongings and personal hygiene were even tougher than in basic training. The training cadre were onery, and the officers in charge took no gaff or deviation from the strict rules imposed on officer candidates.

OCS training included a lot more classroom work than I had experienced in basic training. We studied tactics, artillery calculations (not one of my better subjects), along with military history, use of armor in battle, indoctrination sessions on why America was in the war, and numerous courses on leadership. There was lots of close-order drill, the teaching of command skills,and armored vehicle and tank maneuvers in the field.

There was heavy emphasis on physical fitness, and we had a full schedule each day of calisthenics and double-time running, with several obstacle courses to conquer. Along with learning to operate armored vehicles and firing their weapons, we spent time on our bellies in dirt and mud squirming beneath barbed-wire with machine-gun bullets whizzing about a foot above our heads.

I mean, it was live ammunition that taught you to keep your head and shoulders down.

Our instructors were tough and rough. We expected this and learned not to complain, lest we be assigned to extra duty which took away from study time. We understood the harsh training was for our future benefit.

Our class was fortunate to escape serious mishaps. During the winter, as we rode tanks out to the training areas, there was one steep hill that caused trouble. We had several Sherman tanks slide off the edge of the road and plunge uncontrolled into the rocks and trees.

Fortunately, our company had no fatalities from these mishaps, but other units did. In fact, I heard of several candidates being wounded on the firing ranges, but I never learned how seriously they were hurt.

The food was quite good, a bit better than we expected. There was plenty of entertainment provided, if you had the time from studying to enjoy it. There was an excellent post exchange and recreation center for our use. Had it not been for the worry of completing the course, Fort Knox would have been a far happier memory.

I worked hard in OCS because I knew I must not fail. It was unthinkable I would not be commissioned. I had within me all the motivation I needed. It was spelled K-A-T-H-Y. Little did I know then that a few years later, during the Korean war, I would return to Fort Knox as the Armored Center's Public Information Officer. What a thrill that was for me.

It was Christmas Eve 1942, and I had guard duty at the entrance to

In Officer Candidate School I rode tanks instead of horses, and quickly became convinced that horses were softer.

the headquarters building. Across the parade ground was the officers' club and there was a party going on. It was festive, with colored lights and lovely Christmas music drifting across the field. I forgot, momentarily, where I was and what I was supposed to be doing. I was homesick, pure and simple.

All of a sudden, I was confronted by an officer. I had not seen him coming up the walk in the darkness. I immediately knew I was in trouble, because part of my duty was to challenge anyone who approached my duty post. I had failed to do that. I had failed to shout: "Halt, who goes there?" Then, after verbally challenging the intruder, I was supposed to say: "Advance and be recognized."

I had not done these things. The duty officer, a major, confronted me face to face and, in a terribly stern voice, said:

"What's happening here, soldier, were you sleeping or just not paying attention?"

I answered, a bit shakily and none too confidently:

"I'm sorry, sir. I heard the music coming from the officers' club over there and I momentarily forgot what I was supposed to be doing. I'm very sorry, I have no excuse, and I know I should have remained alert. I guess I was thinking of Christmas."

The major replied:

"Well, soldier, it's Christmas in North Africa, too, where some of our men are dying because somebody wasn't alert. What company are you assigned to? I'll have to make a report, you know, and let me warn you, if you sleep at your post in combat you may wind up dead."

I murmured: "I know you have to report me, sir. It was clearly negligence on my part."

He took notes, and with an admonition to stay alert, he strode off to check other OCS candidates at various duty posts. The next morning, I learned he hadn't relished being duty officer that night, probably wishing he could have been home with his family.

I received five demerits for my dereliction of duty, and also two additional nights of guard duty. I was happy it wasn't worse. It could have been. Fortunately, I hadn't collected many demerits during my time at the school, and my overall record was above average.

Now and then, we would have an opportunity to hear a speech from an outstanding military or civilian figure. They were not always generals, but mostly higher ranking officers or government or defense department officials. Their talks were intensely interesting to me, because at that time I was greatly anticipating my assignment once commissioned.

One of the most inspiring speakers I heard was a one-star general (I wish I could recall his name) who had just returned from North Africa. He told of his experiences there with an armored group that had been battling the Germans.

He made it sound so exciting and adventurous, all of us were ready to stand up and cheer when he finished to great applause. This general obviously was a great motivator and undoubtedly a fine leader. At least he knew how to communicate with young men ready for war and its adventures.

In fact, he told us, for the first time in the war, members of our class would have the opportunity to go directly to North Africa for assignments with units in combat. You should have heard the applause. It was deafening.

We came out of the hall full of enthusiasm and anxious to get our training behind us, put on our lieutenant insignia, and ship out. It is obvious to me today that our training involved more psychological indoctrination than we realized at the time.

I also recall another speaker, a warrant officer, who appeared before an assembly of officers and men to acquaint us with a new tank weapon, or perhaps a gun sight. The front two rows of the audience were composed of bird colonels and generals.

The speaker was introduced, approached the podium, and took a good long look at all the "brass" down front before he spoke. He said:

"I'm sure there are people in this army who know more about this project than I do .... but since I do not see any of them here this morning, I will now tell you about this wonderful piece of equipment."

It was the most artful put-down I witnessed in the war.

Whether I was a bona fide leader of men at this point in my life I wasn't sure, but having closely observed the leadership I had been exposed to at various times, I felt I was up to accepting the challenge and heartache of leadership. It is my conviction that men are not necessarily born with it, but leadership develops as a result of what takes place after you are born, and what role fate plays in your life.

I did fairly well in OCS, but I did not quite rank in the upper ten percent of my class. It was my lack of mathematical skills, in connection with artillery calibrations, that brought my grade average down. Since we were all graded on a class "curve," you had to be pretty dense not to achieve a passing grade, but a few didn't.

Those classmates who didn't make it were given staff sergeant ratings and assigned, not to their old units, but given other military assignments in order to avoid personal embarrassment. A few were sent directly overseas.

At long last, I received my orders and duty assignment. I was to join the 14th Armored Division at Camp Chaffee, Arkansas. My orders said I would become a staff member in the G-2 (Intelligence) Section, with primary duty as the division's public relations officer. Great! I realized then my newspaper background would influence my career path in the army.

I had mixed feelings about that, but as time went on, I realized what a great assignment I had received, one I knew I could handle well and perhaps make a real contribution. Along with my commission in infantry, later armor, I received my Military Occupation Specialty (MOS) number which was 4201.

That number established my specialty as a newspaperman, public information and/or press liaison officer, and it directed my career in the army, both in WWII and, later, in the Korean conflict. That number permitted me to share in some of the most historic events in modern history — and I am forever grateful.

I believe that Justice Oliver Wendell Holmes summed it up when he said: "A man is required to share the passion and action of his time at peril of being judged not to have lived."

Our graduation exercises were held in the fort's fieldhouse. At the conclusion of the ceremony we all threw our hats into the air, cheered and jumped up and down, an old tradition borrowed from the service academies. I had no relatives there to congratulate me, as was the case for most of the others, so we just congratulated one another.

We had each become an "officer and a gentleman."

I had some spare time before going into Louisville, to catch my train to Kansas City, and several days at home before proceeding to Camp Chaffee. I strolled into a building I had frequented a lot while stationed at Fort Knox and ordered a soft drink. I noticed several soldiers, and the waitress, looked at me with some curiosity. Had I been commissioned with my trousers unzipped?

I suddenly remembered: "My God, I'm an officer now. What the heck am I doing in the non-commissioned officers club?" I was plainly embarrassed and left quickly to the smiles of the club staff.

It also occurred to me upon graduation that the main reason I became a "90-day wonder" was to be in a position to marry Katherine Lucille Weide.

My army pay now would be around $200 a month, plus allowances. That wasn't much, even then, but it was just enough. True love minimizes all obstacles.

Kathy and I had been engaged for several months. We had discussed marriage but initially decided it was best to wait until the war was over to tie the knot. For me, though, a few weeks away from each other was pure torture, so I finally suggested to her in a letter:

"Honey, I know it looks like it's gonna' be a long war, but I want to be with you now. I want you to marry me."

Happily, she accepted my reasoning and my proposal in a most sincere, sweet and loving letter. It was the most joyful and sensible thing I had ever done in my life.

We were married in Kathy's church, the Evangelical (now United Methodist) Church on Sunday afternoon, April 4, 1943, in Kansas City. Since I was on a three-day pass, we had to leave our parents, relatives and friends immediately following a reception at Peggy's house. We got as far as Harrisonville that first night and checked in at a small hotel on the town square.

You bet I was anticipating, but I'll never reveal the details of that first night together.

On nervously registering and paying the hotel clerk, I went to our room, and after telling Kathy how much the honeymoon suite was costing, which was minimal, I discovered he had given me a dollar too much in change. I said to her:

"Look, honey, the clerk gave me back a dollar too much. We're beginning our marriage with good luck."

She wouldn't have it that way. Sitting on the edge of the bed, she replied so sweetly and sincerely:

"Joe, you know we can't start our lives together by being dishonest. I want you to go back to the desk and return that dollar. It doesn't belong to us."

I felt ashamed and embarrassed, and knew she was right. Over the years, 54 of 'em, she's been right on just about everything. My love and affection for Kathy is a reflection of her complete honesty and impeccable character that won't quit. Meeting Kathy was my lucky day, and I'm a much better person because of her great and continuing influence on my life.

Armored in Arkansas

Chapter 3

"The Army, for all its good points, is a cramping place for a thinking man. As I have seen too often, such a man chafes and goes — or else decays."

B. H. Liddell Hart

KATHY AND I LIVED in a small but comfortable apartment in Fort Smith, Arkansas, renting from a friendly couple, Mr. and Mrs. Joe Limburg, who knew we were newly married. They went out of their way to make us happy, perhaps indulging us a bit because we were so lovey-dovey. Mr. Limburg was employed by the Camp Chaffee Fire Department. They were very kind and considerate to us.

It was about 22 miles from our apartment to the camp. Most of the time, I rode to work in a car pool since gasoline and tires were not easy to get, even if you were in service. It wasn't an imposition really, because there was always a lot of scuttlebutt going around the division, and the car pool provided the opportunity for exchange of information and education.

My job there was interesting. I came to know all the editors in the camp's general area, with particularly good contacts with the *Fort Smith Southwest Times-Record*, the region's largest and best daily newspaper. The city editor was Ed Barksdale. I could usually count on him to be fair and understanding when soldiers from the camp were involved in auto accidents, tavern brawls, marital strife, rape and other displays of conduct unbecoming a soldier.

There were many such incidents. It was not my job to hide information in such instances, but to cooperate with area media to assist them in gathering the facts, then leave it to them to write their stories as they saw fit. This policy was not always understood and sometimes opposed by some career army people, who believed that only positive and happy things should be printed about the army.

It was also my duty to complain to newspaper editors or reporters,

Fourteenth Armored Division engineers constructed a pontoon bridge across the flooded Arkansas River to connect Fort Smith with Van Buren. This emergency span proved a Godsend, not only for pedestrians, but the bridge also supported vital water lines for Fort Smith residents.

usually at the urging of the commanding general, if he or some other ranking officer took issue with a story about Camp Chaffee or the units stationed there.

Fortunately for me, Major General Vernon E. Pritchard, commander of the 14th Armored Division, was well aware of the value of good relations between the camp and Fort Smith and other surrounding towns. I was not forced to officially find fault with area newspaper stories very often. When I did, however, it was very painful for me since I was a civilian newsman at heart and easily recognized an unjustified complaint — and most of them were.

I soon began to understand the Army did not really want anything printed unless it had a positive slant to it. Sometimes a civilian soldier like myself became a cockle-burr to the career officers, who would have preferred that I disappear into a dark, deep hole.

General Pritchard and the division received well deserved, nationwide publicity in 1943 when a raging flood hit the Arkansas River, destroying the only bridges linking Fort Smith and Van Buren. The general ordered his engineer battalion to construct a pontoon bridge across the swollen river to restore the best possible temporary means of contact between the two towns.

His action created great publicity for him and our division and also provided the engineer troops with invaluable training. They applied this training to good use later on in Europe when an advance armored unit of the 14th captured the Remagen bridge over the Rhine River. This gallant attack provided a great breakthrough for the Allied troops.

General Pritchard, however, found himself in deep trouble with his superiors over a story which I did not originate, but one I was happy to see widely publicized in Arkansas because of its human interest.

A factory near Fort Smith was awarded a contract to supply airborne units with gliders for special combat situations. Somehow the general received an invitation to take a ride in one of their gliders, fresh off the production line. Fort Smith civic pride in action!

The general accepted the invitation, and the event attracted a large crowd. When the news reached the Pentagon, however, the telephone lines between Chaffee and Washington grew hot. According to the secretary in the office of our Chief of Staff Colonel James P. Hill, Pritchard received an extremely harsh and loud dressing-down from a top-ranked general in Washington.

This ranking general obviously did not want to see one of his armored division generals risking his life in a flimsy, assembly-line produced glider, just to get his name in the papers. This was my first personal experience relating to a general being reprimanded, but not the last. I would later witness a two-star general being not only reprimanded, but actually relieved of his command on Bataan.

The glider incident was never brought up in headquarters, and I knew better than to mention it in the general's presence, even though I had a secret desire to see his face turn red. Junior grade officers seldom get to see an embarrassed general.

It was decided to publish a book of photographs of the division in cooperation with the same firm that published the camp newspaper. Our office did the layout work, and I took the mock-up into the general's office for his approval. He took a quick look at the cover and said:

"I see it is to be titled, *The Fighting Fourteenth.*"

"Yes sir," I replied. "We thought that might be appropriate," at the same time thinking to myself: "They sure as heck fight like Burma tigers in the Fort Smith beer joints."

"Lieutenant," he said. "How in hell do we know if this division will be sufficiently trained and how well they will respond before the enemy. Will they be a fighting division or something else?"

I knew I had better be very careful with my reply, although I thought his comment to be a strange one for a general who had been building a fighting machine for months on end. To me it indicated a strange lack of confidence, but all I said was:

"Sir, does the general have a suggestion?"

"Maybe you'd just better call it *The Fourteenth Armored Division*," he replied.

That's what I did. I knew it was just a suggestion, but I also recognized who was making it. I was getting smarter every day and somewhat of a diplomat.

Ironically, General Pritchard did not die in battle but in a post-war explosion in a pleasure craft on the Potomac River near Washington, D.C. For some reason, Pritchard was relieved of command of the 14th prior to its going to Europe. The division was led in combat over there by General Carl Smith, who had commanded one of the division's combat commands.

Colonel Hill, who was an old "blister bottom" cavalryman, died of a heart attack in Germany, presumably from combat stress. I'm proud to say, however, that the 14th performed extremely well against the Germans, and General Pritchard needn't have worried about whether it was ready for combat. It was.

I had my first, but not personal, experience with homosexuality at Camp Chaffee. I shall call the man Lt. Casey. He was a member of the car pool I was in. I had always been rather naive about such things, but others in the car pool had suspected something for some time.

Casey would occasionally place his hand on your thigh. At times, some said he seemed like a "sweet prince." At noontime some of us would go to lunch at the officers' club, and Casey would go over to the record player and listen to Nelson Eddy-Jeanette MacDonald recordings all by himself.

This happened day after day. Not that listening to good music has anything to do with an alternative lifestyle; there was something about Casey that didn't seem quite right, but you coulda' fooled me.

His mannerisms appeared suspect to some, but I was green as a gourd about such things. All I knew about homosexuality was that, as a small boy, my mother told me to stay clear of a man that passed by our house quite often. She said he was "queer." I just thought she meant "odd."

Meantime we had all heard rumblings of a homosexual group

within the division. Finally, it all came out. Homosexual activity was centered in our medical battalion, and at least 20 army personnel were involved; Lt. Casey was included. It was a messy affair and, as public information officer, there was no question I would become involved in the case.

You must keep in mind this incident happened 52 years ago. Attitudes toward homosexuals have changed somewhat. Today there is more understanding and compassion — but not everywhere.

This all happened just after the division had gone through a rape case involving a soldier and an Arkansas girl from a nearby town. In my mind the soldier was guilty, but the army prosecutor from the Adjutant General's office got the girl so confused she finally admitted under oath she could not tell the difference between the young man's finger and his penis.

This incident took place on a car fender, not my idea of comfortable sex, and the girl's admission was hardly a compliment to the soldier's reputation as an army lover.

As expected, the army preferred to keep the homosexual matter quiet, but the press began asking questions, and I told my superiors the best thing to do was to admit there was a problem, give reporters the facts, and assure the press and public that the division would take proper action under existing army regulations.

It was quite a hearing. The testimony was disturbing: several soldiers in the barracks observing two "humping" men in the same cot under a blanket, strange sucking, slurping sounds like, as one GI testified:" ... like a calf suckling its mother." Those involved in the ring were discharged from the service, including Lt. Casey.

I well remember the day following the conclusion of the hearing when Casey walked into my office. I really didn't know why he was there or how I was supposed to react. He spoke first:

"Hey, Joe. If you don't mind, I'd just as soon handle my own hometown story about this."

He smiled, even chuckled a bit. I told him there would be no further releases on the matter as far as I was concerned. I couldn't help but feel sorry for him at that moment and wished him well.

The day came when the 14th left Camp Chaffee for maneuvers in an area around Nashville, Tennessee. Kathy and I stored some things and rented a room in Nashville with kitchen privileges, about 30 miles or so from the command center of the maneuver forces.

The first task for my office, now under canvas, was to publish a weekly newspaper for the troops. I went to Nashville to the McQuiddy Printing Company to contract for printing our *Turret Topics* newspaper. General Pritchard approved the name.

Usually the maneuvers began Monday and continued to at least Thursday. By that time we would have copy ready for that week's edition and McQuiddy would have it printed, sometimes with color, within three or four days. I still have a file of those old maneuver newspapers.

I must tell you that one issue of the paper did not meet the approval of General Pritchard. Each week we filled the editorial space with a "pin-up" photo of a movie star or entertainer. One week a member of the staff suggested we use a picture of Lena Horne, who was a prominent Afro-American entertainer at the time. I saw nothing objectionable about using it. She had a nice figure, was pretty and sang well.

Field maneuvers were serious business. Three soldiers died during nighttime action when their tank rolled off this bridge and fell to the stream bed below.

General Pritchard, however, minced no words in letting me know he did not want to see any more pictures of black girls in his division's newspaper. I was surprised and astonished by his attitude. Perhaps I shouldn't have been surprised since he came from the deep south and old prejudices are difficult to give up; some will always be with us. I would have preferred to forcibly argue the point, but in the Army you do what you're told, and you always know who will win an argument between a lieutenant and a general. Arguing with a superior officer seldom produces promotions. I was a little late learning that lesson, which is one of the reasons I never made it beyond captain.

While in Tennessee I enjoyed some of the best eggnog ever, courtesy of the printing company. In fact, all of Nashville was quite festive over the Christmas holidays, and Kathy and I enjoyed dinner Christmas day at the Maxwell House, famous for its coffee, located in downtown Nashville. It was a memorable experience, one we have never forgotten.

But lest you get the impression maneuvers were all fun for me, let me say that during the conduct of the maneuver war games most of us slept in two-man tents, "shelter-halves" as they were known in army lingo. It was during maneuvers, with the temperature well below zero, I learned how much heat you can get from one or two lighted candles inside a pup-tent.

We also increased warmth by placing cedar tree boughs around the bottom of the tent, packing them in place with snow, to keep the winter gales from blowing us out of the tent. Candy bars provided extra calories and quick energy, but our cooks did an excellent job under the circumstances. One of the cooks made a hit in the officers' mess by cooking an egg in the center of a pancake. It was delicious.

The maneuvers lasted about three months. The division lost a few men either killed or injured in tank or vehicle accidents. One of them occurred near Gallatin, Tennessee, which was the first time I ever heard of a town called Gallatin. Years later, when the postal service issued an Albert Gallatin postage stamp, our Gallatin (Missouri) beat out Gallatin, Tennessee, for the honor of hosting the first day of issue program.

I never understood how the residents of Gallatin, Murfreesboro, Shelbyville and Lebanon — and the area between — could tolerate all the damage our tanks and other vehicles did to their roads, bridges and cropland as a result of maneuvers. Presumably they collected handsomely from Uncle Sam for the damage since patriotism does have its limits.

I had an interesting experience one day while involved in one of the division's maneuver "problems." I and my staff had to move to a new location, and we crossed the Tennessee River on a ferry boat. Enroute to the other side, I asked the boatman how many trips a day he made across that river. He spat a wad of tobacco juice into the water and replied:

"Well, some days quite a few, then again not so many."

Reminded me of a few orders I received during the war. Clear as mud.

Following this field training, the division was relocated at Camp Campbell, Kentucky. Kathy and I finally found a room with kitchen privileges in Clarksville, Tennessee, later sharing a house with another army officer and his wife, which wasn't ideal but we "made do," as my mother used to say during the Depression.

I began getting acquainted with newspaper and radio station personnel in the area, and things were going extremely well. Rumors were the division would be ordered to Europe in the near future. I had already taken and passed my overseas physical exam.

Then I received a bombshell.

Orders came for me to leave for Washington, D.C. and orientation for the army's war correspondent project. I had completely forgotten that I had applied for the project. My orders came as a real surprise, for we had settled in quite well in Tennessee and in the life of the camp's social routine. I had also received a promotion to first lieutenant, more pay and more allowances, but low on authority.

Kathy and I repacked so she could return to Kansas City. Since we hadn't acquired much in the way of household goods, it was not a formidable task, but it was not a particularly happy time.

It had taken the army a while to gear up its correspondent program. It materialized simply because the army wanted to catch up with the Marine Corps. The marines had enjoyed exceptional success with its combat reporters, receiving wide publicity in newspapers, radio and theater newsreels. So the decision was made to let the folks back home know that the army was fighting and bleeding, too.

Leaving Kathy was the hardest thing I've ever done. It was a difficult, tearful farewell, one I will never forget nor, at the time, one I ever thought I would have to endure again during the Korean War. My parents were also shaken by my leaving the country, and my dad simply could not understand why I would volunteer for anything.

Kathy, however, understood that within me was an impatience to get to where the excitement was. I loved her for that.

In Washington I found I was one of about 20 officers who had received the same orders. All of us were volunteers, and we received extensive orientation. We were issued pistols, typewriters and wristwatches, plus the usual gear for combat in the South Pacific. The photographers received cameras and accessories. It seemed to be too good to be true. It was, at least for a while.

Kathy accompanied me to Washington and during the three weeks we were there, we had a wonderful time together. The army had given us a date for leaving, but at the last minute the departure was delayed. In the meantime, Kathy had left the city to visit some old friends in Virginia, not far from Washington. When she found out I was not leaving as scheduled, she returned immediately and, once again, we had to find a place to stay.

Not far from Union Station there was a small hotel which had been taken over by the military to assist servicemen in transit. We went in and approached the front desk where we asked for a room for a week. At that moment the clerk did not have what we desired, and he asked us to wait in the lobby.

Shattering our conversation, the public address system boomed:

"Will the lieutenant who wanted a double-bed please return to the desk."

I don't know whose face was the reddest, but it was a great room, a special week, and well worth the unexpected nocturnal publicity.

The next week I left for the West Coast and Kathy left for Kansas City. Such partings are never easy. We would not see each other again for 18 months amidst all the uncertainties of war. I would be occupied in the South Pacific, and Kathy would be doing her bit for the war effort at Pratt-Whitney in Kansas City.

Now, I thought, I will find out what war is all about. Did I ever!

Bats and Navy Sex

Chapter 4

"October 1, 1916, 150 men waiting at the door of a Calais brothel, each to have his turn with one of the three women of the house; each serving a battalion of men each week for as long as she lasted. Three weeks was the usual limit. After which she retired on her earnings, pale but proud."

— **John Ellis,** *Voices in the Great War*

WHEN OUR SHIP SAILED beneath the Golden Gate bridge headed for the South Pacific I, like many others that day, wondered what the future held for us. My main concern was to get back in one piece, assure my parents that I was fine, and be with Kathy forever.

At that time I did not know our "combat correspondent" project would fall through, and I certainly never dreamed that we would be joining General MacArthur's headquarters within a few months. I did not know even sooner than that, our transport ship would be tracked by a Japanese submarine for several days.

This caused the captain of our vessel to change course, taking the ship down the west coast of California, past Central America, to a point somewhere off the coast of South America. There we made an abrupt turn to the southeast, to our then unknown point of debarkation. There were frequent alerts and "abandon ship" drills, plus a King Neptune ceremony as we crossed the equator. The latter exercise was just an excuse to work off some excess energy. The crew of the ship played a joke on us when an announcement came over the speaker system: "Attention, army personnel. The ship will soon reach a mail buoy a few nautical miles ahead. This will be your last chance to write letters home before arriving at our destination. You have 30 minutes to get them ready."

Well, of course, there was no such thing as a mail buoy. There was a lot of letter-writing done, and I was one of those who bit. It proved to be just a joke, but it didn't help the relationship between the army

New Caledonia was a great place to supplement Army food. I and one of my sergeants purchase an armload of fresh fruit for about 25 cents.

personnel on board and the crew. I thought the "joke" in poor taste.

The voyage took 19 worrisome and tiresome days. Our ship had a Merchant Marine crew, their salaries greatly exceeding ours, plus they received handsome bonuses for taking the ship into "enemy" waters. Worst of all, the crew would not permit army personnel to drink from their cold water fountains, and we had to endure salt water showers.

Their patriotism, comradeship and sacrifice simply overwhelmed us!

None of us knew, other than rumors, where we were going until we sailed into Noumea, New Caledonia. At least the initial view was pleasant. The city overlooked the harbor, situated on green, tree-lined slopes. The prominent feature from my viewpoint was the lovely cathedral, which stood amongst the European-style buildings and dwellings that made up the city.

Later I stood before the cathedral with considerable awe to view a heroic-size bronze statue of Joan of Arc. The interior of the church was decorated in the style of the old French artisans, which not only created a worshipful attitude, but was breathtaking in its beauty.

New Caledonia suffered considerably in two separate phases of the war. The first came when the island suffered great political strife and severe economic losses after France capitulated to the Germans in June, 1940. The people were placed under great stress again when Japanese troops invaded the South Pacific but, fortunately, the enemy advance was halted before reaching their homeland.

My military introduction to the Southwest Pacific Theater of Operations occurred in June of 1944. I, and a few others in our special group, learned we had been assigned to the 25th Infantry Division, currently trying to get itself back together at an upland camp on the island. The division had suffered heavy losses in tough, prolonged combat on Guadalcanal in the Solomon Islands.

Experience gained in fighting there, however, was of immeasurable value in training American troops for eminent combat against the Japanese. Long established military tactics were drastically revised because of painful experiences on Guadalcanal, and those doing the fighting quickly learned that much of their equipment was not suited to jungle warfare.

Guadalcanal supplied most of the news in the early stages of the Pacific war. The Japanese captured numerous key islands in this region after Pearl Harbor. It was in August, 1942, that U.S. Forces, supported by Australian units, attacked positions in the Central Solomons.

The Marines greatly distinguished themselves in jungle fighting on Guadalcanal. Due to heavy casualties, they were relieved by the 25th Infantry Division, and sent to Australia to heal and rebuild their units. As it turned out, the exhausted, malaria-ridden Marine division would take a year to get ready for combat.

The 25th Division completed the mop-up begun by the Marines, but only after many of their own units were severely decimated by the enemy's fierce resistance. Its combat strength had been sapped, crippling both officers and enlisted ranks, and morale was low. Once the island was declared secure, the 25th moved to New Zealand for rest and recuperation.

This was commonly called R&R (rest and recuperation) in the services. Some soldiers said R&R stood for "Rape and Run." As it turned out, New Zealand was hardly the place for soldiers to rest and relax. Few took the opportunity to rest.

All able-bodied New Zealand men had been sent away months before to battle German General Rommel's Afrika Korps in the desert sands of Tunisia. Some had been dispatched to assist their Aussie brothers battle the Japanese in the southern reaches of New Guinea in the Port Moresby region. In fact, all the Australians fighting in Papua New Guinea, were veterans of North Africa. They had been asked to endure to excess.

The GIs found New Zealand women ready, willing and able. Instead of rest and recuperation, great numbers of the Americans quickly dissipated themselves with bedroom acrobatics. It wasn't long until most New Zealanders were echoing their cousins in Great Britain who coined the phrase: "They're over-paid, over-sexed and over here."

The uproar over the issue even reached into diplomatic channels between the two countries. It ended when the decision was made to re-settle the 25th Division on New Caledonia. Peace and quiet? You bet.

New Caledonia's European influence barely extended beyond the borders of its capital city, Noumea. The division settled in an encampment about 60 miles northwest of Noumea, bordering a coastal highway. The camp was located near the highway and the ocean, with 4,500 foot mountains providing a colorful green "backbone" the length of the island.

There were numerous scenic highlights; perhaps it did not compare to the jungle-covered, lush, flowered and palm-tree scenery I was to eventually see on islands to the north and northeast. But it is a lovely island and I was not there long enough to make a critical judgement.

After all, New Caledonia is a semitropical island, lying sufficiently distant from the equator to have two distinct seasons; a humid summer from December to April and a drier mild winter from June to September. The heat in summer was not oppressive. I was told there were 30,000 plant species on the island and one that interested me was unique to New Caledonia, the white-barked Niaouli tree. It reminded me a little of aspens, but still it was different.

There were millions of birds on the island. Their territorial bird, the cagou, cannot fly and makes a sound like a barking dog. I believe I have read that the cagou today is near extinction, an easy target for the hordes of dogs claimed by the natives.

Until the war came along, New Caledonia was little more than a backwater colony. With the fall of France to the Germans in 1940, a pro-Vichy government was established. This government was soon overthrown to put the island on the side of General Charles de Gaulle, Free France and the Allies.

The U.S. presence there began in March 1942, when a Naval armada and the American division arrived at the sleepy port. Noumea quickly became our main South Pacific support base. Believe it or not, Noumea became second only to San Francisco in the amount of war cargo destined for the Pacific. The harbor is fantastic.

The lovely blue-green ocean near the camp offered mostly swampy, rocky terrain where we had hoped to find resort-like sandy beaches, thus providing little recreation. One regimental commander ordered his men to exercise each morning by running halfway up and back down one of the mountains. This had a tendency to limit other physically-demanding activities and sexual forays into Noumea, even when authorized.

A French farmer guides oxen pulling a primitive harrow in the quiet countryside of New Caledonia, not far from our camp.

About the only natural oddity for the unhappy campers to observe were the bat colonies located in caves near the camp. In early evening, almost like clockwork, the bats would come streaming from the mouths of the caves in tremendous numbers. There were hundreds of thousands of them, swarming in such numbers that a part of the sky would be clouded over. It was a sight I hadn't seen before and one I haven't seen since.

New Caledonia has some picturesque rocky shores where numerous caves were located. The opportunities for great pictures were unlimited.

In reality, there was little choice for fraternization. The natives were warm and friendly, and the children curious and sweet.

Some of the half-caste Melanesian families on New Caledonia were quite handsome. Here a mother and her three children are not sure how to react to a picture of them.

The only women in vicinity of the camp were Melanesian, akin to Papua New Guineans, who were labeled "Kanakas."

These local belles wore some clothing, thank goodness, but they chewed betel nuts which blackened their teeth, and they rubbed a certain substance into their hair which bleached it orange. Hardly Dorothy Lamour types!

The natives lived in small villages, housed in conical-roofed houses of thatch which had no windows. They fished in the lagoons and grew taro and other root plants, sometimes on terraced slopes. Each tribe had a chief and its own culture, religion and language. I was told there were 20 different languages, none of which was understood outside the tribal group.

Thanks to the U.S. Navy, however, there was a place in Noumea for sexual adventures. It was called the "Pink House" and was Navy sponsored and Navy operated. The girls were mostly French and not unattractive to those men who had a terrible urge after months in the jungle. The girls were regularly examined, and treated if needed, by Navy doctors.

While there might be room for criticism of a branch of our government operating brothels, the Pink House did offer servicemen controlled sexual release, perhaps reducing desertions and rapes of innocent women. It definitely assisted the medical corps in controlling sexual diseases.

It was not unusual during the late afternoon and evening, to see long lines of army and navy personnel waiting to get inside the pink-stuccoed building for service. It was my understanding the Navy supplied condoms; patrons did not have the privilege to choose their sexual partner. It was sort of potluck and there were normally eight to ten prostitutes "on duty." One could compare the operation to an auto production line, sort of piece by piece.

A soldier in division headquarters had an affair going with an army nurse. He received a letter from his girl friend back home and in it she questioned why she had not heard from him. She wrote: "Have you found someone over there. If so, what's she got that I haven't got?"

The soldier wrote back: "Honey, she don't have anything you haven't got. The difference is what she's got, she's got over here."

The "Dear John" letters were the roughest. A soldier would receive a letter from his stateside girl, only to learn she had decided not to wait for him to come home. She might reveal she had fallen in love with someone else. Her excuse for abandoning her GI boyfriend was not often true love, but simply social and sexual needs. The impact on the GI was terrible.

Such letters caused many a soldier to blow his brains out, or else become so depressed he was no longer of any value to his unit. I doubt the writers of such letters really understood how demoralizing such news was to soldiers cut off from their friends and family back home. To learn the "girl they left behind" was no longer waiting for them was devastating.

Make no mistake, women played a huge role in the war. In some instances, prostitutes were on military intelligence payrolls. The military discovered that most men like to talk and brag when enjoying themselves socially and sexually, even to the extent of revealing classified information.

Now and then to relieve boredom, several of us would finagle a Jeep for a tour of the island which was 250 miles long and 38 miles deep at its widest point. At various points along both coastal highways, there were decent roads which bisected the island and led into the interior.

Normally we would turn off the coastal highway at the town of Burail, turning inland on a route that took us past lovely waterfalls, green slopes, singing birds and tiny native villages. Now and then we would see Sumatra deer, which provided residents with palatable food. These were rather small animals, with antlers seldom exceeding six points.

There was a tiny French restaurant along the way. I can't recall its name, but I do remember the sign outside which read: "English spoken." Once inside, you quickly learned the other words of English spoken, and those were "Staik an' eggs." The meals there were a pleasant respite from the camp's bill-of-fare, and the scenery was a soothing change from the tent community and its monotonous routine.

Oh yes, three other English words were spoken in the cafe. "Two dollairs, pleece."

At the inland villages we could load our jeep with fresh tropical fruits. One could buy an armload of bananas for 25 cents. Tangerines and coconuts were also quite cheap. These visits helped augment our rather bland GI diet in the division headquarters mess hall.

On one of these jaunts into the interior of the island, Lt. Ron Mears and I found an old fort. We had stopped to view a roadside waterfall, when we spied the ruins near the bottom of a hill. The date, 1878, was carved into the well-preserved tower, and there were dungeon-like rooms in an opening below. The walls of the fort were still standing in many places. One could only wish those old stone walls could talk.

Sometimes, just to be doing something, we'd take our .45 caliber pistols and go fishing. We'd find a shallow spot in one of the many streams on the island and wait for a meandering fish. "Pow!" We'd have fish for dinner. I was never one to kill anything, being rather tender-hearted, and shooting fish was more like target practice than anything else.

I haven't intentionally killed any fish or wildlife since.

Occasionally, the USO would supply us a stage program. Some of the entertainers who put on a show for us included Bob Hope, Jerry Colona and Frances Langford. Even Joe E. Brown, the comedian, provided some great entertainment for us. We enjoyed frequent movies as well, often sitting in heavy rain, covered by a poncho, to see them.

Movie star Errol Flynn showed up one time with a small troupe of entertainers, but spent most of his time with his female counterparts and a few nurses. That figured. His reputation had preceded him.

My time with the 25th Division was not by choice. I didn't appreciate being stuck with a combat-weary outfit at a time when exciting events were taking place on island battlefields all over the South Pacific. About all I and my two sergeants were doing was writing "hometown" news releases by the hundreds.

Such stories were important to all newspapers, of course, but were especially welcomed by small city and hometown newspapers. The stories were great moral boosters to those who had fought for America anywhere during the war and those mentioned in them certainly deserved mention for their selfless service. The short little items were pridefully shown around town by parents, who later put them in scrapbooks.

I recall that the one item found most often in the effects of our war-dead were souvenirs of my profession — a worn, much-folded and faded clipping from a small-town weekly newspaper. It may not have excited the public when they read it; it may not have meant much to the editor who used it, but the human being it was about carried it with him to eternity.

It was General William Tecumseh Sherman who described the infantry soldier best when he said they were the kind of men for whom their best reward was "to be shot on the battlefield and have his name misspelled in the newspaper."

I came home from the war with the deepest respect for the infantry. They risked their life for little pay and deplorable living conditions, and faced indescribable terror, with the odds good they would wind up dead. One has to take his hat off to those who made the transition from the protected to protector, and from civilian to military in 13 short weeks.

Perhaps that's why the slogan, "You haven't lived until you've almost died," became so pertinent. Another quote, not as humorous as you might believe, was appropriate as well: "We are the unwilling, led by the unqualified, to do the unnecessary, for the ungrateful."

The GI quote I liked best was: "Last to know, first to go."

While with the 25th, a few of us became acquainted with a couple of "coastwatchers" who had accompanied the division back from Guadalcanal. These brave men, usually Australian, conducted one of the most valuable operations of the war. There had been a similar organization of "watchers" in the South Pacific for years, simply to keep an eye on vast, unguarded territories.

These watchers might be planters, missionaries, government officials in remote regions, plantation operators or miners. These men were supplied with special battery-powered radios, designed to withstand the rigors of the extreme tropical heat. They had a range of 400 miles for voice broadcasting, a bit more for telegraphic use.

The radio equipment was quite heavy and required a platoon of native bearers to move them from place to place. The two watchers who, for whatever reason, came south with the 25th, had many a harrowing tale to tell, having barely escaped capture and death several times. The Japanese hunted for them constantly, since the watchers were sending intelligence information on a 24-hour basis.

Quite often these coastwatchers operated from behind enemy lines in coastline caves, or huts hidden in the brush. There is no question the watchers on Guadalcanal saved Allied troops from disaster time after time. They frequently were able to assist in the rescue of downed pilots, in addition to keeping top army and navy "brass" informed on enemy movements. Their network covered thousands of square miles of ocean.

Meanwhile, I was missing Kathy very much and it was agonizing not to know if, or when, I would see her again. As it turned out, I didn't have to mark time in New Caledonia too long, because after three months on the island, orders came for us to report to MacArthur's headquarters in Brisbane, Australia.

The Brisbane headquarters was designated the General Headquarters of the Southwest Pacific Area (GHQSWPA), hereafter referred to as GHQ. Our job there would be to assist war correspondents. Glory be!

At last, I was going to war with one of the most decorated generals in U.S. history. Best of all, I would get to work with famous reporters and experience exciting events in some of the world's most exotic regions; ones I had only read about in books. I was ready to go!

MacArthur's Press Section

Chapter 5

"I am convinced that without press censorship, and with unlimited television, we would have lost World War II. There is nothing that looks quite like blood on color television. You can't have scenes of American bodies, thrown on trucks like cordwood, served up with dinner night after night, and expect the American people to support the situation."

— George Jacobson, *Newsweek*

IT WAS JUST A SHORT FLIGHT from New Caledonia to Brisbane, Australia. What a glorious sight the city was after being virtually isolated for three months in comparative desolation. I was finally getting closer to the war, for better or for worse.

General MacArthur's press staff was composed of about 30 officers at the time his headquarters was located in Australia. As the war progressed into the largely unknown islands to the north and west, the Southwest Pacific theater of war became more active, and battle lines extended farther and farther into the vastness of the region. The meager press staff was being stretched far too thin.

U.S. forces had begun assaults on the southeast tip of New Guinea, and on other isolated islands in the area, and more newspapers were sending reporters over to report the war for "the folks at home." The reason the press section was able to expand so quickly was because our band of "combat correspondents" had arrived overseas and nobody knew what to do with us. The Pentagon had failed to follow through with proper orders to insure the success of the project designed to write battle stories from combat areas.

It was a typical army "snafu," and if you don't know what those letters stand for, ask any old World War II combat soldier who will be glad to explain. Snafus weren't confined just to the Army's coverage of news, either.

All of a sudden, MacArthur discovered he had this group of well-

MacARTHUR'S PRESS SECTION

This is our press group, both officers and non-coms, on board the ship that carried us to islands of adventure in the South Pacific. Little did we know what might lie ahead, or when we'd get home again. I'm second from right in Row 2.

trained reporters and photographers scattered all over the place with various units working, if that is the correct word, on very trivial projects. So it wasn't long until orders came and most of us were on the way to either Brisbane, Australia or Hollandia, New Guinea, where the advance GHQ complex was under construction.

Within weeks, the press staff had swelled to about 45 or 50 officers. Sometimes we were referred to as press staffers, sometimes as press relations people, other times as public relations guys, even press liaison officers. Often, we were referred to in terms I do not find pleasant to recall or repeat.

On occasion we had to act as censors. Newspapermen simply don't like censorship, but most reporters understood the reason for it during the war. Others understood but still did not willingly accept it. There is little doubt in my mind that some important stories were withheld from the public because of this tight censorship. Management of news in wartime has its place, but it can be abused and it was on occasion, particularly when it suited the general's inner circle of command.

Neither Japan nor the Allies liked to report atrocities, so the censors didn't give such stories their stamp of approval. At no time during the war did any Japanese newspaper print stories of atrocities committed by Japanese soldiers. Likewise, I do not recall our censorship people allowing any reports of atrocities by U.S. soldiers to reach U.S. newspapers or radio. Both sides, however, emphasized such incidents by the enemy.

We enjoyed an advantage in this because we could use the brutality of Japanese soldiers to stimulate hate against them, but the Japanese could not contrive stories about our GIs mistreating Japanese prisoners. This was because the Japanese assured its citizens that none of their soldiers ever surrendered to be taken prisoner — they were supposed to die fighting, or commit suicide.

One of Japan's most bizarre weapons was kept under wraps for years. They put into the air nearly 10,000 paper balloons which the trade winds carried across the Pacific to the U.S. The balloons were about 35 feet in diameter, and each carried a small anti-personnel bomb. Some landed in Alaska and Mexico, but several came down in the Midwest.

The balloons created considerable concern and killed at least six people. They stopped coming only after our B-29 raids disrupted Japan's supply of hydrogen gas. Very little about this threat was published until well after the war was over.

The Navy was guilty of suppressing the extent of damage from the Kamikaze suicide planes. These attacks began at Leyte (how well I know), and greatly increased up to and including the battle for Okinawa, where the damage was nearly catastrophic. The Navy finally permitted mention of these attacks, but never the extent of damage.

One nationally-known reporter, Homer Bigart, had covered the war in Europe for *The New York Herald-Tribune,* and won a Pulitzer Prize for his work before coming to the Pacific. He refused to shake hands with anyone he thought had ever censored one line of his copy. He was wary of Army personnel meddling with his copy. He and I got along fine and he was with me on two or three excursions to battle sites.

Bigart was unquestionably one of the best in the business, and felt he was just as intelligent as MacArthur's censors. Further, he believed he was sensible enough, and patriotic enough, not to write anything that would jeopardize a single U.S. soldier. He never did and, besides, who was I to tell him what and how to write?

A censor once told me he was once handed a story to clear from Australia that read: "There was a parade in downtown Brisbane today and the marchers responded smartly to the playing of "Stars and Stripes Forever." The chief censor cut out the reference to the band because "it told the Japanese that American troops were in Australia."

This was absurd reasoning. The Japanese had known about the

presence of U.S. troops there for months. This is just one example of how poor judgement gave wartime censorship a bad rap. Most censors I knew did not enjoy their assignment. It wasn't easy to satisfy anybody. I had been instructed that my job was basically to assist correspondents, not impede their performance. There were numerous times I witnessed censorship and distortion that was absurd, unnecessary and arbitrary. As an example, GHQ once issued a communique to the effect that troops in New Guinea on Christmas Day had performed only routine safety precautions so they could hold "divine services." The truth of the matter was, there were no services.

Soon after arriving in Australia from Bataan, General MacArthur gathered civilian correspondents in his headquarters to present his views on press coverage and censorship. He began by getting up and pacing the floor, which was his style, answering frankly and with openness all the questions he was asked.

Officers who were there (I was still in New Caledonia, twiddling my thumbs) said the general had the press "eating out of his hand" by the time the session concluded. I was told the general's comments commanded such interest the grand entrance of the American ambassador to New Zealand largely went unnoticed. MacArthur talked, or lectured, for an hour and 45 minutes and then abruptly left the room.

Perhaps the most reassuring words he uttered during the meeting were:

"I am an old censor myself. My main purpose will be not to suppress news from you, but to help you get the news."

During his talk, he promised to provide as full disclosure as he could, emphasizing emphatically that in a democracy people must know the truth so they can understand why the nation is involved in war. If they are not informed, he said, they will be more inclined to believe whatever they happen to hear. He did ask the reporters present to be sure they had all the facts before they criticized him or his press staff.

"I am well aware of the value of good press relations," he said.

The record shows when MacArthur was Chief of Staff in Washington, he frequently cut through red tape to insure cooperation between the Army and newsmen. It seems he always managed to secure good relations with most reporters. There were times, however, despite his eloquent and effective style of speaking, when the publicity was not good.

Certainly this was not the fault of many staff members, who would not let a word of criticism about him pass censorship — if they could help it. It was their intent to present him always as an infallible, invincible, error-free general. It appeared those who dealt with him face-to-face on a daily basis had a special mission to "sell" the general to the world. They didn't trust newsmen to interpret the general's remarks and his battlefield strategies correctly or, more likely, to their liking.

On one occasion Colonel LeGrande Diller, who headed the GHQ press section, was somehow moved to issue a photograph of MacArthur and General Eichelberger sitting in a Jeep. The caption read: "Generals MacArthur and Eichelberger at the front in New Guinea."

The photo, in fact, was taken at a training camp in Australia. In a corner of the picture could be seen the radiator of a Packard motor car. Troops in New Guinea had a field day with that one, urging correspondents: "Try and find a Packard on the Kokoda trail."

The decision to popularize the phrase, "I shall return," came from his inner staff. It was not only repeated countless times in news stories, but was printed or stamped on thousands of matchboxes, blotters, buttons and even bars of soap, which were air-dropped on the Philippines. I have one of the matchboxes among my souvenirs.

Some analysts believe MacArthur eventually did grow and mature in his command function to fill the void or image his publicity created for him. I choose not to believe this theory, because long before World War II he was known as an egotist. One wonders why MacArthur was singled out when so many career officers of that era were egotists and tyrants?

Sometimes heated arguments would erupt when worshipping censors refused to pass negative statements in a newsman's story. It was my feeling this attitude on the part of staff caused harm to MacArthur's image. It only resulted in charges in the states that MacArthur was "trying to apply dictatorial powers to the world's press."

It was my impression the general never instructed the staff to provide such image protection, but it simply was not his nature to limit their doting over him. He relished adulation.

Although MacArthur himself told reporters they were free to write whatever they wanted about him, Diller made certain that all criticism was deleted from their stories. Those who meekly permitted this, and often praised the general's leadership in their copy, were repaid with special interviews and tips on what to watch for as the war progressed.

As a result, dispatches from "Somewhere in Australia" often quoted "authoritative military sources" as saying the war could be won more quickly if supplies were diverted from the Central Pacific (Navy) Theater of Operations and sent to the South Pacific. That was true but hardly served the spirit of cooperation between Army and the Navy.

A story made the rounds in the Brisbane press section that the general slid into bed with his wife, Jean, one evening and she said: "God, your feet are cold." Her husband replied: "Dear, you can call me Douglas when we're home alone."

Many dispatches sent from the South Pacific rivaled drama notices. Few reporters could resist the charm and charisma of the general which moved one correspondent to report: "He could talk for hours and never grope for a single word." Others described him as "both a cold-blooded strategist and an impelling, controversial personality." Another wrote: "He considers himself a child of destiny, likes the spotlight, and thereby sets a lot of teeth on edge."

A correspondent sits in rubble to type his story for U.S. readers. This scene was repeated endlessly during the war.

Emphasizing the publicity consciousness of MacArthur, one of his ranking press officers once said that another ranking general in GHQ said to him:" I would prefer to have you put a rattlesnake in my pocket than to have you give me any publicity." I believe most generals in GHQ headquarters realized it did not enhance or advance their careers if they received personal publicity.

Still, MacArthur was highly respected and immensely engaging. In fact, he was normally irresistible, convincing and exhilarating. Some said even if the general wore civilian clothes, most people would know he was a soldier, capable of creating a special presence.

As a civilian newspaperman serving in Army news work during

the war, I was frequently embarrassed by press staff policy. There were times when I was torn between my personal feeling about the free flow of information and obnoxious censorship, and my responsibility as an officer to follow orders.

It seemed to me that GHQ censors intended to depict all Americans as wonderful fellows, and all Japanese devoid of courtesy or compassion. All Filipinos were loyal allies and not one single Japanese PW was ever subjected to torture, and no American officer ever led his troops unnecessarily to certain death.

Thus you never knew about Japanese being tied to trees and tortured to death by guerillas. Or Mindanao guerillas fighting on the side of the Japanese, or the robbing of Japanese corpses by U.S. soldiers for watches, swords, gold teeth and jewelry. Nor did the public know that one of the first acts of the command on Leyte was to set up a brothel. The lines were two blocks long with the MPs allocating five minutes to each man.

I tried to avoid conflict but on occasion I would offer suggestions which, coming from a lowly lieutenant, carried little weight in an office where senior grade officers were a dime a dozen. I know my promotions were jeopardized, one delayed, because of my "inappropriate" comments, made in the interest of giving the public news, which in no way could have adversely effected the outcome of the war or a single soldier.

As an inactive reservist during the Korean "police action," I was called back to active duty. After a few months as The Armored Center's Public Information Officer at Fort Knox, Kentucky, I was again assigned to MacArthur's staff in Tokyo, later being attached to IX Corps in Korea. I presume my record of service wasn't all that bad, or I wouldn't have been assigned to Mac's headquarters a second time.

The Corp press section's CO in Korea was a reserve colonel from Chicago. In civilian life he had been a minor-league opera singer. What he knew about news, briefings, and handling war correspondents, you could stuff in an eardrum. He and I were at odds quite often, and I cringe when I recall him singing operatic arias in his tent night after night. It got to be a joke around headquarters, but he blocked my promotion to major which wasn't funny to me.

I doubt that relations between reporters and the military were ever better than they were right after the start of World War II. The entire nation, including news organizations and reporters, were focused on one goal, the defeat of Germany and Japan. It was a demonstration of patriotic purpose and spirit not likely to ever occur again.

I would be remiss, however, if I did not point out that none of the hundreds of reporters who came through our press section during the war ever deliberately attempted to bypass censorship. Colonel Diller once told us that not one correspondent "had to be sent home" for ignoring censorship that affected security. He did not say "resisted" censorship, for there were numerous times when they had legitimate gripes.

On the other hand, reporting of military operations could be greatly enhanced if correspondents assigned to combat units had some awareness of the conditions they would face in the field, seasoned perhaps from their own past military service or attendance at training sessions arranged by the military. A few correspondents were not emotionally or physically prepared for combat situations and became burdens to the units to which they were assigned.

The military, as well, has a responsibility to teach commanders how to deal with reporters in the field. I know of instances where officers were very nervous about talking with reporters, fearing they would say too much and jeopardize their future in the military. Some commanders felt reporters shouldn't even be there, and could not be trusted, ever. A few hot-shot, ambitious officers actually used reporters to get "lots of ink" and thus improve their image and, presumably, lock up future promotions.

Realistically, the military during wartime needs the media to achieve its goals, and the media cannot perform its mission of information satisfactorily without the military. In a democratic society, the media must be able to "tell it like it is." That may not smell sweet to some arrogant commanders, but eventually the people back home must be given an honest accounting.

It's ironic there exists the notion that the military and the press have little in common. In battle they quickly understand how much alike they are, living dangerously to enhance their respective careers.

Had I known I would ever be writing about my experiences in the war to this extent, I would made some notes. I sent many letters home to Kathy about my work, but somewhere during our several moves they were lost. The information in those letters would have helped me recall many interesting facets of my experience.

A number of correspondents were killed or injured during the Pacific war. I have been told that the casualty rate for them was three times that for soldiers in combat. My memory tells me we lost a number of war correspondents during the fighting in the Pacific but I can recall only a few.

I certainly remember Ernie Pyle, the shy, bald idol of GIs, who made history with his front-line reports from Europe. Pyle came through our headquarters in Manila just prior to his leaving for Okinawa.

His career ended on the small island of Ii Shima with the 77th Infantry Division. A Japanese machine gun opened fire and everybody went into a ditch beside the road. Pyle raised his head to see if anyone had been hit, and three bullets hit him in the right temple.

Pyle was the star reporter for the infantry. "I love them," he once said, "because they are the underdogs. There is an agony in your heart and you almost feel ashamed to look at them. They are boys from everywhere but you might not remember them. They are too far away now."

Pyle missed death by inches at Anzio in Italy, a place he called Shell Alley. In Naples he survived artillery fire which killed three other reporters. Hitting the beach on D-Day he wrote: "I think our chances are very good."

After ten days under fire, he confessed: "I'm so sick of living in misery and fright." He knew better than most what war was really like. He was my favorite war correspondent, despite being in Europe most of the war.

I recall John Cashman, reporter for *International News Service,* who had a burning desire to experience a bombing run over Japan for a personal account of what it was like. He received permission from GHQ and headed for an airstrip on Okinawa. The plane he boarded, loaded with bombs, crashed on takeoff and Cashman was killed. I had become acquainted with him during the battle of Zig-Zag Pass on Bataan.

There was an incident in Manila before I arrived there, involving a Filipino reporter who, with some other newsmen, had taken refuge in a building since the street fighting was still raging. A tremendous explosion ripped through the building. The source of the blast was a mystery. It could have been an older bomb or an artillery shell that suddenly detonated.

The blast's concussion stunned those inside. Damage was considerable and the room they occupied was in shambles. The dust made it impossible to see much of anything. Rescuers made their way inside, where it became obvious the bomb had been very destructive. Somebody shouted: "Everybody okay in there?"

Other reporters indicated they were relatively unhurt, but the Filipino cried out: "I think I'm hurt. I'm standing in some kind of a hole and can't get out."

At that point, other army personnel had reached the building and came in to assist. One produced a flashlight and its beam focused on the reporter in trouble. He was not in a hole as he had thought. The bomb had taken off both his legs and he was trying to move on the bloody stumps. He died of his wounds. For the life of me, I cannot recall his name, nor can I find any record of this incident anywhere.

There was an incident involving the late John De Passos. He came into the area as a reporter for *Life* magazine. While in the Philippines he was involved in a rather odd accident. He was strolling along the beach when he accidentally wandered onto a small airstrip used for the small L5 observation planes. He was nearsighted and failed to see the Piper Cub aircraft taking off. His hearing wasn't so good, either.

A wing tip struck him on the forehead and left quite a cut. He also had a swollen eye for several days. He could have been killed but ended up more embarrassed than anything else.

There was a famous personality on our press staff. He was Colonel Phil LaFollette, who had been governor of Wisconsin three times and was a member of a prominent political family. He became second in command of our group and was said to be greatly admired by General MacArthur and Colonel Diller. This view was not shared by everybody; many wondered how this man even qualified for his position. Most of us figured it was Republican politics.

On one early island invasion, LaFollette was the escorting officer for a group of correspondents. They had given him their stories for delivery to GHQ for censorship. One writer even gave him his typewriter. Somehow the colonel slipped between two boats and lost all the copy and the typewriter. From then on, his official name was "Fumbling Phil" but not when Diller was in earshot.

One of my associates in GHQ was Selwyn Pepper, who, before and after the war, was on the staff of *The St. Louis Post-Dispatch*. He had a personal and disturbing encounter with LaFollette. In early 1944, one of MacArthur's many targets was the small island of Biak, north of New Guinea.

By the third day of the fighting, communiques issued by GHQ, drawn from intelligence reports from the field and written by Diller and LaFollette, made it appear that Japanese opposition had all but ceased and that our forces were in full control.

Associated Press reporter Spencer Davis witnessed the battle. He returned to the press camp at Port Moresby with a full account. He turned in his story to Pepper, who was serving as a censor. It was 2 a.m. and Pepper realized at once that Davis' account went well beyond the official communiques in telling the truth about just how fierce the fighting was.

Captain Pepper, in a post-war news story in *The Post-Dispatch* wrote that he felt, as a newspaperman in uniform, the American people deserved an accurate account from a reliable witness. Pepper says he didn't wake Diller to consult with him about the story, but instead put his No. 28 GHQ stamp on it and handed it to the cable operator for transmission to the States.

The next day, Davis' story was displayed in newspapers all over the country, and he received cable congratulations for his story. Then an investigation began in the press office and Diller and LaFollette found that Pepper had approved the story.

Not one word was ever said to him about it, but later Diller awarded Bronze Stars for meritorious service to everyone who had served on the press staff for two years or more. Pepper did not receive a medal. It was his punishment for passing the Davis account of the Biak fighting.

Another mutual friend, Major Jack Cross, told LaFollette that if Pepper didn't get one, he didn't want his either. Others joined in, and the rebellion succeeded. Pepper later pointed out the Bronze Star is usually given either for bravery or meritorious service.

"None of us could claim bravery," Pepper said.

It was true the Bronze Star was often called "the officers' good conduct medal." Later, on Corregidor, I received this medal for valor and I was pleased the recommendation for it came from civilian war correspondents who believed I had risked my life to help them. Actually, I was more scared than brave, and ran headlong down a dock at Corregidor with a reporter to avoid becoming a casualty.

Pepper retired from the newspaper in 1982 and still lives in St. Louis as far as I know. He has a daughter currently on the staff of *The Kansas City Star*.

Novelist Richard Powell, a member of the press staff, began writing another book while he was overseas. As a lieutenant colonel he was my immediate superior but I can't recall ever getting a direct order from him, except a dumb one at the surrender ceremony. Since the war, Powell has written two dozen novels and five have been made into movies. "It's terrible to be rich," he says. Yea!

Another officer on the staff worth mentioning was Lt. Sanford Terry, who was decorated for communications work. Terry was the mastermind of a 100,000 watt radio ship which brought the news of the Leyte landing directly to the States from Leyte Gulf. He was aboard the 55-year-old converted army transport ship Apache for the Philippines D-Day assault. At that time only about 50 radio stations in the U.S. had more power.

Terry planned, begged, borrowed and sweated out the old ship's conversion. He stole the equipment required on a rush-rush basis to have it ready for MacArthur's long-awaited return to the Philippines. He scrounged it and everything was ready on time. At last report he was alive and well in Richmond, Virginia, following a distinguished career in developing FM and television stations.

I had the pleasure of assisting a reporter for *The Kansas City Star*, Ira McCarty, who was in the Pacific Theater several months. Ira had been a top political writer for the paper and he sent back some excellent stories from our region.

It was a real pleasure for me to aid Ira, because he was one of several reporters on *The Star*, who had been considerate and helpful to me in my early days on that newspaper.

Cruise Palmer was another *Star* staffer I was able to befriend. He was a Naval officer who, for some reason, had lost all his clothing and personal effects. I found him wandering around our headquarters area in New Guinea and, after exchanging greetings and news from home, took him to our supply sergeant. There he received new clothing and the basic necessities of life until he could get back with his unit.

I cannot recall the names of all the reporters I worked with in the Pacific, but some are forever imbedded in my memory. They were the ones who, like Ernie Pyle, got their stories first-hand, "up there" with the infantry, armor and artillery units, facing the enemy. Some accredited correspondents wrote their dispatches from GHQ handouts and spend much of their time in the nearest tent or town, guzzling beer or booze, or both, seeking out pleasures of the flesh.

I have always told people I received my college education during World War II. I feel indebted to the Army for the opportunity it provided to learn my craft and gain respect and credibility from my peers. My education, such as it was, came from reporters who wanted to tell it like it was, and went there to get it. They were an inspiration to me. My honor roll includes James Hutchinson, Frazier Hunt, H. R. Knickerbocker, Clark Lee, Howard D. Quigg, Frank Roberts, Ralph Teatsworth, Richard Tucker, Theodore White, Howard Handleman, Homer Bigert, Stan Troutman, Frank Kluckhohn, Richard Harris, Bob Shapler, Dick Tregaskis, Russell Brines, Frank Kelly, Bill Dickinson, Ira McCarty, Merlin Spencer, Fred Hampson, Frank Hewlett, Yates McDaniel and a few others whose names I wish I could recall.

My time with MacArthur's press staff was well spent. It bolstered my pride and self-esteem, and increased my fascination with the printed word. The only gripe I had is that those assigned to GHQ headquarters received promotions with regularity. Those of us assigned to corps or division headquarters for escorting reporters on invasions, remaining in the field for lengthy periods, were often forgotten.

I suppose I did fairly well going from buck private to captain, but I discovered it was easier to "brown nose" promotions in headquarters than it to be on detached service with a combat outfit on some God-forsaken island. More positively, today I understand that had I not been fortunate enough to have been assigned to GHQ in the first place, I likely would have missed the greatest adventure of my life.

Plus, a priceless education in news work.

MacArthur, One-of-a-Kind

Chapter 6

"The soldier, above all men, is required to practice the greatest act of religious training — sacrifice. In battle and in the face of danger and death, he discloses those attributes which his Maker gave when He created man in His own image. No physical courage and no brute instinct can take the place of Divine help which alone can sustain him. However horrible the incidents of war may be, the soldier who is called upon to offer and give his life for his country is the noblest development of mankind."

— **General Douglas MacArthur**

IT NEVER FAILS. Once somebody learns I was a member of General Douglas MacArthur's press staff during World War II, they inevitably ask the question: "Were you required to embellish the general's ego and image?"

"No I wasn't. It wasn't necessary," is my carved-in-stone reply. "The old boy handled that pretty well himself."

No one was more surprised than I when, due to an administrative snafu on my original overseas assignment, I wound up on the press liaison staff of General MacArthur. As it turned out, this assignment introduced me to some of the most gripping, interesting and educational adventures of my life.

It proved to be an opportunity for both rare excitement and service to my country. I wouldn't have missed it for the world!

Not that I had not already been involved in Army news work, but to serve under one of the most honored and controversial generals in U.S. history was beyond my wildest dreams. An added and most beneficial plus for me was an opportunity to assist, and observe first-hand, the work of some of the finest war correspondents in the annals of newspaper history.

And when I say served "under" MacArthur, I echo the quote of former Secretary of Defense Caspar Weinberger, who spoke at the rededication of the Battleship USS Missouri held in San Francisco in May, 1986. Kathy and I were fortunate enough to have been invited by the Navy to that unique ceremony.

In the speech Weinberger delivered there, the one-time GHQ first lieutenant mentioned he had also served "under" MacArthur but hastily added "way under." Thus it was with me. The general may have not even known I was on the press staff roster.

I joined the GHQ press staff early in April 1944, at the time the main headquarters was being moved from Brisbane, Australia, to newly conquered territory along the northern coast of New Guinea. Even as fighting progressed in areas in and around New Guinea, and not far from Hollandia, construction on a new headquarters complex was begun.

The headquarters occupied a slope of a 6,000 foot mountain, overlooking Lake Sentani, dotted with cone-shaped green islands with native houses on stilts crowding the shoreline. There was a backdrop of peaks and deep ravines covered with jungle growth and tropical blossoms. Deadly scenery to be sure, but unquestionably lovely.

MacArthur's own quarters were quite impressive, but hardly overdone for the top general in the Southwest Pacific. It consisted of three pre-fab buildings joined together with furnishings flown up from Brisbane, the architecture reflecting the tropical environment in which it was situated. There was an abundance of natural light, numerous open spaces with high ceilings so typical of humid climates.

The building was the creation of the general's adoring inner circle. MacArthur never requested such lavish surroundings for a temporary headquarters and, as a matter of fact, he spent relatively little time there.

A few correspondents wrote stories hinting of the excesses involved in placing GHQ headquarters on such a high hill, actually a small mountain, requiring extensive clearing of the site. It was a massive earth-moving project to construct the hairpin curved road that led from the bay up to the headquarters complex.

The reporters' criticism made barely a ripple and was hardly noted even by the headquarters hierarchy. It was war, and most people assumed MacArthur had ordered this elaborate structure because of a need for it. This just wasn't true. The general's inner staff never missed an opportunity to stroke the general's ego. To them, he was a king.

GHQ had been in Brisbane since early in 1942, when Bataan defenses collapsed and Corregidor Island was under siege. Facing a hopeless situation, President Franklin Roosevelt ordered MacArthur back to Australia because he did not want the general to be killed or captured by the Japanese.

This decision was not likely based upon personal admiration for MacArthur but rather because Roosevelt feared a barrage of unfavorable public reaction if he did otherwise. The general was very popular in the United States at the time and entrenched politicians were not inclined to boost his popularity because there had been some evidence of a "MacArthur for President" movement.

Contrary to some accounts, MacArthur did not want to leave Corregidor and even considered resisting the order. Actually, the general was very reluctant to abandon the cause, but eventually was convinced of how hopeless the situation had become. It was with great reluctance and sadness he agreed to leave, after having resigned himself to dying on the island.

In fact, MacArthur, back in February, had sent a footlocker full of personal things to a Washington, D.C. bank for safekeeping. Included were his medals, his son's baptismal certificate, some stocks and bonds, the MacArthur's wedding certificate, wills, and some clippings his wife, Jean, had collected from newspapers.

MacArthur, speaking to General Jonathan Wainwright on March 10, 1942, said:

"Jonathan, I want you to understand my position very plainly. I'm leaving for Australia pursuant to repeated orders from the President. Things have gotten to such a point that I must comply with these orders or resign from the army. I want you to make it known throughout all elements of your command that I am leaving over my repeated protests."

Instead of waiting for a submarine which was scheduled to reach Corregidor by March 15, by which time the Japanese might well have set up a blockade, the general decided to head for Mindanao by PT boat. There he would transfer to B-17 bombers for the remainder of the journey. Four boats were assigned for the perilous journey.

There were 21 persons to be transported including the general, his wife and son, Arthur, and a nurse for the child. In addition, key members of his staff including Lt. Colonel LaGrande Diller, his public relations officer and later my commanding officer in the South Pacific, were aboard when the boats departed.

The general gave General Wainwright a box of cigars and two jars

PARA(GRAPH) TROOPER FOR MacARTHUR

Douglas MacArthur was controversial, and you either liked him or you couldn't stand him. Yet no other general in U.S. history equalled his record of military achievement. This photo was taken before he received five-star rank.

of shaving cream and tried to appear cheerful:

"If I get through to Australia, you know I'll come back as soon as I can with as much as I can. In the meantime, hold on as long as you can."

On March 12, as darkness settled in over the island, the group left with meager possessions and limited rations. The PT boat commander, John Bulkeley, idled away from shore as quietly as he could with the boat's powerful 4,050 horsepower Packard engines barely in check for security's sake. The general, as senior commander, was the last to board and he did so reluctantly after stalking up and down the dock, scanning the horizon.

Two hours later they had cleared the mine fields and headed for Mindanao, reaching there on the 14th. Of four B-17s dispatched to carry them to Australia, one had crashed and two failed to arrive. MacArthur refused to fly in the fourth - and who could blame him.

Incensed, the general radioed Washington for safe and reliable aircraft and experienced crews, which were quickly made available, and the journey was resumed.

General Wainwright was left to salvage what he could from his rag-tag, ailing forces, and to await the inevitable Japanese invasion and ultimate surrender of U.S. Forces there. By the time the surrender came, Wainwright's garrison was suffering intolerable conditions involving lack of food, medicine, ammunition and other supplies. The garrison had been under intense bombardment for weeks.

Later, MacArthur made the comment:

"I was the leader of a lost cause, and from the bottom of my heart I pray that a merciful God may not long delay their redemption."

When the general received word that Bataan and Corregidor had fallen into enemy hands, he issued a statement from Australia:
"The Bataan force went out as it would have wished, fighting to the end its flickering forlorn hope. No army has ever done so much with so little, and nothing became it more than its last hour of trial and agony. To the weeping mothers of its dead, I can only say the sacrifice and halo of Jesus of Nazareth had descended upon their sons, and that God will take them unto himself.
"Corregidor needs no statement from me. It has sounded its own story at the mouth of its guns. It has scrolled its own epitaph on enemy tablets. But through the bloody haze of its last reverberating shot, I shall always seem to see a vision of grim, gaunt, ghastly men, still unafraid."

It was a typical bit of prose from MacArthur, reflecting his faith and, in my opinion, a sincere demonstration of his personal grief and concern for those he had been ordered to leave behind.

Bataan and Corregidor became an obsession with him, and he maintained a constant desire for revenge. Each time his headquarters moved forward, he named it Bataan. His personal plane was also named Bataan and it was that plane the press followed as we landed in Japan following the cessation of hostilities.

After the difficult victory at Buna in New Guinea, the general was heard to say:

"The dead of Bataan will rest easier tonight."

This brilliant defense of the Philippines by poorly equipped U.S. and Filipino forces will always be considered a magnificent defeat but not, of course, by MacArthur haters or detractors.

The anger within him, which reached scorching bitterness at times, was based on his belief that his own leaders in Washington had let him down by failing to provide men and material to assist the stubborn defense of his command. His feelings were understandable, but the reality was a decision had already been made in Washington that the war in Europe would have priority.

Unfortunately, on MacArthur's arrival in Australia, newspapers gave the impression that Roosevelt had given him command of a mighty army to drive the Japanese out of the South Pacific.

The facts were different. There was no mighty army. The air force consisted of a few battered planes with war-weary crews. Of the 11 Australian divisions, less than three were effective, only one was approaching combat readiness, and the balance were militia units. The Royal Australian Air Force had little but obsolete aircraft and was short of engines and spare parts.

The Australian Navy did not have a single aircraft carrier. In short, as MacArthur reported to President Roosevelt on May 8, 1942:

"At this time, there are present all the elements to produce another disaster."

MacArthur's command at that time included Australia, the 1,500-mile-long island of New Guinea, the Philippines, the Dutch East Indies, Borneo and the Malay Peninsula. He would not receive his first American infantry division until April 1942, and his air force was not created until the following September.

Those fighting in the Southwest Pacific would have to get along with whatever Washington felt they could spare. The result was Allied and American troops in the South Pacific fought for months with one hand tied behind their backs. It did not help morale. Infantry soldiers in most units were never issued the new carbine rifles which were particularly suited to jungle warfare,

For months there never were sufficient small boats on hand to carry out assault landing operations. In many instances, boats were purchased or confiscated from natives or settlers, or wherever they might be found.

The Joint Chiefs gave the general staggering goals, but he was given pitiful little with which to reach them. At no time was the Southwest Pacific allocated more than 15 percent of the war effort. I was told that when U.S. troops invaded Africa, Eisenhower was provided fifteen tons of supplies per man. MacArthur received five tons per man.

Even worse, during the first year of the fighting in Italy, American supplies to needy civilians there were about equal to all the shipments sent to MacArthur that year. Our State Department was quite proud of this, but their message was poorly received by soldiers in the South Pacific

MacArthur summed up his military philosophy this way:

"It doesn't matter how much you have so long as you fight with what you have. It doesn't matter where you fight as long as you fight. Because where you fight, the enemy has to fight too, and even though it splits your force, it must split his force also. So fight on, whatever the scale, wherever and whenever you can. There is only one way to win victories. Attack, attack, attack!"

Another factor in the war in the Pacific was the intense rivalry between the Army and Navy "brass" over strategy. The biggest point of argument was over the "path" to victory. The Navy wanted to bypass the Philippines and attack Formosa, while MacArthur held firm on honoring his promise to the Filipinos.

His vow: "I shall return," was a personal commitment he would not barter. He persevered and the Navy reluctantly gave in, but the issue remained a festering sore throughout the war.

One can understand the Navy's reasons for challenging the general. The Pacific Theater was nearly all water and, as history shows, was largely an amphibious operation. So in the Navy's eyes it should have been directed by the Navy and its admirals. In addition, the Navy felt it was under a cloud from the Pearl Harbor disaster and anxious to achieve redemption.

For all his purported flaws, no other general in all history did so much with so little. At the general's death in April 1964, even former President Harry S. Truman, who fired him during the Korean War, had this to say:

"I am deeply sorry at the passing of General Douglas MacArthur, who has given of himself with exceptional strength and valor and will be remembered as one of the great military men in our history."

I think highly of Mr. Truman as well, but I have always found it hard to accept the abruptness and lack of respect with which Truman brought an end to MacArthur's long and distinguished career. There is no question in my mind the general had, not unknowingly, intruded into political decisions affecting the conduct of the Korean "police action," which was not his prerogative.

In view of MacArthur's service to his country, however, I felt his shabby, abrupt banishment from the Army could have been handled more appropriately, with a bit more dignity, in recognition of his achievements and stature.

After all, he was first in his class at West Point, setting new records for academic achievement. He was the youngest brigadier general in World War I, the youngest superintendent in the history of West Point, the youngest major general, the first field marshal of a foreign nation, the Philippines, and the only American officer to serve as a general in three wars.

I was personally thrilled to be working for the general, even in such a minor position. I saw him in person numerous times during the war. He was always present to view the assault landings and usually went ashore shortly thereafter. I saw him, of course, at the surrender ceremony and at a distance several times in Tokyo after the war.

He was very loyal to those around him. He never released a member of his staff for making a mistake; he took the blame. But if a commander in the field made a serious command error, he was booted out. One thing he could not tolerate was disloyalty, and he could never hurt an old friend. Perhaps that's why he kept some old timber around who actually caused him to be misunderstood and embarrassed from time to time.

Some detractors spread stories that MacArthur wouldn't take advice. Others said his staff was filled with "yes" men. Neither was apparently true if one can believe the stories I heard from those who should have known. I know personally he asked for and received advice from Colonel LeGrande Diller, who headed the press relations staff all through the war.

I have heard many people speak about General MacArthur, not always favorably. It was a case of either like or dislike; there was no in between, but there was much to like and admire about him. He was

President Sergio Osmena of the Philippines reads the headline good news in his office at Malacanan Palace in Manila. Note the photo of President Harry S. Truman on his desk.

dashing, handsome, eloquent, and a brilliant soldier. He did have a tendency toward showmanship and, I think, a sense of the role he was playing in history.

In nearly every military operation in the South Pacific, MacArthur was habitually near the front. His continual exposure to enemy view, and fire, was a constant source of worry and concern to his staff. On one occasion when he endangered himself to enemy fire, his G-2 (intelligence officer) remonstrated to him about appearing on the front lines. The general replied:

"Thanks, Charlie, but I can't fight 'em if I can't see 'em."

When he appeared before his troops, he wasn't nearly as flamboyant as General George Patton, who featured boots and breeches with inlaid pearl pistols at his side. It was never his intention to portray a "gung-ho" figure, yet he was treated with great awe and respect in the field. The lowest in the ranks could appreciate the difference between oratory and bombast.

And that's not to take anything away from General Patton who, because of my service in the horse cavalry and the armored forces, was my favorite field general of the war. If you wanted excitement, he could supply it. Patton was not a political personality in the manner of, say, Dwight Eisenhower, and it was never Patton's goal to become one.

MacArthur never over-dressed. He always wore a plain khaki uniform with his shirt open at the neck, with freshly - pressed trousers. He never wore his medals, only the stars on his shoulder, and that rumpled cap with all the "fruit salad" on it. He nearly always had a corncob pipe around someplace, and now and then one might see him with a swagger stick, a carry over from the glory days of World War I.

MacArthur had a sense of drama which made him "noticeable." At the surrender ceremony on the USS Missouri, he was the center of attraction, standing very erect behind the table upon which the documents were signed, his field marshal's cap at a rakish angle. His over-emphasized gestures toward the Japanese dignitaries as he directed them to sign the document, spoke more loudly than words and left little doubt in anyone's mind who the victor of the war was.

To many people, he appeared friendly but aloof. He displayed those traits at West Point. He was popular but never "one of the boys." He was held in esteem for his academic brilliance but appeared to lack intimacy with most of his classmates and, later, his fellow officers. He was not a back-slapper but was highly disciplined, always.

While not over-zealous, everybody who knew him well understood he would do his duty. He accepted responsibility, was very determined, and had unbridled zeal for excellence. His classmates appeared to understand that down the line, MacArthur was destined for greatness. How perceptive they were.

Perhaps no other general in our history could speak as eloquently as he. Some of the phrases he coined remain classics: "Only those are fit to live who are not afraid to die for their country." Once when he came across the body of an American soldier killed in action on Leyte, he proclaimed: "I do not know the dignity of his birth, but I do know the glory of his death."

One of the first things MacArthur did when he arrived in Manila in 1945 was to go to the army hospital where some of the rescued veterans of Bataan and Corregidor were being treated.

"These are my own men," he said, "and I am one of them. I owe them a lot. I promised I would return, and I'm long overdue."

As he went down the line of beds, he stopped at each one. Tears appeared on the faces of these unfortunate GIs who had suffered beat-

The general gets the big news, but was less than pleased when Russia entered the war just before it ended, and the USSR began scrambling for political advantage.

ings, malnutrition and disease.

"I tried to get here as soon as I could," he told them. "I am going to see that you get all the medical attention America can provide. Then you're going home."

Some of his statements were almost theatrical, made with wild gestures, striding back and forth, rippling the air with oratory concerning God, the flag and country. He spoke as if possessed with such assurance that listeners felt that, indeed, here was a man who believes what he is saying. Few people who knew MacArthur doubted his sincerity.

General Dwight D. Eisenhower, who was likely the most effective politician the Army ever had, had this to say about MacArthur:

"I don't think he ever had a conscious egotism. He has a tremendous amount of self-confidence and he's damned able; there's no mistake about that. I would never be party to criticism of General MacArthur."

Yet on another occasion, Eisenhower had this to say: "I studied theatrics under MacArthur for 12 years." This was a rather spiteful comment.

I believe the general's greatest speech was the one he gave to West Point cadets following his dismissal from service and prior to his final retirement. It was a masterful piece of work. Its theme, "Duty, Honor, Country," will ring in the hearts of patriotic Americans for generations to come.

As for his personal courage, the record is clear. Time after time during the war, he took risks even to the point of being foolhardy. At the beginning of the battle for Corregidor, he had his headquarters on a hill above Malinta tunnel with the flag flying in front of it. His staff became concerned and asked if the flag could be lowered. He replied:

"Take every precaution, but keep the flag flying."

On Leyte, I saw him endanger himself during an enemy bombing raid. Everyone else, including me, took cover. The general remained erect, using binoculars to search out Japanese gun positions. When most of the men saw this they began climbing out of their foxholes, perhaps a little embarrassed although they had done the sensible thing.

His philosophy seemed to be that when it is your time to die, you will die.

"The bullet meant for me has not yet been cast," he would say.

MacArthur's bravery in combat is a part of American history from the time he received his commission. If he had been forced to wear all his medals, including the Medal of Honor (which his father, Arthur MacArthur, also won), he could have hardly walked. No other officer in American history won as many decorations as Douglas MacArthur.

The great respect MacArthur had for demonstrated courage was made clear in remarks he made to a soldier who had just been awarded the Congressional Medal of Honor:

"Of all military attributes, the one that arouses the greatest admiration is courage."

The assault force for recapturing the Philippines in 1944 was huge. The fleet exceeded 600 ships with 200 million tons of supplies and equipment. As the force prepared for the landings, MacArthur stood at the rail of the command ship, getting an overview of this great armada that stretched across the sea as far as the eye could see.

"General," his aide, General Courtney Whitney, said: "It must give you a sense of great power to have such an assault force under your command."

"No, Court", MacArthur replied, "it doesn't. I cannot escape the thought of all those fine American boys who will die on those beaches tomorrow morning."

Cardinal Spelman once said of MacArthur:

"Despite his intellectual abilities, he was characterized by directness and simplicity. He will always stand as a towering symbol of what it means to be a loyal American."

I remain very proud of my service under MacArthur's command. The nation, unfortunately, is running out of men of such character and devotion to duty in the service of their country. The nation could use a few today.

New Guinea Jungles

Chapter 7

"We call Japanese soldiers fanatics when they die rather than surrender, whereas American soldiers who do the same thing are called heroes."

               Robert M. Hutchins

I REACHED HOLLANDIA via a C-46 transport plane from Brisbane, and it was a very rough and scary ride. As the plane bounced and fluttered over jungle-covered Papua New Guinea, I thought sure we would go down a time or two and I asked the struggling pilot what the score was. He yelled back:

"Don't worry. I'm worrying. There's no sense in both of us worrying about it. This old heap will get us there."

I hoped he wasn't kidding. Before long we touched down on an airstrip still under construction and it was a bumpy landing. My personal introduction to New Guinea was a heck of a lot better than that accorded those who arrived in that remote region of the world earlier to thwart Japan's plan to take over Australia.

My arrival there, however, was not without a degree of unpleasantness. When I climbed down out of the truck that brought me from the airstrip into my bivouac area, I discovered my luggage was missing. I was devastated. I lost everything I had except the clothes on my back. I asked some other soldiers in the truck if they could see my luggage. They said it wasn't there.

I was aware, of course, I could replace the clothing and personal items. What I couldn't replace, however, was my favorite picture of Kathy, and that distressed me greatly. After the truck had departed, I became angry with myself when I finally realized that I had probably been intimidated by the other guys on the truck who knew a "90-day Wonder" when they saw one.

I finally figured it out. My bag wasn't really lost, but was now plunder being divided up by some American soldiers who considered their prank just plain fun. I had no way of knowing who was responsible, but I never forgave them for the loss of Kathy's picture.

I made a hurried visit to a nearby supply depot and was re-supplied the necessities to carry me until I checked in to the new GHQ Advance Headquarters at Hollandia.

Hollandia boasted little prominence before the war. At one time, it was the center of trade for bird-of-paradise feathers, but such commerce had diminished before the war began. The government had promoted colonization and agriculture there but labor problems and tropical diseases resulted in these ventures being abandoned by 1937.

The town had never been more than a cluster of bars, supply stores and a rag-tag hotel or two, inhabited by the riff-raff of the region. The natives did most of the hard work, tourism to the region hadn't been invented.

Hollandia was attractive to the military, however, because of its anchorages in a sheltered bay and the ability to load and unload several ships at the same time. It became a staging area for several subsequent landing operations to the north and west. In a matter of weeks it became a community of over 50,000 support troops, and a busy base for Army, Navy, and Marine personnel.

While still in New Caledonia, we had heard of terrible combat conditions and tough Japanese resistance in New Guinea. The Allied offensive had earlier been directed from an advance combat center set up on the southern shores of the island at Port Moresby. As the battles moved north and west, so did the logistical and combat commands.

MacArthur's strategy sent troops to strange and exotic islands and coastal regions. The place names read like an explorer's log: Bouginville, Finchhafen, Salamaua, Itapi, New Britain, the Admiralty Islands, New Ireland, the Solomon Islands, Vella LaVella, New Georgia, Wewak, and other far-off places, hardly common topics of conversation to most Americans.

Before the war, these dots on the map were known only to traders, expedition leaders, bar-bums, and a few miners. The war had re-introduced geography for millions of Americans, most of whom probably didn't even own an atlas. If they had, they would have known that Papua's most prominent feature was a razor-back range of high mountains that stretched down the peninsula like the vertebrae of a pre-historic monster.

New Guinea was a hellish place. It is a region of heavy rainfall, with some areas recording as much as 200 to 300 inches a year. This quagmire of muck, insects, disease, jungle and torrential rain was a military nightmare. I don't believe God ever intended such a harsh, punishing landscape to be used as a battleground by human beings.

There were 10,000-foot saw-toothed mountains covered with forest, flat, malarial coastal areas, but mostly matted jungle, coconut trees, mangrove swampland and patches of high, razor-sharp kunai grass. It was easy to get lost in this maze of vegetation and some soldiers did, indeed, get lost. Little light penetrated the swamps and the clumps of bamboo and palm trees. Sometimes the trails were covered with knee-deep slop formed by too much rain and rotting debris.

These posters were plastered everywhere to remind soldiers to take their Atabrine pills as protection against malaria and other diseases.

One soldier was apparently carried away from his guard post by a giant crocodile. You could see its tracks, and we found the remains of the soldier alongside a small river in tall grass, eight feet high. The air reeked with terrible odors.

The humidity sapped one's energy, and near the rivers the fringes of lush growth become interwoven with vines to form an almost solid mass of vegetation that had to be cut with a machete to pass through. The troops here had to battle two enemies: the Japanese and the jungle. Both were tenacious and unforgiving.

It was in New Guinea that I was introduced to Atabrine, a synthetic drug to prevent malaria and other tropical ailments. Signs were posted all over the camp areas, warning everyone to take a pill a day. In some combat units, the men would have to line up each morning and pass in front of their sergeant who would toss an atabrine pill into their open mouths and make sure it was swallowed.

Quinine was the preferable drug for malaria, but the Japanese expansion in the South Pacific cut off the supply for Allied troops. Some soldiers could not be convinced of the importance of atabrine, or the danger of contracting malaria, and many became seriously ill. Some died of it. Other medical problems involved cholera, typhoid, encephalitis and trench foot, made famous by the trench warfare in World War I.

New Guinea made famous another malady during World War II. It was those terrible tropical ulcers that constantly formed on your feet, stomach, chest and armpits, and which became known as "jungle rot." Waving away the constant irritation of the everyday swarms of flies and mosquitoes became known as the "New Guinea Salute."

Unless you experienced it, you cannot imagine how savage the mosquito attacks were. They would all of a sudden swarm over an entire company of soldiers. They were not easily discouraged and would bite through clothing. Insect repellant, when available, was the only real protection the troops had. For every soldier who was wounded by gunfire, there were five put out of action by insect bites or a tropical illness.

There is no way to describe how difficult life was for Australian and U.S. troops. Their mission was to go from Port Moresby, over the Owen Stanley Range via ancient trails, to reach the Buna area on the north shore. At one point, the trail rises 6,000 feet in less than 20 miles and the soil in the valleys could be 20 feet thick with humus and leaf mold.

While this trek was going on, other Allied forces were working their way up the northwest coast of New Guinea. Their objectives were Buna, the village of Gona, and between them, Sanananda Point. Every action was targeted toward the capture of these villages and the construction of a military base at Hollandia.

Fifteen thousand Japanese soldiers died in defending Sanananda, but it was described in a MacArthur communique as a "mopping-up" operation. General Robert E. Eichelberger, commanding the forces there, took issue with the communique, saying it was "disconcerting" in view of the danger and casualties involved in the victory.

Eichelberger later wrote: "If there is another war, I recommend that the military, and the reporters, and everyone else involved, drop the phrase 'mopping up' from their vocabularies. It is not a good enough phrase to die for."

There were three major objectives overall: encirclement of the enemy stronghold at Rabaul, New Britain, tighter control of enemy movement throughout the Bismarck Archipelago and, most of all, boosting MacArthur's promise of returning to the Philippines. It was all part of the high command's strategy of "island hopping."

The general considered his strategy sound. It was its flexibility that captured his imagination. He deployed sufficient troops to make an impact and draw out enemy defenders; few enough so we could withdraw if the response was overwhelming, but in sufficient strength to hold until reinforcements arrived should enemy response prove ineffective.

It was this theory of island hopping that worried Washington. The Joint Chiefs of Staff worried about the thousands of Japanese who were being by-passed and thus *behind* MacArthur's line of advance. The general's reply to the Pentagon emphasized the saving of lives and minimizing casualties:

"The enemy garrisons which have been by-passed in the Solomons and New Guinea represent no menace to present or future operations. Their capacity for organized offensive effort has passed. The various processes of attrition will eventually account for their final disposition.

"The actual time of their destruction is of little or no importance, and their influence as a contributing factor of war is already negligible. The actual process of their immediate destruction by assault methods *would unquestionably involve heavy loss of life, without adequate compensating strategic advantages.*"

MacArthur had a difficult, if good, reason for subjecting troops to the horrors of New Guinea. He needed to push the Japanese back and, at the same time, cut their supply lines. It wasn't easy. No other area of the world presented as many military obstacles as did this mountainous and jungle-covered island.

While most of us had what was considered standard equipment at that time, much of it proved unsuitable for this daunting region. Radio equipment, so vital in dense forests and swampy territory, had not been designed for such a hostile, humid climate and could not always be depended on.

Early battles in New Guinea and the Solomons proved to be a testing ground for military equipment, and that proved a godsend to those who arrived later. In that climate it did not take long to discover weaknesses or flaws in clothing, medicines, ammunition, foods and all other equipment. My boots rotted off my feet in less than a month, but it was even worse for the soldiers who had to stay in the jungle for weeks at a time.

On my arrival there, I discovered that the first units battling the Japanese, had been given none of the specialized apparel which later became standard for jungle operations. Their clothing, camouflage-dyed for concealment, caused great discomfort. The terrible heat caused the dye to run and the residue blocked the cloth fibers and made them nonporous.

Lieutenant Colonel Robert Darwin Suffcliff, commanding an Australian infantry battalion, had this to say: "If those idiots who ordered these outfits had to wear them in this jungle, we'd quickly get some decent duds."

This clothing became unbearable to wear in the intense heat and caused painful body ulcers. Although the Army was aware these units were to become engaged in tropical warfare, few men had been issued either insect repellant or machetes to hack through the dense undergrowth. Perhaps this could not be helped due to the special requirements of jungle warfare, and the emphasis on the European front.

No one had thought to issue our troops waterproof containers to protect personal effects or medical supplies, atabrine, aspirin, salt tablets, cigarettes and what-have-you. All these items began to disintegrate once in the GI's pocket. Even water chlorination tablets, so important in the jungle, could become useless from the stifling heat.

Medical units used canned heat, gas stoves and kerosene burners to sterilize instruments and provide the wounded with nourishment. Hot food and liquids for the wounded could not always be guaranteed. Medical personnel, however, performed yeoman service and suffered from the tropical environment along with everybody else.

I did not have a prior assignment with any particular unit in New Guinea. The press assignments had been made by GHQ long before my arrival there, so I was free to roam around and experience war in New Guinea with several different outfits. So I gained an overall view of combat conditions and the hardships faced.

Front-line troops had very few convenience or comfort items. They used tin containers of all kinds to heat up rations, prepare coffee (if they had coffee), and wash mess gear. Since it rained nearly all the time, there were few opportunities to wash mess kits in hot water. Because of this lack of sanitation discipline, dysentery and diarrhea were widespread.

I joined a patrol one day for the fun of it and, fortunately for me, we were not ambushed.

The hills became steeper, and harder to climb. Leeches and insects got worse. The GIs began tossing aside personal items, even equipment, to lighten their load. Upon reaching a stream they would rush headlong into it to drink, ignoring that upstream wild animals might be fouling the water, or other soldiers might be defecating in it. Such contamination made many a soldier ill or, even worse, lose his life.

The Kokoda trail, south to north across Papua New Guinea, became littered with stragglers, many panting for breath from the heat, exhaustion and lack of proper food. Such patients had to be taken care of immediately because, as darkness came, it was feared they would be killed by Japanese patrols. The farther north the troops moved, the more active the enemy became.

Many New Guinea natives provided invaluable assistance to American and Aussie troops during this operation. Hundreds were used to carry supplies and also to bear the litters upon which the wounded were taken to medical stations. Conditions would have been much tougher without their help; overall progress markedly slower.

At one time, the tribes in this region were among the most ferocious savages in the South Seas. Head-hunting was practiced, along with head-shrinking. There were tribes of "big people" and also some villages of Kukukukus, jungle nomads who were less than four feet tall, quite a contrast.

Some of New Guinea's finest, perhaps members of the Papuan Chamber of Commerce, floated in to look us over and to scrounge what they could around camp sites.

It appeared some natives had never before seen people with white skin, but none were threatening or menacing; merely curious. I noted tribal women carried huge burdens on their heads, often with a baby slung over a shoulder. Clothing was minimal. I realized I was as curious about them as they were about us.

Soldiers in the opening engagements of any war are often ill-prepared to wage the kind of war they must fight. That was the case for several U.S. units committed to battle in New Guinea. Sometimes the failures could be traced to command; in other situations, lack of time for adequate training.

I recall the fear and sense of hopelessness about my own chance of survival the first time I and a few correspondents came under fire. All my training in the army had been with units destined for battle in the fields and hedgerows of Europe, not in jungles where often you cannot see an enemy within 10 feet of your position.

There is no such thing as silence in the jungle. It is a nerve-wracking experience when you feel isolated, yet know you are less than five feet from a friendly soldier. The worst thing about combat is that you don't always know what certain sounds are. You listen and focus your hearing to try and pick up the least little sound, and you strain your eyes to try and see things that often are not there. It can drive you nuts.

You know the enemy is somewhere out there ahead of you, but the problem becomes how can you locate his position? You know he intends to kill you.

Handling that kind of fear was not an easy thing to master. Learning to live with it took time, and I realized I was lucky compared to the GIs and the junior officer squad leaders who had to face such sinister, insecure dangers around the clock.

Experienced soldiers learn to distinguish the sounds of enemy weapons from their own; they know the satisfying whine of friendly artillery overhead, and easily identify friendly aircraft as they pound enemy positions. They understand the excitement of battle but there is always that lingering feeling of loneliness and danger that is always present.

Maybe, as one experienced sergeant told me:, "It pays to be a little crazy. It is easier to cope," he said, "if you do not think about your future for the next ten years or the next ten minutes. You do what you can to survive and hope the next body bag doesn't have your name on it."

I will never forget the faces of the wounded, nor the tenderness with which the medics attempted to care for them, often under extremely hazardous conditions. When a buddy was "hit," everybody was sorry, truly sorry, but everyone knew nothing could be done about it.

At one medical station, it became obvious some of the wounded were past saving. The official position was these men would not survive and doctors' time must go to those with a chance to live. Fatally wounded GIs often seemed aware of their fate as the surgeon passed them by with a meaningful pat on the shoulder, and perhaps a cheering word. There was seldom any reaction, only blank stares through dull eyes dimmed by shock, pain and medication.

Casualties are the saddest reality of war. A father's "rainbow gone to smash" and a mother's heart broken forever.

Since the water table was high, there were no underground defense systems. What the men faced were coconut-log bunkers. If the terrain was favorable, the Japanese would construct huge blockhouses, each holding 20 to 30 men. All the bunkers were placed to command favorable fields of fire.

Most were covered with earth and then camouflaged with fast-growing plants. In a few days the bunkers would be completely swallowed up by the jungle and you would not know they were even there.

Such conditions did not take long to tire and dispirit U.S. troops. A medical officer, after one exhausting fire-fight, described the men he had treated as looking like "gaunt animals looking for a den to hide in."

Actually it was just as bad, if not worse, for the Japanese. Many units had been cut off from their supply sources and were in bad shape. A diary obtained off the body of a dead Japanese officer noted that his men had been reduced to eating roots and grass. Two days later he wrote:

"The food shortage has caused some of my men to eat human flesh."

Another enemy notebook captured read: "No medicine for malaria, no food for the company for a week. Went to collect bodies of enemy dead. Ate human flesh for the first time. It tastes comparatively good."

There was considerable evidence that Japanese soldiers literally were starving to death. Captured documents revealed time after time that they sought out insects, small animals, tree bark or varieties of vegetation including grass, to try to keep themselves alive. In such instances, I suppose cannibalism could be forgiven.

One incident occurred in a native village after those who lived there were driven off by the enemy. Returning two days later, they found one of their neighbors dead, flesh having been cut from his chest, thighs, calves, buttocks and back. His shoulders had been cut through and his forearms were missing. The top of his head had been cut off and his brains removed.

In another instance, I went with several correspondents and photographers to a spot about 35 miles from Hollandia, the site of a deep ravine. There we observed one of the consequences of war and attrition. There was a gentle slope leading into the ravine, but once at the bottom the only way out was a 30-foot bluff.

The Japanese at some point had constructed a ladder which was used to climb out of the gully. At the bottom of the ladder was a heap of rotting bodies. These unfortunate soldiers had tried to climb out but were so weak they finally lost their grip and fell to the bottom. I guessed there was at least 25 bodies lying there in a tangled pile.

The New Guinea campaign was a real test of human endurance and character. Perhaps in no other place were fighting and survival conditions worse. I believe I may have said that about later battlegrounds as well. How does one distinguish between such miserable surroundings?

It was in New Guinea I had my first experience with leeches. On one short trek into the jungle, to view a former Japanese bivouac area, I looked down at my boots and saw what I thought were pieces of moss. A staff sergeant with us quickly said: "Scrape them off right now. Sometimes one bite will lay you up for a month."

"Where are the leeches?" I said, looking at the jungle floor. "I don't see any."

One of the GI's took a stick and struck the ground. All of a sudden hundreds of little thin objects sprang from the grass. All it took to get them up was the vibration of our footsteps. Those under your feet would fasten themselves to the edge of your boots. I had heard of leeches, of course, along with jungle snakes, and knew that they had been a problem. They were among the most disgusting creatures I ever saw.

Communications were always a problem. Radio equipment was subjected to extreme abuses and stress. There were also instances where Japanese commanders intercepted our battlefield messages. As a solution, the Army recruited some American Indian radio operators who transmitted messages in Navajo code.

That must have driven the Japanese crazy. It is doubtful anyone in the Japanese army at the time knew that the oral Navajo communication system is an unwritten language. There was no way they could "break" that code.

This campaign was noteworthy, however, because it was at Buna that the Allies, for the first time in World War II, engaged and successfully overran a fortified area defended in depth by the Japanese. Its success was a great boost to morale for soldiers in the field, as well as the military strategists who had conceived the plan.

The mostly-Aussie thrust from Port Moresby that came over the mountains was accomplished at great sacrifice. This does not mean the predominately U.S. assault from the sea onto the north shore of New Guinea was any less heroic or hazardous. The pinchers movement worked because every soldier involved did what he was supposed to do.

The Australians suffered heavy casualties - 5,698 including 1,731 killed. American losses totaled 2,848, including 827 dead. I'm sure the Australians required little motivation in this battle because they were fighting to protect their homeland, just south of New Guinea.

I remember an Aussie reporter discussing the campaign, and he remarked how casually our troops had treated the war early on. He said:

"The Americans went into action laughing and joking. Didn't they know what they were getting into?"

I explained to him this was what most Americans do to try and hide their fear and nervousness. As a matter of fact I came across a few Americans during the war who actually enjoyed combat and the killing. I had been trained to hate the enemy, but I always felt a twinge of sorrow when we'd come across dead Japanese soldiers. I figured

These local beauties, and others like them, were frequent visitors in the camp areas. They did no harm but appeared to have a great curiosity of Americans and the devices of war used to drive the Japanese from their homelands.

they were in a strange place, too, perhaps homesick, and had family who loved them as much as my family loved me.

One Australian war correspondent was killed in action in New Guinea. I believe his name was Pendil Raynor who had served with Aussie troops in World War I and had been overjoyed to join that same unit in World War II as a reporter. Fate does play dirty tricks.

Our side had some senseless casualties when the pilot of a transport plane reported he had seen a unique village and some unusual-looking "fuzzy-wuzzy" natives in a remote valley. His story was so fascinating several American officers decided to "borrow" a plane and take a look.

This was against regulations, of course, but in a combat zone such things went on occasionally.

The plane had been airborne for about an hour when an incoming pilot from Port Moresby reported a fire and debris near the "hidden valley." Sure enough, the sight-seeing escapade had ended in tragedy and 23 people, including some nurses, lost their lives on a lark. It took a week to get the bodies out.

On the fun side, you cannot believe the decisions made by people in authority now and then. For many Americans, New Guinea must have appeared like a page from *National Geographic* magazine. After

NEW GUINEA JUNGLES

the worst of fighting was over, natives began coming out of the jungle. The men wore loin cloths, women a sort of sarong-like wrapping.

It was a topless paradise with an assortment of breasts in all sizes bouncing and sagging all over the place. Finally, a quartermaster colonel decided it was bad for morale to have these nearly unclad females frequenting the camp. So he placed an order for brassieres, and in a few days they arrived via air freight. High priority stuff!

The native women seemed very happy to receive them and they quickly melted back into the jungle, presumably to put them on. The next morning, they came back all decked out in their new brassieres, except they had tied them around their waists and were using the cups to carry trinkets in!

The colonel's plan had just gone bust.

The Papuan battles were not cheaply won, but it provided lessons and experiences of great value in succeeding battles. The U.S. had just made a 600-mile jump along the New Guinea coast which isolated some 40,000 enemy troops. Having taken Hollandia, construction of air fields could begin in earnest to provide support for the Marine assaults in the Marianas and Palau.

Unfortunately, the airstrips for big bombers could not be built at Hollandia as planned because the soil was too soft and moist. The bases were subsequently built further north up the coast.

It was in New Guinea I learned Japanese troops take baths according to rank. They would heat up a large tub of water and the highest ranking officer would bathe first. After he was done the next ranking officer would jump in, etc.

By the time the privates' turn came, the scum was about four inches thick. They simply pushed the debris from the center to the edges of the tub, slid in and lathered up. Banzai!

As successful as the Hollandia area conquest had been, there were rumors around GHQ that not every staff officer approved of it. But the general's strategy in leap-frogging over intermediate areas went so smoothly and, in retrospect, seemed so logical, what criticism there had been disappeared.

All of a sudden the Philippines were not as far distant as once supposed.

My Life is Spared

Chapter 8

"There is always inequity in life. Some men are killed in war, some men are wounded; some are stationed in the Antarctic, some in San Francisco. It's very hard in military or personal life to assure complete equality. Life is unfair."
                                        President John F. Kennedy

SEPTEMBER 15, 1944, was quite likely the day when many people in the United States irritably and understandably exclaimed: "Where in the world is Morotai?"

Well, they weren't alone. Most of us involved in the landing there had never heard of it either until two weeks before we arrived. Located a few hundred miles from the Philippines, and nearly 300 miles northwest of Sansapor, New Guinea, Morotai was an insignificant dot on the map, the poor stepchild of the Dutch East Indies empire.

The island was MacArthur's answer to the Japanese who boasted the Americans would never get past Halmahera, the largest of the Spice Islands, lying 14 miles north of Morotai. The enemy had a strong defense force of over 50,000 men there, but not all of these were trained soldiers. The Japanese hadn't given the Halmahera-Morotai area a high priority until early in 1944, when they began to develop Halmahera as a southern strategic point of defense for the Philippines.

Halmahera was a big, mountainous island, its scenic centerpiece being Gam Konora, the first active volcano I had ever seen. It wafted smoke and red-tinted debris during daylight, and projected a faint orange glow on the sky at night.

The only major eruption on Halmahera occurred, however, when the Japanese garrison realized MacArthur had cut them off from their homeland with the invasion of Morotai. His leap-frog strategy had succeeded ... again.

U.S. forces invaded the island to obtain airstrips closer to the Philippines and simplify future air operations in the region. Another huge benefit was that disabled aircraft, returning from bombing runs on the Philippines and unable to make it back to their home base, would now be able to land on Morotai. This eliminated ditching or crashing into the sea, thus saving aircraft, the lives of crewmen, and a lot of U.S. dollars.

MacArthur's forces were on the move. They had completed their advance across Dutch New Guinea, seizing sites for airfields near the town of Sansapor at the northeast corner of the world's second largest island. It had taken his armies six months to retake Papua, and only nine months to cut off the Japanese stronghold at Rabaul on New Britain, east of the Solomons, and to clear the bulk of northeast New Guinea.

The price tag on the New Guinea operation was high, even though GHQ attempted to minimize the losses. Most everyone was aware how costly the battle for Guadalcanal had been, claiming nearly 6,000 dead and wounded. The casualty toll for New Guinea, on the other hand, was 8,546, of which 3,000 were killed in action.

Thus, one in eleven combat soldiers lost his life in New Guinea compared to one of thirty-three on Guadalcanal. Both battles took nearly the same length of time to win. In truth, it was one of the most costly victories of the war, certainly one the general was not counting on when he answered Washington's inquiry pertaining to his leap-frog strategy.

Just "clearing" a region did not necessarily mean that our forces controlled the area. For example, many of the islands U.S. troops had recaptured, and a good portion of New Guinea, were not entirely free of Japanese opposition at the time MacArthur declared the battle over. Many enemy soldiers continued fighting in several localities until they were finally convinced the war was actually over, years later.

Yet in less than three months, MacArthur's forces advanced nearly 1,400 miles from the Admiralties to Vogelkop, the tip of New Guinea, and north into the Moluccas, a group of Dutch East Indies islands located between New Guinea and Mindanao. He was getting closer to the biggest prize of all, the Philippines.

Morotai will always remain vivid in my memory because it was on this tiny, obscure island I experienced an incident with religious overtones that has been a part of my life and my faith ever since.

Little opposition was expected from the Japanese, and on September 15 the main force comprising the 31st Infantry Division, commanded by Major General John Persons, plus a combat team from the

Landing sites on Morotai proved troublesome, but they did not long delay the assault on the island, nor the re-supply of our troops there. We'd seen worse.

32nd Infantry Division, hit the beaches in two places. This was my first assault landing and I was surprised to discover there had been no preliminary air or naval bombardment of the island prior to D-Day.

However, for 14 days prior to the landing, Allied planes carried out heavy raids on Japanese bases within range of Morotai. As a result, the island was nearly isolated from possible Japanese air counterattacks. Two hours prior to the landings, however, naval fire support gave us one heck of a show with five and eight-inch shells, rockets, and plenty of 20-mm, 40-mm and three-inch fire right up to time we off-loaded for the beaches.

The naval armada that took us there was commanded by Admiral Daniel Barbey, who was involved in more combat landings than any other admiral who served in the Pacific. The invasion force, labeled "Tradewind," had been assembled at Hollandia and that's where I and the war correspondents assigned to this landing boarded Barbey's flagship for the voyage.

This was probably the first time in military history an invasion site had been sprayed for insects from the air. Apparently, medical staff had learned the island was infested with disease-carrying insects. The spraying of DDT all but eliminated insects on the island for about three weeks, and greatly reduced illnesses from bites. Malaria and other diseases carried by insects were not only a health problem in the South Pacific, but a tactical hindrance as well.

Within a six months period, nearly one-third of all U.S. troops in the region had to be evacuated because of malaria, dysentery, or some other tropical disease. It seemed bugs were everywhere: giant chiggers, ants of various species, poisonous spiders and other large, mysterious, brightly-colored insects that would land on your body and begin sucking blood like vampires.

These bug bites often turned into festering sores, and often produced fever. Most GIs, at one time or another, suffered from yaws, scrub typhus, ringworm, malaria, dysentery, ringworm, plus the threat from snakes, wild pigs and, in some instances, crocodiles. Medics were often kept so busy that only those with very high fevers would be given time off from duty.

Reporters along for this landing included Spencer Davis, *Associated Press*, Howard Handleman, *International News Service* and Jerry Thorpe, *Chicago Daily News*. Each of them were great to work with and observe because each one was an outstanding war correspondent.

I heard one of them say one day: "GHQ is often like a log going down the river with 25,000 ants on it, each thinking he is steering the log." I made no comment but I think I could agree.

It was always exciting to "join the Navy" for an assault landing. For one thing, I would be in the company of competent newspapermen. From them I could learn more of the craft of writing and, better still, all of us were guaranteed excellent food and a hot shower, plus a clean place to sleep.

If after death there is a hereafter, and I find myself back in a world where wars are fought, I plan to join the Navy. They live very well even in the midst of battle. I envy Air Force pilots as well. They bomb, strafe and battle the enemy in aerial combat in the midst of danger, to be sure, but once their mission is successfully concluded they return to clean beds, good food, relative safety, plus ice cream machines.

We on the ground never had it quite that good. Once an island had been invaded and the airstrips were usable, we'd watch our rich cousins from the Air Force fly in and begin unloading their air mattresses, refrigerators, frozen steaks and other goodies. This didn't set too well with the infantry guys, for whom luxuries were few and far between. I suppose it was envy. Heck, I know it was.

Correspondents were usually placed on command ships in order to get the "big picture." Other reporters, seeking first-hand combat material, were most often placed on troop transports for the first part of the journey, then placed in landing craft for the beach assault. Usually by the time the second wave of infantry had hit the landing zones, all the reporters were off the boats and onto the beaches.

It was a good thing the Japanese did not attack in force at the breaches, because nearly all the vehicles off-loaded from the landing craft bogged down in the exceptionally treacherous mud on shore. It was a real mess and had there been any opposition of consequence, casualties would have been substantial.

Getting troops from the landing craft to the beaches was worse than expected. The depth of the water near the beaches was far greater than had been anticipated. Infantry soldiers had to wade in water up to their necks to get ashore, holding their rifles and packs above their heads.

Although I did not witness the incident, I learned later that MacArthur, who came up from New Guinea aboard the cruiser *Nashville*, came ashore after the first wave reached the beaches. His Higgins boat grounded offshore and when he stepped off the ramp, he found himself chest-deep in sea water. Concerned staff officers quickly decided that from now on, someone else would test the depth of the water.

Disgorging of vehicles, ammunition and supplies from the landing craft was a real test of human endurance and quality of equipment. In some other areas, the depth of water was far less at high tide than had been predicted. The situation became so bad, alternative landing sites were quickly selected. Misinformation on landing sites throughout the Pacific war caused far more casualties than the services cared to admit.

The only serious opposition to the arrival of U.S. troops came from a few Japanese Zero fighter planes which strafed the beaches and caused the infantrymen to take shovels from their packs and begin digging foxholes. As far as the Japanese defenders on the ground were concerned, they initially displayed little inclination to defend anything but themselves.

Most chose to run for the hills rather than attacking, or even defending, well-prepared strong points near the beaches. This situation was to change later when the Japanese managed to put an infantry colonel from Halmaherea ashore who began reorganizing the scattered forces there. The Navy had pretty well managed to prevent reinforcements from reaching the island.

As if the landing site problems weren't bad enough, preliminary sites for airstrips had to be abandoned because of the viscous mud and required building materials. Morotai's coral base proved to be too sandy and the coral rocks were as hard as granite. Heavy rains the first 10 days didn't helped, either. Other airstrip sites were quickly located, however, and it wasn't long until fighters and bombers were flying off the island around the clock.

It has always seemed ridiculous to me, if the story told me was true, that the United States had to pay the Dutch government $10,000 for every coconut tree felled in the building of the airfields. Those damaged by our troops during the occupation of the island also carried a price tag. It was Dutch property, of course, but they had lost it to the Japanese.

We got it back for them with blood, sweat and tears, then had to pay them for the privilege! That's real appreciation.

Less than two hours after the troops landed, MacArthur knew he had secured another advanced base of operations, although not as cheaply as once thought. He had isolated thousands of Japanese, and was only 300 miles from the Philippines. Invasion Forces had relatively light casualties.

It is said that the general, as he gazed through the mist towards the Philippines, said: "They are waiting for me there ... it's been a long time."

For this landing, I had been assigned to Major General Charles P. Hall's 11th Corps headquarters, which was in command of the Morotai invasion. Eleventh Corps had already been exceptionally successful in its mission at Aitape, southeast of Hollandia in New Guinea.

I greatly respected General Hall, who was more of a regular guy than most other generals I ran across during the war. He had another side, however, and later on Bataan I saw him summarily remove a division commander from his post for lack of leadership during the famous battle of Zigzag Pass. He could have overreacted at the time, but it was not my prerogative to judge and I considered him to be a fair and understanding commander.

General Hall was not a tall man, but stocky and square-shouldered. He was always well-groomed, his mustache neatly trimmed, and uniform pressed and immaculate. His West Point buddies called him

"Pinky" but I was never brave enough to ask him how he acquired such a nickname.

The XI Corps engineers did a great job. The airfields were carved out of the coconut groves and jungle in record time. Landing strips were surfaced with coral, a technique utilized frequently on islands in the South Pacific that were little less than atolls themselves.

Many of them cleared the surface of the ocean by only a few feet and during frequent rain squalls or storms the troops waded through flooding surface water blown in from the sea.

It wasn't long until aircraft were flying on and off the island in swarms. Morotai made one think of a beehive, with planes buzzing in and out around the clock. As expected, crippled bombers that had been shot up in raids over the Philippines began crash-landing there.

Such landings were spectacular, made usually with the landing gear retracted, the plane sliding on its belly for hundreds of feet. I happened to witness one where the pilot lost control. A wingtip hit the runway and the plane cartwheeled a couple of hundred yards before bursting

A gouge is taken out of a huge coconut grove on Morotai in order to get a quick landing site for aircraft. Later on, a huge airfield was constructed farther inland.

into flames. Only two members of the crew managed to escape.

Later on, the airstrips served an important role in the tactical support of the Leyte landings, and again in April of 1945, for the Australian invasion of Borneo, which was also under the command of MacArthur's headquarters, and in which I participated as the GHQ press officer.

Morotai was not a place to compile "sack-time" or meditate. For the infantry, of course, sleep was always marginal. In many headquarters sections, however, staff personnel, unless on duty, could get a fair amount of rest.

They could sleep normal hours if, and that "if" was, if "Washing Machine Charlie" did not fly over the island in the wee hours and drop his bomb. This persistent Japanese pilot usually called about midnight, coming from Halmahera, just a couple of minutes away by air. His nickname derived from the sound of his engine, which reminded many soldiers of their grandmothers' gasoline-powered washing-machine engines.

We had several batteries of anti-aircraft guns on the island, along with a number of powerful searchlights which would sweep the sky every time Charlie showed up. Now and then they would frame his aircraft in their lights and the anti-aircraft guns would "pum - pum - pum - pum" and the noise of all the guns would eventually rise in a thunderous chorus of harsh, angry discordant sounds that seemed a violation of the lovely South Pacific scenic paradise we had intruded upon.

In the weeks I was on the island, despite all the effort by our artillery, I never saw Charlie hit once. By the time our fighters roared into the sky, Charlie was long gone. It was as if he owned the sky and was letting us know that the Sons of Nippon would not be easily intimidated.

Charlie's persistent effort paid off one night. There was to be a raid on the Philippines early the next day and the Air Force had their planes all lined up in a neat row along the runway. Not only were they aligned in a straight line, they were fully loaded with bombs for the early-morning strike.

Charlie dropped his bomb and it magically hit one of the bombers on the ground. That plane disintegrated in a fiery explosion, the flames and smoke rising several hundred feet. That explosion spread to the next plane, and from that point on it was just like knocking down dominoes on a table.

One bomber after another exploded. I was in my tent when the explosions began but I ran outside, and looking toward the airfield, I saw huge flames with pieces of aircraft sailing in all directions. There was no way to control the destruction. The island fairly shook from the multiple, continuous explosions. The Air Force lost a dozen bombers from Charlie's one little bomb.

It is my guess he laughed all the way back to Halmahera.

Our corps headquarters was set up on the beach near the airfield. It was like a small tent city. We ate our meals in the open, some distance away, thank goodness, from the so-called latrines. They consisted of bamboo tubes stuck in the soil for urination and a slit-trench for bowel movements. We took showers in a canvas enclosure, but all of us who could dipped in the nearby ocean once or twice a day.

Our stretch of beach was breathtakingly beautiful. The white-tipped waves rolled in on music all their own, the huge waves breaking against the coral and sandy beach like great cymbals clashing together during a dramatic symphonic finale.

This beach was a wonderful place to find colorful sea shells. I mailed a box of them home as souvenirs to Kathy and my parents.

I bunked in a tent with another captain whose name was John Edwards, a native of Pennsylvania. John was assigned to the G-4 Section of 11th Corps, involved in maintaining supplies of all kinds. He was a great guy, had a wife and two children back in Pittsburgh, and he and I would sit in our tent during the evening and dream about getting back home.

He would tell me of the tremendous joy of having children, and the blessings they brought to his life. It was obvious he loved his wife very much and that missed all of them terribly. He explained that he accepted being called into service because he felt he was going to help make the world a safer place for his kids. I must admit his philosophy didn't sound a bit corny to me.

At that time Kathy and I didn't have children, of course, but that did not keep me from dreaming of the day when we would become a real family. It was at times like these that I yearned for home and the war seemed to drag along so slowly. I missed Kathy and the folks so very much.

I was also aware that my parents worried about me all the time. Sending sons and daughters off to combat certainly qualified most par-

MY LIFE IS SPARED

ents as the true unsung heroes of the war. My parents had a little flag in their window so people would know they had a son in the war. They had so much pride in me that I knew I had to justify it somehow.

One afternoon, Edwards asked me if I would like to go along on a re-supply mission in the interior. It developed that two platoons of infantry, sent on a search and destroy mission in the hills, had been temporarily cut off by a band of enemy soldiers in well-placed fire zones. The Americans were running low on food and ammunition.

In the early days of my war experience, I sought out excitement of this nature. It was like a big adventure to me, and so I told Edwards I'd love to go along. We took a corps Jeep to the airstrip where a C-46 transport plane had been loaded with supplies to be dropped by parachute to the isolated infantrymen. It was gung-ho as Edwards boarded the plane so I could follow him.

As I approached the steps into the plane, I suddenly heard a voice. So help me it was a voice! And words came: "Don't go, Joe, don't go." I couldn't believe my ears. In the first split seconds upon hearing those words I wanted to pretend I hadn't heard anything at all. So I lifted my leg, placing a foot on the plane's ladder.

Again, this time very clear: "Don't go, Joe."

I could not take another step. I was dumbfounded. I was confused. I was frightened. The crew chief aboard the aircraft hollered down in frustration:

"Hey, Cap'n, you gonna' go with us or not?"

I was so shaken by my startling experience, I could barely respond. Greatly embarrassed, I replied:

"No thanks, sergeant .... tell Captain Edwards I've changed my mind."

The aircraft roared off the runway. I stood there immobile for a moment, trembling, shaken, my brain whirling, pondering this strange encounter with the unknown. It was mind-boggling.

I had been a Methodist Sunday School boy and had sung for several years in the boy choir of an Episcopal Church. I had maintained a casual interest in religion all the way to adulthood, but I had never publicly professed any particular commitment to religion, much less God.

How was it I had heard this voice out of nowhere? Were my ears playing tricks on me? Did I actually hear someone speak? Was God actually talking to me or was I hallucinating? Was I suffering a form of combat fatigue?

I returned to camp and went to our tent where I looked out over the beautiful ocean tapestry; no painter could ever quite capture all the color, all the magic, all the beauty that stretched from the beach to the distant horizon. I thought of Kathy and my parents and wished they were with me so I could tell them about my strange experience. My hands were still shaking, my brain in a whirl.

I was startled out of my contemplative shock by another officer who came dashing by and said:

"Hey, Snyder! You hear what happened? That cargo plane with the drop for the infantry guys has crashed. The word is it swooped down into a small valley to drop the stuff and as it zoomed up the other side it didn't clear the mountain. It's still burning ... everybody's presumed dead."

As it turned out, everyone aboard was dead. I was devastated by the news. Captain Edwards was gone. His wife no longer had a husband and his children no longer had a father. It had happened so quickly, so unexpectedly. I was stunned, grief stricken.

I excused myself and put my face in my hands, threw myself down on my cot and went through an agony of guilt and soul-searching like I had never done before. I thanked God over and over again. As I think about it today, I'm sure the feeling I experienced then must have surely resulted from God's presence.

Tears came, then I underwent a sincere rebirth of my long-dormant faith there in the jungle on one of the earth's most remote green cathedrals, little Morotai Island.

I assure you, it really happened. I heard a voice. It had never happened before and it hasn't happened since. I am often reminded of that old hymn:

"I know not why God's wondrous grace to me he hath made known, nor why, unworthy, Christ in love redeemed me for his own."

For whatever reason my life was preserved, I do not know. I am thankful I was spared for my wife and family-to-be, and for my mom and dad. For that I will be eternally grateful.

For years I never told anyone about the incident for fear I would be ridiculed. During nearly every communion service, however, the incident always comes to my mind and in those quiet moments of prayer and contemplation at bedtime, Morotai is seldom far away. If the Lord saved me only to direct my path to Gallatin to publish a small-town weekly newspaper, I sometimes wonder if that was a favor or a punishment.

Captain Edwards died near Nill 40 where elements of the 33rd Infantry Division, brought in to replace the 31st Infantry Division, ran into fierce enemy resistance. Two columns of the 136th infantry regiment were ordered to reduce the threat which developed into a terrible battle.

The jungle of Morotai had been underestimated. Men carrying heavy weapons quickly tired. Radio equipment often failed which forced Colonel Ray Cavenee, regimental commander, to utilize an artillery liaison plane, flying from one column to another relaying messages.

Approaching enemy lines, the troops came under heavy fire from snipers in trees. Visibility was about 20 feet at best. Supplies became a major problem of Cavenee, ammunition and food were particularly short. Native bearers used to carry supplies could carry only limited amounts as well.

The evacuation of wounded was a nightmare, some situations requiring eight men for each casualty because of the terrain and the distance from the front lines to the aid station. Eventually bamboo rafts were constructed and the wounded were floated down the Pilowo River. The trip to the aid station was thus reduced from two days to one.

When combat units got lost, the artillery plane would come to their aid. Though the pilot could not see the troops beneath the jungle canopy, they would direct him via what radio communication they had working at the time.

Meanwhile the infantry and artillery was taking a huge toll on the Japanese defenders, but the going was hardly easy for our infantry. Company B of the 136th, for example, found a quiet moment suddenly erupted by a well-placed enemy machine gun. Without realizing it, a squad had moved into its line of fire. Barely a dozen feet from the squad, the machine gun spat out its death-dealing lead and within a few seconds eight soldiers lie dead. The gun and its crew were finished off with grenades, but too late for the dead.

This battle last over two weeks, and GIs would never forget the impenetrable jungle, fighting the enemy where often there was no daylight under the trees. They will always recall hacking their way through dense growth where covering a 1,000 yards a day was maximum. Unit histories later recorded many heroic deeds in the taking of Mortai, a task that had once been considered a breeze.

One morning a Jap plane came roaring down the beach and I ducked

"HOT MEALS AT ALL HOURS"

This photo made the rounds in the South Pacific, originating from New Britain island. We did not think of it being particularly disrespectful or degrading, because such scenes were commonplace in the tiny villages we passed through.

into a nearby bunker. This was nothing more than a simple hole in the ground, covered over with coconut logs, with sandbags on top. This time, one of our anti-aircraft gun crews scored a hit, and the plane crashed about half a mile down the beach.

Out of curiosity I ran to the scene of the wreck, which did not burn. The pilot appeared extremely young although it is not easy to judge the ages of Oriental people. He was still strapped in his seat, and his face did not have a mark on it. His right arm, however, had been severed by metal fragments, and it was obvious his lower body was badly mangled.

I picked up two pieces of metal from a wing which had part of the red circle "rising sun" emblem painted on them. I mailed them home to my two nephews, Don and Bob Alber in Kansas City, who were quite small at that time. Their souvenirs likely made a worthwhile subject for "show and tell" at their elementary school.

In talking with some infantrymen one afternoon, they mentioned they had found several women in the wilds of Morotai. Anyone who served in the Pacific has not been surprised by post-war revelations that the Japanese army imported Oriental women for the purpose of providing sexual pleasure for their troops.

Perhaps I became more aware of the so-called "Comfort Battalions" because I moved around a lot in connection with my assignments. It was not uncommon as our troops overran Japanese positions, or camps, that they would wind up with female prisoners. After a while we understood what was going on.

The Japanese rarely used Japanese women, usually "recruiting" from Guam, Saipan or Formosa, the latter known today as Taiwan. I do not recall seeing any foreign women in New Guinea, but if a soldier was driven to have sex with New Guinea women, he deserved what he got.

In the Philippines, for example, they conscripted women from rural areas who were usually poor and uneducated. Quite honestly, none of the troops serving in the Philippines, including Americans, had any difficulty in relieving their sexual urge because prostitution was widespread and it was neither encouraged nor discouraged by the military.

It was not unusual in most Philippine barrios or cities to be approached openly on the streets, most often by relatives of the girls who were willing, even anxious, to go to bed. The youngsters would walk with you down the street, making a pitch for the services of their sister, which might go something like this:

"Hey there, GI!. You want pom pom? My sister is only 15, very nice, very hot, and not used much. She make good time for you. Only 20 pesos, sir."

Having been carefully taught about such things, and with a new wife in Kansas City who was working hard to help us save money to buy a newspaper when I got home, I never indulged in extramarital sex — the term in use today. I do admit, however, to a certain ache in my groin which I didn't get rid of until I arrived home.

I'm not judging those who did or didn't. I knew Kathy would be faithful to me and I wasn't about to dishonor her trust in me. Guess we were old-fashioned, even back then.

I have no intention of dignifying the Japanese custom of borrowing women for immoral purposes. A few years ago some of these women began speaking out about this abuse during the war. Following the end of hostilities, many of these women (many had died from disease and beatings) tried to return to their villages, only to meet with scorn and disgrace from their families, treated as outcasts by society.

I can't forget how these girls, some quite young and pretty, came running to meet our troops. They threw themselves on the ground, wailing loudly in both anguish and unbridled happiness at being rescued. Many were starving, some pregnant and often diseased. Help for these victims of war from the Japanese government is long overdue. I have no idea what disposition was made of the women found on Morotai.

Unknown to us ashore, a prime casualty of the Morotai landings was an American submarine, the USS Seawolf, which was attacked and sunk by U.S. Navy escort ships in error. All aboard the sub were lost. The mishap occurred after one of our escort ships had been sunk by a Japanese submarine which got away. Seawolf was mistaken for it, and the tragic mistake was very painful to all concerned.

As the battle for Morotai came to an end, it became obvious some of us would be moving again soon. MacArthur's return to the Philippines was fast approaching. He wasn't the only soldier anxious to get there.

Invasion of Leyte

Chapter 9

"There is no such thing as getting used to combat. Each moment of combat imposes a strain so great that men will break down in direct relation to the intensity and duration of their exposure."
J.W. Apple in *Journal of the American Medical Association*

AT FIRST GLANCE, a map of Leyte resembles a large tooth. It is about 114 miles long and ranges from 15 to 45 miles in width. At the time of MacArthur's invasion the island had a million inhabitants, yet its capital, Tacloban, was its largest city with only 30,000 residents.

It is a mountainous island covered with jungle and rice paddies, with two great agricultural valleys. MacArthur chose Leyte for his initial thrust into the Philippines because of its location in the center of the archipelago. It was also favored because Leyte Gulf provided one of the best anchorages in the Philippines, and the beaches were favorable for assault landing sites.

The general also wanted the airfields the Japanese had built during their occupation. These strips would help support future offensive drives, now on the planning board, designed to reclaim all the Philippine Islands and fulfill his promise: "I shall return."

The fleet of ships that returned MacArthur to the Philippines was believed the strongest in the history of the world at that time. Under Admiral "Bull" Halsey's command, the task force included 738 ships, including 105 combat ships and 18 Navy carriers. It was rated the most powerful force, firepower-wise, ever assembled.

With 160,000 men to be put ashore, this total exceeded those put ashore in the opening phase of the Normandy invasion in Europe. MacArthur was finally getting the men and equipment he had long needed. I had the pleasure of seeing this great task force from the air, and it was one of the most breathtaking views of my life. As far as the eye could see, ships were dotted across a wide expanse of the South China Sea like tiny black islands, all the way to the horizon.

This tent was our first press office in the Philippines. At right is our first native pet, "Condition Red." We later added a parrot and a monkey.

As serene as this scene was, aboard the ships nervous soldiers, sailors and marines paced the decks or peered over the railings into the sea, thinking about what lay ahead. Below in stuffy quarters, men cleaned and rechecked rifles, machine guns and equipment. Last-minute letters home were written; several were reading their Bibles.

Those with special missions to perform studied plans — again and again. There was the usual nervous laughter and the inevitable card games with high stakes. Tension was high. For many GIs, it would be their first experience in landing on an enemy-held island.

Earlier I mentioned how much I enjoyed going aboard Navy ships because of the creature comforts the ships offered: hot showers, decent food, even steak and ice cream, and a bed with a mattress. This trip was no exception and the Navy guys did all they could to make us feel comfortable. It certainly beat army rations, showering infrequently in the open, and sleeping in a tent with all those crawling things.

I envied the Air Force fly-boys, too, who took off, dropped their bombs, and came back to base — leaving the misery on the ground behind.

In Tokyo, ranking Japanese officers were meeting to coordinate plans for smashing the invasion fleet. There was disagreement, but the Imperial Navy appeared to dictate strategy. It was a historic, fatal decision, but we would soon be hearing much more about the "Divine Wind" attack units.

At 6:30 a.m., October 20, 1944, the battleships, cruisers and destroyers opened fire on Leyte's beaches. From our transport ship, the horizon appeared as a solid ring of flashes. Smoke, dust and flames obscured the landing sites. The bombardment, complemented by air force bombing runs, continued unabated in all its thunderous, earth-shaking terror and death.

At 10 a.m., four divisions of infantry landed simultaneously, two near Tacloban, two near Dulag, everyone scanning the skies for enemy aircraft. There were more than expected; the enemy air response was not as weak as our intelligence units had predicted.

The troops encountered only scattered opposition as they rushed inland, but the going was far from easy. Beyond the beach we discovered a deep swamp. The cogon grass bog was almost waist deep in places, even up to the armpits, and many in the advancing line of troops employed some choice profanity, hoping it might make the going a bit easier.

A couple of enemy pillboxes nearby were knocked out, with about a dozen enemy killed in the process. Nearby Filipino houses posed a threat and each one had be searched in case they shielded Japanese defenders. Actually the initial assault could have been much worse. The enemy allowed about three assault waves of troops to land virtually uncontested, but when the other waves reached within a few hundred yards of the shore, they unleashed a strong mortar and artillery attack.

By this time, nearly everyone was struggling through the swampy ground and into the dense, wet jungle, still not too distant from the beach, and discovering some Japanese snipers had been tied in trees to pick off as many Americans as they could.

Under such conditions, the infantry could not carry all their gear. It required three trips to get it all and every soldier was happy that enemy resistance was light. By evening, most units were well dug in along their assigned sectors. Mechanized units of the 7th Cavalry units had moved quickly inland and they were followed by division engineers who immediately began work on the airfields.

This landing attracted a great number of reporters who were assigned to various assault units. For this initial phase, I was with the Major General Verne Mudge's First Cavalry Division, but in the next month I escorted reporters to a variety of units within the 24th and 77th Infantry Divisions.

Among them were William B. Dickinson, *United Press;* Robert Donovan, *Reuters*, Walter Simmons, *Chicago Tribune;* Richard M. Johnson, *United Press;* Merrill Mueller, *NBC News,* and Lindsay Par-

An assault landing is a mixture of bravery, foolhardiness, exploding bombs, naval projectiles, rifle fire — soldiers often frightened and confused. The landing sites quickly become littered with the tools of war and can quickly become a junk yard if the lines on a map in a commander's hand prove utterly useless in the intensity of combat.

rot, *New York Times.* William Dunn, *CBS Radio,* who was as close to MacArthur as any "outsider" could get, was also in our group.

This was one of my three amphibious assault landings. Three of the reporters wanted to go ashore with the initial line of infantry. We entered the landing craft, climbing down cargo nets from the transport ship's decks. The net swayed to the extent that I thought some of us might be tossed into the ocean. I suppose you could say we descended "crablike," clutching weapons and other items of necessity.

The boat below us lifted and bounced down, straining its lines against the rolling seas. Someone cussed and I saw that he had dropped something into the water. The officer in charge yelled to the GI: "Forget it; get in this God-damned boat. You're holding up the show."

We headed for the shore amidst the greatest din of assorted noises I have ever heard. Thank goodness, there was far more firing from behind us, than came from the shore. The assault wave of boats was forming now, but the waves were making people sick. One GI said to his buddy, "I just knew you'd puke before we got ashore."

The coxswain, in a Navy pea jacket at the stern, called our attention to puffs of smoke, pointed to them, and said: "They've seen us!." Our air force was now strafing the landing area, shooting at anything that moved. Someone shouted: "A hundred yards to go." It was then I saw the surf — heavy and boisterous. The closer we got to shore, the heavier the enemy fire appeared to be, but actually it was not as bad as predicted.

A platoon sergeant shouted: "Load and lock; get at it, load and lock." Everybody on the boat began nervously fumbling with his rifle, carbine or pistol. You could have cut the tension with a dull knife.

One soldier asked another: "Do you think we'll get a hot meal today?"

The other GI responded: "Hell no ... the smoke will draw fire."

The other soldier retorted: "Hell's Bells, that's a bunch of shit. You can wiggle your butt and draw fire."

Just as our little group left the boat, a ponderous wall of water swept over our heads. I lost my balance and got a salt water bath. I was shocked the water seemed so cold. I hoped my weapon would fire if I needed it.

Two other boats were ashore. Everybody ran for what cover they could find, firing their weapons in response to some sporadic firing from just beyond the landing sites. An infantryman, cowering behind a tuft of grasses, yelled: "Where in hell are they?" The Japanese defense was surprisingly weak. Thank God, in our sector the defenses were negligible and casualties were light.

Little did we know Japanese generals had decided not to oppose the initial landings in order to prevent another bloody "last stand" on the beaches. They had learned by the blood of their own soldiers that defenders, no matter how loyal and indoctrinated, could not withstand the massive, punishing pre-landing "softening-up" bombardment strategy developed for the Pacific war.

We were to learn the real battle for Leyte would be fought in the interior — and that it would be extremely costly in time and casualties. The light resistance near the beaches didn't mean the enemy wasn't going to make us pay for every inch of ground gained.

Later, the great wave of battle would wash through the jungle and up the rugged hills, embracing in its fury platoons, companies, regiments and divisions of brave men who pressed forward into battle because they felt what America had was worth saving. They fell on the beaches, the mountains and the paddies, because of an allegiance, not just for a flag, but because of an ideal of human dignity that alone was worth the walk into withering enemy fire.

Great men, men with futures and dreams, men of promise, the

sturdy oaks of America as well as the thorny scrub, were swept by the fury into a soldier's grave alone in a strange and faraway land. A pang of sorrow for the tragedy of war will ever remain in my heart.

General MacArthur returned to his beloved Philippines on the light cruiser USS Nashville, from which he watched the initial assault. He came ashore with senior commanders and the new Philippines president, Sergio Osmena. The general waded ashore, even though he could have waited a few moments and then easily stepped over the boat ramp without getting his feet and pantlegs so thoroughly soaked.

On the other hand, he'd been waiting to set his feet on Philippine soil for a long time.

Pictures and newsreels (remember newsreels?) of the general wading ashore became so famous that some of his detractors thought the whole thing was staged. It was not staged. What was planned, however, was a convenient microphone and radio transmission system installed on the beach. Once ashore, he strode to the microphone in his freshly-pressed uniform, ignoring his dripping pantlegs, wearing sunglasses and a cap. After a dramatic pause, he said:

"People of the Philippines, I have returned! By the Grace of Almighty God, our forces stand again on Philippine soil."

That was the theme of his address but there was much more of the typical MacArthur oratory, not uninteresting, but much too long to be repeated here. It was obvious the general was emotionally moved and, after all, the speech was not written for Americans, but for the Filipino people.

Following his remarks, the Stars and Stripes and the Philippine flag were raised on two of the tallest coconut trees left following the invasion bombardment. It was, after all, a momentous event.

Later the general endangered himself as a conspicuous target by smoking his famous pipe and wearing his braided cap into the jungle. At that time Japanese snipers, some in trees, posed a real threat to unsuspecting Americans. Japanese commanders later said they were astounded that MacArthur came ashore so soon. Had they known, they said, a suicide squad would have greeted him.

The beachhead was quickly expanded over the next two days and the First Cavalry Division entered the outskirts of Tacloban October 22, where they had to conduct a house-to-house search for concealed Japanese. They received a tumultuous welcome from the Filipinos, who lined the narrow streets waving American flags and presenting gifts of eggs and fruit to the soldiers. It was a great feeling, believe me.

To the south the 96th and 77th Divisions slogged through swamps and mud toward the airstrips west of Dulag. Japanese resistance was gradually stiffening for all our units. I noted increasing numbers of body bags headed toward the beach. This was always a sobering sight, graphic blood and bones evidence of the price of any battlefield victory.

The difficult terrain, plus a formidable enemy, slowed the advance. There were many hills that had been fortified by the Japanese, which presented formidable obstacles to the advance. Numerous tunnels had been constructed and were so interconnected that infantrymen didn't know from one moment to the next from which direction a Japanese soldier might pop up and take a shot at them.

The men were hampered also by the tall Kunai grass, which cut off every breeze as the GIs struggled up steep slopes and over sharp ridges. It didn't take long to become exhausted in the extreme heat. In one area a detachment of enemy soldiers unexpectedly appeared, approaching the hill from the opposite side. A fire fight resulted and about 40 enemy soldiers were killed.

As if they hadn't worked hard enough, elements of this regiment were sent to Tacloban the next day, October 23, to act as an honor guard for General MacArthur. As the old saying goes, rank has its privileges.

A special ceremony was held that day on the front steps of the capitol building, where MacArthur and Osmena announced President Roosevelt's restoration of civil government to the Philippines. Out at sea, Admiral Halsey's flagship, USS New Jersey, began flying warning flags. A large Japanese fleet had been sighted, headed for Leyte.

We were subjected to a heavy air attack on the 24th, when an estimated 200 twin-engine bombers approached the area. Our side knocked down 66 planes with 18 "probables." Our losses were minimal, which was fortunate because most of our Air Force was out at sea attacking the main Japanese fleet.

Air raids are spectacular. Would it be honest if I said I enjoyed them? Perhaps not, but they were always interesting and exciting. During this raid, two of our aircraft crash-landed on the Tacloban airstrip. These are high drama in slow motion, and no two are ever the same. If there is anything more spectacular, it has to be the crash-landings on the big carriers, with planes sometimes careening into the sea.

(Please note: It is not my intent, nor my capability, to write a complete account of the Leyte campaign. I saw only a small part of it, and I mention only what I witnessed. Now and then I include events like the naval battle of Leyte Gulf only to provide some continuity.)

The Battle of Leyte Gulf took place over three days beginning Oct. 23 and proved to be one of the greatest sea battles in history. It was a great victory for the U.S., because our Navy had unmasked the main enemy fleet and sent many of its units to the bottom. After intensive at-sea fighting, the Japanese fleet was virtually annihilated and would no longer be a major factor in the Pacific war.

Those of us on shore could not see the actual battle, but we could hear the sounds of the big guns, and the bombs and explosions that resulted. The sky was aglow at night during the massive engagement.

It was a horrifying event from a tactical standpoint, because we all knew that if even one enemy battleship or carrier broke through into our beachhead area, our losses in men, material and shipping would be devastating. It could set back the general's conquest of the Philippines by many months.

Happily, it proved to be a lopsided encounter. The Japanese losses

A Japanese airfield is bombed as the invasion of Leyte begins. The "parafrag" bombs descend slowly and detonate on contact with the ground to spread the destruction over a wider area. You can see Japanese fighter planes in their revetments.

in ships, submarines and aircraft were staggering; our losses relatively minor. The enemy lost 10,000 men while our losses were 1,500. It was the last major naval battle in the Pacific, and with 282 ships involved, the biggest naval engagement in U.S. history.

This battle reflected the difficulty correspondents often encountered in trying to obtain the facts. Following the Battle of Leyte Gulf, the results were greatly understated because the Navy and MacArthur did not know themselves what a great victory they had achieved.

George Jones, correspondent for *United Press*, wrote a story on the basis of what he had been told, but it was highly inaccurate because the Navy itself could not assess the extent of its victory, days after public interest in it had died away.

It was also in October that Japanese generals ordered the first "Kamikaze" air attacks. It was at Clark Field on Luzon that the first group of suicide pilots was organized from volunteers, their planes loaded with 550-pound bombs. Incidentally, their commander was General Onishi Takijiro, who would never ask a man to do anything he wouldn't do.

Later, when Onishi learned Japan had surrendered, he disemboweled himself in a suicide ritual with his own sword.

The suicide pilots created havoc with the U.S. fleet until the war ended. Hundreds of our ships were sunk or disabled, and for a time both west coast and some east coast naval shipyards were jammed with repair work. Toward the end of the war, the Japanese built crude wooden planes with one-ton bombs for the one-way trip. The Kamikaze philosophy was also applied to suicide boats and human torpedoes.

By chance, I picked up a piece of film on Luzon with several frames obviously depicting a farewell gathering of Kamikaze pilots with an officer addressing them. All volunteers were promoted two ranks for a successful mission. I never understood how this could be considered a benefit, but their passion for victory and love for their country was unsurpassed. Their average age was only twenty.

Naval losses from Kamikaze attacks at Leyte were so severe that MacArthur and Admiral Nimitz issued a complete blackout of news about the attacks. The reasons were that they did not want the enemy to know how successful their attacks had been, and how great the losses were. It was also feared the public might panic if they knew how severe such attacks were.

Still, the attacks threw light on the Japanese character. It was supposed to be a privilege for Kamikaze pilots to volunteer for the suicide missions. Apparently the pilots believed in it, because they flew and fought with courage and honor, crash-landing their planes on the decks of our ships and carriers, and into our planes in aerial combat.

Before Onishi died, he wrote an apology to the souls of the Kamikaze pilots and also to their parents. In it, he took blame for his part in Japan's failure to achieve the victory his pilots had given their lives for.

During one Kamikaze attack on Leyte, I was in a camp area at mealtime when my attention was directed toward the ocean. Here came a supply ship, without escort, sailing into the bay. The scuttlebutt was this ship was loaded with a beer ration for our troops.

While standing in the chow line, a roar went up from the soldiers nearby when they saw a plane with the rising sun on its wings head for the cargo vessel. The plane dived into the ship, creating a huge explosion. The concussion could be felt ashore, and the ship began to sink.

All of sudden the troops around me began shaking their fists and hurling insults toward the ship: "You SOBin' bastards!" "You f—— — Nippon a—holes," etc., etc. I had never heard such profanity in chorus. The GI's assumed they had been robbed of their beer, and they weren't about to let it happen without relieving their frustration.

I always figured one of the big reasons the Japanese lost the war was the sinking of that "beer ship." I'd never seen soldiers get that mad over beer before. Women, yes, but not beer. In addition, while this was going on, someone tossed a cigarette butt into the rolled-up cuffs of my fatigues. I began to smell something, looked down, and my pants were on fire. Only my pride was scorched!

It became obvious the Japanese intended to fight the decisive battle for the Philippines on Leyte. They took advantage of the geography of the archipelago to reinforce their troops. Our side was unable to prevent it because the soil there made it difficult to maintain and build sufficient airstrips and the Navy's airpower was either over-extended or tired or both. In a matter of days, the Japanese had moved two fresh divisions onto the island.

The fighting was made even more difficult by a typhoon which marked the beginning of the rainy season. The entire area was lashed by tropical downpours that turned roads into quagmires, the soil into deep mud, drenching all humans from head to toe. I know it is hard to believe, but 35 inches of rain fell during our first 40 days on the island.

This deluge further delayed construction of airfields. You can imagine what it was like for soldiers slogging their way in the jungle, onto the cultivated fields and over the slopes of defended hilltops. Frontline units had to be supplied by native bearers who, on the return trip, carried the dead and wounded.

I don't know how to describe a typhoon. The rain reaches earth in horizontal sheets. The palm trees bend low to the ground, if not uprooted and hurled away. In the tall grass, the howling of the wind is magnified to the intensity of a thousand freight trains roaring down the tracks.

The planes can't fly, and ships at sea become haunted things looking for refuge in utter blackness. Trails are washed away and you can't see the enemy ten feet away, but, fortunately, he can't see you either.

The struggle for Leyte soon hinged on the battle for Ormoc, also in the mountains, and Leyte Gulf to the east. Stiff resistance in the hills, particularly around "Breakneck Ridge," forced MacArthur to postpone the invasion of Mindoro by ten days. This action occurred early in November near a fishing barrio called Carigara.

The 24th infantry division had run into one of Japan's finest divisions, the 1st, rushed into battle from Manchuria. This led to some of the most intense combat in the Pacific. The typhoon had not yet ended when the battle began. It was my luck, I suppose, to get this assignment, shepherding three correspondents to cover Breakneck Ridge: Yates McDaniel, Clark Lee and Lindsay Parrott.

The Japanese called this the "Yamashita" line. Peacetime maps did not show the jumble of razorback ridges, shoved there by volcanic upheavals of long ago. As the battle progressed, individual ridges and summits were named by the GIs who fought for them, a privilege paid for in blood.

On these ridges many savage battles were fought. From their maze of tunnels and holes on and between the hills, the enemy had cut narrow, interlocking fire lanes through the jungle and Kunai grass. Machine-guns covered these lanes and snipers fired from hidden perches. Enemy mortar squads dug into cleverly hidden sites, firing deadly patterns of bursts. Japanese artillery roared from distant ridges.

American GIs faced four Banzai attacks in less than 24 hours. Units that had entered the battle 160 strong found themselves down to 60 men on their feet by the time they had broken the back of the Yamashita Line.

We joined an infantry regimental headquarters unit which was located about a half-mile behind the lines. This permitted reporters easy access to action zones and yet gave them an opportunity to rest and compose dispatches in relative comfort and safety. Division artillery had already pounded Japanese positions to make the job easier, if that is the right word, for the infantry.

The ground soldiers always bear the brunt of any battle. You see them bearded and mud-caked, near exhaustion, bodies marked by cuts and bruises, jungle rot and insect bites. The veterans of combat sorties nearly always acquire that tell-tale vacant stare after terrifying encounters with an enemy for too long a time.

They have seen their friends spun around by enemy bullets to fall into the mud and slime. They have seen many die, crying out in agony as their life's blood spilled out on the green matted jungle floor, or in a muddy foxhole.

There is no question the American soldier is courageous; yet as I watched our troops in combat I was driven to think that while they were most always brave in battle, many remained impulsive individualists. I recalled my leadership training in OCS where we were indoctrinated in the philosophy that everyone must operate as a unit with a specific purpose.

As a result of violations of this doctrine of battle, some men became heroes, while others became casualties because of this individualistic effort. While aggressive conduct on the part of one soldier might appear commendable, and sometimes was, such boldness often endangered the lives of his comrades.

The reporters and I spent two days near the main line of defense, and it was a harrowing, exciting experience I shall never forget. We witnessed a "fire fight" at close range which included the foxholes we occupied, and we saw a number of combatants from both sides fall either dead or wounded.

I did not know it at the time but a fellow townsman, Jack Brown, who attends the same church I do, could have been just a few yards away at that time. The Japanese were pouring murderous flanking fire into Brown's forward positions, but despite this he walked around, directing fire into the Japanese emplacements, all the while encouraging his men.

The record shows that Brown also helped remove wounded men to the rear. He was not always lucky, however, and was severely wounded in action on Mindanao, shortly before the war ended.

In one instance, a squad flushed several Japanese out of a cave with a flame-thrower. They were on fire from head to toe. The GI manning the nozzle cried out: "Burn, you SOB's, burn." His buddies cheered as a mother's son burned to a crisp..

The nighttime hours were nerve-wracking, one's ears fine-tuned to catch every minute noise; the sound of a footstep was enough to put one on alert. A tinkle of metal against metal would raise the hairs on your neck. You've never really seen a fireworks display until you've witnessed a night-time artillery barrage, combining concussion shells with white phosphorus projectiles.

It was here I learned what it takes to become a Congressional Medal of Honor winner. Three companies of Japanese moved toward American positions and had pushed to within a few yards of the Americans holed up there. They quickly killed or wounded everyone in the first two positions except one, Pvt. Harold H. Moon, Jr.

The enemy soldiers then centered their fire on him who, although wounded, responded with his submachine gun. An enemy officer attempted to lob grenades at Moon's position but he was killed. The Japanese then brought up a light machine gun to within 20 yards of where Moon was lying. Moon then called back coordinates to friendly mortars which knocked out the machine gun.

For over four hours, he held off the attack. Finally, an entire enemy platoon with fixed bayonets charged toward him. From a sitting position he fired into the Japanese, killing 18 and breaking up the attack. He then stood up and threw a grenade at a machine gun that had begun firing from his right side. He was hit again and instantly killed.

The Japanese then resumed their advance, but those left in Moon's outfit, inspired by his courageous stand and determination, launched a bayonet attack and succeeded in breaking through the enemy line.

Private Moon was posthumously awarded the nation's highest honor, his heroism substantiated by stories in three of the finest newspapers in the country. After observing Moon's performance under fire, I spent some time trying to understand what motivates such courage and sacrifice.

Where do we get such men? I'm sure they were not born heroes, but whatever it was deep inside them is sufficient to cause them to make the supreme sacrifice. How could any act be more noble or reflect all that is best in the human spirit? In battle, the man next to you may be today's hero — you just never know.

The poor dogfaces encountered such situations daily. I didn't want to trade places with any of them. Concerned with the fearful tasks of fighting and trying to stay alive, these guys weren't interested in the so-called Big Picture. They were willing only to contemplate what they saw and heard in a firefight, and to protect the little piece of earth they occupied at the time.

I could normally break away when I or the reporters chose to; the infantrymen had to stay there and pray for survival. Then, too, part of my job was to protect the reporters as best I could. A few didn't need protection; they weren't interested in becoming a statistic. Others insisted on getting right up there where the action was.

In another incident, our infantry met stiff opposition from a group of about 100 Japanese. After a short fire-fight, the Japanese began waving a white flag, sign of surrender. Heavy machine guns were positioned, and the GIs motioned for the Japanese to remove their clothing to prevent them from concealing weapons.

At that point, the enemy soldiers opened fire and wounded five GIs. The infantrymen unleashed their machine guns and hurled grenades, killing at least a dozen of the enemy. The remainder of the Japanese withdrew over a nearby hill. Often such trickery worked, but it didn't take many such encounters for our troops to wise up and remain alert.

The Breakneck Ridge battle began November 7 and lasted well into December. Two thousand Japanese died defending the position, and the Americans were only a mile closer to Ormoc.

Medical care for the wounded was exceptional on Leyte. Medical platoons accompanied the assault waves on the beaches. Wounded men were immediately given treatment on-site and evacuated to designated ships by landing craft. As the battle moved away from the beaches, additional medical personnel came ashore and field hospitals were set up.

As the troops moved inland into difficult terrain, medical evacuation became more of a problem. With few exceptions, however, all casualties were treated within one hour after being wounded. Surgical operations were done only if the medical examining officer concluded the wounded soldier could not withstand the arduous trip to the rear, or decided his condition was critical.

The wounded would come back a trail toward the nearest medical aid station, sliding, falling, staggering in the mud; stretcher bearers straining, cussing, weary under their load. One soldier held his face which was a bloody mass of torn flesh; another in obvious great pain gripping his stomach, the blood running down his arms and onto his boots. On another stretcher a figure lay on his stomach with a huge red hole in his back. Such scenes became commonplace, but to me never routine. What a waste!

In subsequent U.S. wars, the helicopter would save many a wounded soldier who in World War II would have died before reaching field hospitals or a hospital ship. It's sad but true: medical and surgical skills, and new techniques in surgical procedures, flourish during war due to the high numbers of available patients. Medical advances are thus passed on to the civilian population at a great saving of lives in the future.

But war, overall, is a terrible waste. I am not an authority on the matter, but there are few heroes by nature. Battle pits life and death against each other. When all is said and done, life, no matter how miserable, is better than death that ends everything. The worse thing about combat is the never-ending suspense.

Meanwhile, GHQ had set up its headquarters and the general was provided quarters in a rather ornate structure known as the Walter Price mansion in Tacloban, not far from the capitol building. Price was an American businessman who had been taken prisoner and placed in Santo Tomas prison in Manila. His wife, a native islander, was living in the jungle. The Japanese had used the mansion as a recreational center.

When I returned to GHQ for further orders, the white-stuccoed mansion was scarred from repeated strafings. There were shell-holes here and there. The Japanese had tried to destroy it, hoping to get MacArthur as well. A dozen Filipinos in a building next door had already died from the air attacks.

If that wasn't bad enough, three correspondents died as a result of these air attacks: Ashel Bush, of the *Associated Press;* Stanley Gunn, *Fort Worth Star-Telegram;* and John Terry, of the *Chicago Daily News.* Bush died during the attacks, while the other two died later of their wounds.

They were billeted in a house on the other side of the Price mansion, which we had taken over for use as a press center. Fortunately, I was not "at home" when this attack occurred. My good luck was holding.

One day, as the general sat at his desk, a flight of Zeros came in at

This was once an Army truck whose driver struck a Japanese mine in a road near Tacloban. If you look closely, you can see a leg and foot with a boot on it just to the right of the wheel rim, below the truck frame.

low level and riddled the house with .50 caliber bullets. A staff officer rushed in, fearing the worst:

"Are you okay, sir?"

The general, pipe between his lips, replied: "It was not my time," and motioned toward a hole in the wall a couple of feet above his head. The enemy attacked Tacloban 30 times during the last week of October.

The Japanese tried trickery at an airfield near Tacloban one Sunday night. It was just after supper, when in the growing darkness several soldiers and airmen noticed a small formation of transport planes approaching the field. The planes made a half circle and prepared to land. It was quickly discovered, despite the bogus U.S. insignia on the wings, that they were Japanese intruders.

Anti-aircraft batteries went into action and quickly blew one from the sky; another was hit upon landing. The third rolled to a stop. Enemy soldiers piled out of the latter two aircraft and began attacking nearby gun emplacements and installations. The battle did not last long and little harm was done.

Some of the invaders appeared to be drunk or drugged. Some blew horns, whistles; others had gongs, wooden clappers, flares, and some were even singing. Documents recovered from enemy dead revealed the surprise attack was based upon a Japanese theory that "the Americans are notoriously sluggish following the evening meal."

The Japanese did land several hundred men on an airfield at Buri, December 5. They reaped havoc there and caused heavy losses to aircraft, supplies and installations before being wiped out. The casualties on our side were relatively light, however, and I never learned how this sizable enemy force managed to slip in undetected.

The final push on Leyte began December 5 with offensives toward Ormoc and in the central highlands. My group of reporters joined the 77th division in an unopposed landing south of the city. A week later, after overcoming stiff defense in the city, Ormoc was taken, along with vast quantities of supplies and equipment.

The Japanese on Leyte were now divided and isolated, cut off from reinforcement. Fighting would continue awhile, but the real contest for the island was over.

The city suffered great damage. GIs entering Ormoc found much of it in flames, a massive inferno fed by bursting white phosphorus shells, with homes and business buildings in utter ruin. A great pall of smoke hung over the city, mixed with the dust of buildings blasted by artillery, mortar and rocket fire.

Infantrymen supported by tank units began compressing the remainder of enemy resistance off the ridgelines of Ormoc Valley. Some made a last stand on a highway south of the city but eventually abandoned their positions and fled into the hills.

Organized resistance on Leyte ended as a Christmas gift, December 25, 1944. MacArthur's communiqué said the battle was over except for "mopping-up" operations. This was a laugh to the commanders whose troops had to do the "mopping up," which resulted in another 27,000 Japanese dead. In fact, when the war ended, thousands of Japanese soldiers still occupied much of the countryside on the island.

MacArthur called the six-month battle for Leyte "perhaps the greatest defeat in the military annals of the Japanese Army." In Japan, top military leaders recognized they had lost the Philippines at Leyte. The battle cost us 5,000 dead and 14,000 wounded in action, plus 89 missing in action.

While MacArthur was on Leyte, he received word he had been

promoted by President Franklin Roosevelt to a five-star general. There were no insignia for this newly created rank readily available, so his staff found a Filipino artisan who created a few sets out of silver.

As far as I know, there has yet to be publicity about the Japanese Army's use of Formosan citizens as pack mules on Leyte and, in New Guinea, as food for the table. As U.S. forces tightened the noose around Japanese troops in several localities, and their supplies of food ran out, we discovered that an undetermined number of Formosans (Taiwanese) had been killed and eaten.

A few Australian soldiers in Papua, New Guinea, deep in the interior to prevent enemy soldiers from entering areas bordering Northern Australia, are believed to have eaten Japanese flesh. Some enemy dead were found with special cuts of flesh from their remains, but I prefer to believe their own countrymen were to blame, not the Aussies.

Cannibalism, of course, was common in many South Pacific cultures. The arrival of missionaries nearly eliminated the practice. One can only imagine the plight of Japanese soldiers as they were forced to eat insects, tree bark, grasses, jungle rats, snails and snakes in a desperate effort to survive.

In such instances, human beings can resort to shocking measures to sustain life. Believe it or not, there are a few recorded instances of American GIs consuming human flesh during the war. I've never been that hungry.

MacArthur's return to the Philippines was now history, and with memories of Leyte, New Guinea, and Morotai forever etched in my mind, I began to anticipate my role in the forthcoming invasion of Luzon. I had now become almost oblivious to the sight of army trucks carrying loads of body bags to ships or burial grounds. I had found it best not to grieve or worry too much over things I couldn't control.

I now could bear, but still not without sorrow and pain, the agonizing cries of the wounded and maimed. Most of all, I hated to watch a dead soldier being placed in a body bag. There was no dignity to it, no reverence, just a dirty, heart-wrenching job I'm glad I didn't have to do.

Since Morotai, I had steeled myself against being too close to a man who might become, unexpectedly and quite suddenly, a casualty. Yet I did not want to ever lose those memories, as painful as they were, because I wanted to be forever reminded of the great spirit, courage and acceptance of sacrifice, that lies within us all.

It was President John F. Kennedy who said:

"Today as never before responsibility is the greatest right of citizenship, and service is the greatest of freedom's privileges."

I agree with that and most of who served in battle recognize its truth.

It has become very clear to me in my twilight hour that the blessings of life, liberty and the pursuit of happiness have been the product of God-fearing, honorable men. Who else could have provided the heritage for which men give their lives, their fortunes and sacred honor? Has it worked in America? You bet it has!

I would be remiss if I did not mention Sergeant Milton Kutcher, who was my public information assistant in 11th Corps headquarters. He was of invaluable help to me each time I had been assigned to General Hall's corps, and he was particularly helpful during the Leyte operation.

Milt was from near Liberty, New York, and his family owned "Kutcher's Country Club" in the Catskill mountains. It was a multi-million-dollar resort, and I was his overnight guest there during the Korean War when, prior to going overseas, I was sent to an army censorship school at Fort Slocum, near New York City.

It was really ironic. I was his so-called "boss," and my only income was my army pay. He was a sergeant who ran the PIO section in 11th Corps and was already a millionaire! I have never forgotten my friend "Milt."

While on Leyte 11th Corps press section acquired a green and yellow parrot, along with a monkey whose tail was about four inches short. Our photographer, Jim Simmons, named it Myrtle, I asked him where the name came from and he replied: "I had a girl friend named Myrtle once, and she didn't have much tail either."

I knew better than to attempt a reply.

Bataan Retaken

Chapter 10

"Now I want you to remember that no sonuvabitch ever won a war by dying for his country. He won it by making the other poor dumb sonuvabitch die for his country."

— General George Patton

AS THE LENGTHY CAMPAIGN FOR LEYTE came to a close, and with the realization the island's value as an air base had been greatly overestimated because of tricky soil and topography, MacArthur still lacked bases for the air power he believed he would need for his attack on Luzon.

Even after the airfields he could complete on Leyte were ready for use, the general would lack sufficient land-based air power within range of Luzon, Formosa, and other enemy air fields needed to adequately support the landings north of Manila.

The Luzon invasion, originally set for December 20, was rescheduled for January 9 in order to give the Navy's big carriers time to make repairs and re-supply after their extended use in the Leyte campaign. Weather and tide considerations were also factors.

Meanwhile, planning for the invasion of Mindoro, just south of Leyte, was underway. The airfields there would be used in support of the Luzon invasion and protect shipping. About all MacArthur had left for Mindoro were the escort carriers that had been severely tested during naval action off Leyte.

None the less, six of the small carriers, three battleships, six cruisers and some smaller warships formed the Mindoro invasion fleet which sailed from Leyte December 13. The Kamikazes would show up, but a far more powerful enemy, the weather, would endanger the invasion fleet.

Two days later, the troops went ashore at Mindoro with practically no opposition, but the Navy vessels at the landing site came under heavy attack by Kamikazes. The flagship Nashville was hit by a suicide plane and lost over 125 men killed and nearly 200 injured. The dead included the landing force commander, Brigadier General William C. Dunkel. Subsequent air attacks damaged numerous other ships, several severely.

The weather was an even more ferocious enemy. A typhoon blew in December 18 as the larger ships were refueling the destroyers who were there to protect them. Forecasters had misread the track of the storm and Task Force 38 Commander, Admiral "Bull" Halsey, the Navy's answer to the Army's General George Patton, had little advance warning. His ships were soon scattered over 2,500 square miles. The wind reached 90 knots and 70-foot waves rolled and tossed the vessels like toys in a bathtub.

Men were washed overboard; planes became loose from their moorings, some falling into the raging seas. Other ships caught fire; destroyer smoke stacks were sometimes nearly horizontal; water poured into ventilators and intakes, shorting power lines and cutting off power, steering and communications. Three destroyers capsized and most of the crews were lost. It was a terrible and costly nightmare, but 12 hours later Halsey began pounding Luzon with all the firepower at his disposal.

On Mindoro, both American and Australian engineer battalions worked at top speed to ready airfields. One fighter strip was completed in five days, another ready in 15 days, both ahead of schedule. From these bases the air force could support the Luzon invasion, attack Kkamikaze planes at their bases, and attack Japanese shipping. MacArthur would now have the air power he had long sought.

I was not personally involved in Mindoro. By that time, most of the reporters had phased themselves out of Leyte, finding some rest wherever they could, a few flying out to Hawaii for its attractions. I knew I would be assigned to some phase of the Luzon landings and, indeed, the invasion force was already being assembled, not only at Leyte but from other ports as far away as New Guinea and Morotai.

Finally my orders came, and I learned I was to be assigned to General Hall's 11th Corps once again, which suited me fine. I must admit I was somewhat disappointed at first, because I would not be part of the main thrust of the Luzon drive south toward Manila. Instead, I would be part of a smaller invasion of the west coast of Luzon, just above the Bataan peninsula.

When I heard the name "Bataan," however, I immediately swelled

PARA(GRAPH) TROOPER FOR MacARTHUR

with pride. I was gung-ho in anticipation of joining the force that would retake Bataan and Corregidor Island. I vividly recalled the angry reaction of my parents, friends and neighbors back home when word came that Bataan had fallen and Corregidor was under relentless siege.

News reports from Bataan relating to the infamous "death March" really enraged the public, including those of us who had just entered the army weeks before December 7, 1941. The brutal and inhuman treatment of our captured soldiers by the Japanese military in the Philippines remains an ugly memory yet to be erased.

MacArthur chose Lingayen Gulf, halfway down the west side of the mitten-shaped island, for the primary assault. This involved more troops than ever before used in an invasion landing: 175,000 to be put ashore on a beachhead 20 miles wide. Eventually, ten-plus divisions were engaged on Luzon but even with such strength, total victory would not come until June 30, 1945.

Except for a few Japanese stragglers who fired wildly before fleeing into the jungle, there was little organized resistance at Lingayen Gulf. At sea and at the landing beaches, however, it was a far different story. Kamikaze aircraft swarmed all over the fleet of ships and created major havoc. Many ships were damaged, a few sunk, and loss of life was heavy.

It was at Lingayen that U.S. forces were first introduced to Kamikaze boats on a large scale. The tiny plywood craft were a major surprise when they began ramming into the sides of the larger landing craft and naval vessels. The prow of these tiny ships were filled with explosives and detonated upon impact, also blowing up the Japanese

In the battle for Bataan, many Japanese soldiers blew themselves up with grenades, or disemboweled themselves with a sword or bayonet, to escape capture. Infantrymen of the 38th division sift through the belongings of one such soldier who used a grenade to join his ancestors.

patriots guiding the boats. These pesky boats continued to be a problem for the rest of the war.

The Kamikaze Shintoist philosophy convinced men of all grades and ranks that they were invincible, that defeat was not thinkable. Their suicidal mind-set was evidenced in one of their war songs which contained the following words:

Across the sea, Corpses in the water. Across the mountains, Corpses heaped upon the field; I shall die only for the Emperor, I shall never look back.

Despite the suicide threat, the Lingayen assault force pushed inland, over sand and marshland, consolidating their two beachheads. They quickly captured the Lingayen airfield and began to set their sights on Manila, 125 miles to the south. It wouldn't be as easy as it then appeared.

At about this precise time, a large formation of American planes fanned out over Luzon to drop leaflets. They read:

"In a series of brilliantly conceived blows, General MacArthur's forces of liberation have successfully, in but a short span of time, destroyed the enemy army defending Leyte, seized firm control of Mindoro, and now stand defiantly on the soil of Luzon at the very threshold to our capital city. Thus are answered our prayers of many long months — thus is the battle for the liberation of the Philippines fully joined and the hour of our deliverance is at hand."

The message was signed by President Osmena, but to many it sounded like a product of the GHQ psychological warfare staff, with a few choice phrases taken from MacArthur's writings.

Twenty days later, another U.S. Armada was off the west coast of Luzon near the small barrios of San Antonio, San Miguel and San Narciso. General Hall's XI Corps had 40,000 men aboard, including me and five reporters. Admiral Arthur Struble's warships were set to pound the beaches when a "Hold Your Fire" order was given.

What an unexpected but welcome surprise!

Several small boats loaded with Filipino guerrillas were sailing out to greet us. They had been sent by Lieutenant Colonels Gyles Merrill and Ramon Magsaysay, leaders of area guerrilla groups, to report the Japanese had abandoned their defensive positions near the beaches.

I cannot honestly say I was unhappy that the excitement of another assault landing was not to be. I felt something was not quite right; I knew the enemy was awaiting us somewhere. Later, we learned the Japanese had withdrawn their troops into the interior, where they now occupied even stronger defensive positions. We wouldn't miss the excitement, nor the battle. We'd would just have to walk farther to find it.

General Hall called off the bombardment and ordered the troops ashore. The landing force was composed primarily of the 38th Infantry Division, a National Guard outfit from Indiana and Kentucky, and the 34th Regimental Combat Team, plus additional support units. It was known as the "Cyclone" division, presumably on the basis of its service in World War I.

The soldiers were greeted by cheering Filipinos and the only casualty was sustained by one GI who attempted to ride an ill-tempered caribou and was gored. This was not considered a battle wound, just a big pain in the rear, with no Purple Heart.

It was a day or two following the landing I was nearly "wounded" — not from an enemy bullet — but from a caribou, or water buffalo. A native had driven his oxcart up a road near our area and had stopped to water it. I got up close to give it a pat or two, but when I stepped too close to its head it nearly ran its horn through me.

The apologetic driver managed to tell me in broken English that the buffalo wasn't really mad at me, he just didn't like the way I smelled. It seems one must never get close to a buffalo's head unless he is familiar with your body odor. I decided to keep my distance, since I didn't care if the animal liked me or not.

I didn't blame the water buffalo; he was pretty intelligent, for in truth I had not had a bath for a couple of days and deodorant was something we didn't carry around every day. There were times when I could barely stand myself, but body odor was the least of our worries.

The happy natives assisted in removing supplies from the ships, but, unfortunately, movement of supplies was impeded by the throngs of joyous people who jammed nearby roads. The people were anxious to help and grateful for food and cigarettes. For one of the few times in the war, we sensed how it felt to be "liberators."

The Filipino people were exceptionally friendly and mostly attractive. They led quite a simple life, however, and few had anything except family, a few hogs or caribou, perhaps a rice paddy or two, and their tiny house.

Their barrios, or villages, were merely clusters of thatched-roof houses on stilts. The livestock were kept beneath the floor, and the stilts also protected the dwellings from the heavy rains of typhoons. The air was always filled with the smells of charcoal heating up the cooking pots. The beads of light one saw from outside were from candles or oil lamps which produced a minimum of illumination.

Each barrio offered the same scenery: The women carrying water from the town well; an abundance of bicycles to dodge. Here and there old men were sitting on their haunches in doorways, others straining the morning light to read a newspaper or book. Sometimes one might see a small lad, or even his grandpa, standing against the wall of a house taking a leak.

The Filipino family had a certain formation when they walked down the dusty street. The husband walked in front, sometimes holding a youngster by the hand. Next, the wife with an infant on her hip, and bringing up the rear another small child or two. It was interesting to see the villages come to life in early morning. They enjoyed a simple life, but, aside from the effects of war, occupation and another invasion, they appeared happy.

The 38th Division had seen limited action in New Guinea and at Leyte. The division recorded its first Japanese soldier killed in New Guinea on December 7, 1944, when Sergeant Bill Steward raised his M-1 and fired. An enemy soldier fell from a coconut tree "deader 'n hell," as Steward described it.

Little did he and his buddies know that within hours the division would be engaged in some of the toughest fighting in the Philippines, and the 38th would go down in history as the "Avengers of Bataan," an honor they richly deserved.

After the invasion confusion settled down, a ceremony was held on the grounds of the provincial capitol in San Antonio. General Hall presented medals to the guerrilla leaders, Magsaysay and Merrill, for their service to America during the Japanese Occupation. I was able to attend this ceremony, along with other Corps personnel and reporters.

Also present were several members of the Negrito tribes, rather diminutive, pygmy-like warriors, who were heavily involved in the guerrilla movement. These small but sturdy tribesmen wore loincloths and primitive jewelry and carried bows, arrows and spears. Most were bearded but appeared reasonably clean considering their primitive and isolated environment.

Each one was given an appropriate memento by General Hall, who bowed low before each one as he presented the gift. They deserved this recognition, for many had put their lives on the line against the Japanese invaders, and many died in the effort.

In fact, these people, and another tribe known as the Igorots, often exposed themselves to enemy fire to carry ammunition, food, water and even mail, to our troops in remote jungle regions. Their bravery was legendary.

General MacArthur once praised them, saying: "For sheer, heart-stopping, desperation fearlessness, I have never seen the equal of these people."

The Negrito warriors who assisted our cause were an exception. Most of the tribes considered any human being outside their own tribe an enemy and fair game to kill or torture. They would risk their lives without hesitation to obtain guns or women, or even a pig.

Strangely, however, if another man fell in love with a tribesman's woman, even a man in the same tribe or blood kin, that man was permitted to commit adultery with her. If the husband found out about it, though, he then must kill the intruder even if he didn't want to. That is because, Tolandian, the Negrito high god who lives in the earth, doesn't approve adultery. If Tolandian gets angry, he might just destroy everybody.

Earthworms were said to be Tolandian's messenger. The Negritos never display disdain for them and the worms are always thanked before being placed on the fishing hook. Even worse, if this god is displeased, he may turn the world over so the trees are upside down. The Negritos believe monkeys convey information to Tolandian. Fascinating philosophy.

Later that evening, several of us were invited to a feast at the barrio where Captain Magsaysay was staying. The dwelling he occupied there was perched on high ground overlooking the scenic China Sea. To me it was like something out of a primitive Arabian Nights.

There we were, beneath a cluster of palm trees with a full South Pacific moon painting thin lines of orange striping on the incoming waves. Our host had a local instrumental group playing traditional music as we sipped coconut milk mixed with a mild liqueur of some sort.

I was surprised how relaxed Ramon appeared to be. After all, he and his guerrilla army had been on the run since the Japanese captured the Philippines. He had been ambushed and nearly captured several times. He had seen many of his followers captured and tortured, and others killed or wounded in hundreds of skirmishes.

Before us was a large shallow pit and over the glowing coals was a sizeable pig, roasting to a delightful degree of moist tenderness. Smoke from the embers curled lazily skyward until it disappeared in the lush canopy of palm leaves. About a dozen natives, mostly women, worked furiously to complete the lavish menu of Filipino specialties one of which, I was informed, was reserved for only the most honored guests. This dish was served on small sections of palm leaves and the portions were not too large. The main ingredient came from the very top of the coconut tree, right where the top branches divide to form a small pod of tender shoots. I was told that removing this pod destroyed the entire tree, so you can understand how unique this delicacy was. It's flavor and texture was simply fantastic.

It took nearly 53 years to learn the name of this delicacy. In November, 1996, quite by chance I sat down at a table with a Filipino Methodist minister, the Rev. Cesar O. Paniamogan, of King City, Mo. In telling him of my war experience in his homeland, I mentioned the banquet with Magsaysay and the delicious food from the top of a coconut tree.

He knew at once what I had eaten. It is called *Ubod,* and he affirmed it was served only for very special guests and, indeed, killed the tree it was taken from. Cesar also told me of his family's plight during the war. The Japanese plundered and destroyed his barrio and drove his family into the jungle where they barely survived by eating and clothing themselves from the jungle habitat.

The meal ritual lasted several hours. Nothing ever tasted better than that roast pig, especially after spending months on sand beaches and in dense jungle where K and C rations were the standard fare. The meal embraced at least eight courses; exotic, exciting, mysterious, delectable; each tasty dish an adventure for army guys away from home in a strange land. I thought of Kathy and wished we had this special night together.

I became well acquainted with Magsaysay, who later became president of the Philippines. He was one of the few real patriots I have ever known. Upon his election I wrote him a letter, never expecting to receive a reply. He did write back, on official government stationery, thanking me for my friendship and reflecting briefly on our meeting in Zambales province.

Sadly, Ramon died in a mysterious plane crash, presumably the target of Filipino insurgents, while still in office. I will never forget him. He and his bands of guerrillas kept hope alive for millions of their countrymen during the oppressive occupation until MacArthur could mus-

PARA(GRAPH) TROOPER FOR MacARTHUR

This pristine scene, featuring a coastal lighthouse, was only a few miles from the horrors of the interior of Bataan Peninsula. Not far away was Zig-Zag Pass where some of the toughest fighting on Luzon took place and cost a general his career. Believe it or not, there was a Japanese defensive position built into the cliff below the lighthouse.

ter sufficient forces to return the country to its rightful owners.

It was my good fortune recently to meet retired Col. Price Ramsey, a distant relative of mine through marriage, whose exciting book, *Lieutenant Ramsey's War*, is in its second printing. Ramsey was in a Cavalry unit on Bataan and had the choice of surrendering to the Japanese, or joining Filipino guerrilla forces in the jungle. He choose the later, and became a highly decorated and respected officer as a result of his heroism.

The fun and honors over, our effort was directed toward the pending battle for Bataan. Before the war, Bataan was an obscure province in the islands; strategically, however, it became important because of its proximity to Manila Bay and its value as a military base.

Perhaps a little geography is in order. Bataan is bordered on the west by Subic Bay and the South China Sea, and on the East by Manila Bay. It is mountainous and jungle-covered and sparsely populated. The natives made their living fishing or growing rice. There were two fairly good roads, one crossing the peninsula at its base and another south to Marivales at the tip, just across the bay from Corregidor Island.

It was along these roads the thousands of defenders of Bataan and Corregidor were forced to participate in the infamous "death march" in 1942. These same roads would play a key role in Bataan's liberation and the restoration of peace and honor.

For Americans, the peninsula was a symbol of defeat, of a painful retreat, and a death march that prickled the U.S. conscience to the boiling point. Bataan was a place of humiliation and grief, of heroism and sacrifice. It was in all our minds: the enemy had to pay for its treachery. The 38th Infantry Division would avenge the shame and sorrow of Bataan for all Americans.

General Hall once confided to correspondents gathered around his battle map that back in 1930, as a junior officer, he had the opportunity to observe the territory that would soon be under attack. His report to his superiors at that time indicated his belief that the terrain there provided natural defense and would be "virtually impregnable."

Thus he now had to prove, as a major general and corps commander, that no defense could stop the American advance into Bataan. It wasn't easy, but Hall refuted his earlier prediction. Bataan proved to be tough going, but it proved not impregnable, just extremely tough.

Though tough, our troops knew they were far better off than the defenders of Bataan in 1942 when there was little to defend it with. Everything was in short supply — particularly food. Commanding General Johnathan Wainwright found himself even worse off when MacArthur ordered half-rations for the Bataan and Corregidor garrisons.

He immediately ordered his men to supplement their scanty food supply by killing every carabao they could find. This tough meat had to be soaked overnight in salt water and pounded before being cooked. It was edible, but stringy and chewy beyond belief. Still, it was nourishment. Later on, the survivors of the battle would resort to eating dogs, monkeys and lizards.

All normal combat supplies were in short supply: gasoline, barbed wire, trucks and communication equipment. There were no telephone lines and few radios. The Japanese attack began January 9. They dropped thousands of leaflets from planes, warning MacArthur that the end of the fighting was near, and that his troops on Bataan and Corregidor were doomed.

The fate of most of those troops is a painful memory to Americans. There was much contempt toward General MacArthur within his command at this point. The feeling was there was no rhyme nor reason in sentencing a small group of Americans to a hopeless task that had no chance whatsoever to succeed.

The Japanese were surprised that U.S. defense forces surrendered.

This violated their code of *Bushido*, the way of the warrior. The code said Japanese soldiers could not surrender because it would bring disgrace to their country, family and self. It was far more honorable to die in battle, or commit suicide.

This feeling was responsible, in part, for the treatment our soldiers received once captured. The enemy considered them dishonorable for having surrendered, and they were shocked that our men wanted their loved ones to even know they were alive. In some instances the Japanese offered pistols to their captives so they might shoot themselves. They were stunned when our men refused.

A Philippine scout watches for mines as a jeep-load of U.S. soldiers prepared to enter Zig-Zag Pass. A quarter-mile beyond this point the road nearly disappeared in a lush green canopy of jungle growth.

The battle for Zigzag Pass was the key to the re-taking of Bataan, and it developed into one of the most difficult struggles of the Philippine campaign. Officially the pass was highway 7. It crossed the lowlands of Zambales through Olongapo, site of a huge U.S. Navy base before and after the war, into a tight defile leading into the mountains of Northern Bataan. Eventually the highway reaches Dinaluphan on the west side of the peninsula.

The highway twists and turns like a writhing snake. One GI truck driver said: "The curves are so sharp I can see my spare." The road was seldom level either, rising and falling with every ridge, bordered on both sides by steep cliffs and thick, nearly impenetrable jungle.

Later on, I ran across a Filipino school teacher who said the highway route had in much earlier times been a path established by wild pigs. I could believe it! One trail, about 700 yards north of Highway 7, was known only to Negrito tribesmen of the region. This trail was utilized by our forces, with the help of Negrito bearers, to carry essential supplies to forward areas since the highway was so often exposed to enemy fire.

I doubt our troops ever fought in a region where natural obstacles were greater, or the close-in fighting more ferocious. The terrain was not easily adaptable to armored vehicles, artillery function was limited, and often could not be used at all because jungle growth detonated projectiles before they ever reached their targets.

I can tell you that in some places you could step five yards off the highway and not see the road. I am not exaggerating.

The Japanese had honeycombed every hill and knoll in the pass with foxholes linked with tunnels or trenches. At certain key points, they had built strongpoints of log and dirt pillboxes. All these defenses were well camouflaged because the lush jungle growth covered virtually everything.

The fighting in the pass began January 31. I accompanied INS reporter John Cashman, the AP's Jim Hutchison, Homer Bigart, of *The New York Herald-Tribune,* and Stan Troutman, *Acme News.* There were other correspondents with the 38th Division from time to time, but I wasn't always aware where everyone was at any given time.

The 38th Division had its own press officer, Major Peyton Hoge, who in civilian life worked as a public relations person for the Brown-Foreman Distillery in Louisville. He was a congenial fellow and provided correspondents with all the help he could in the way of food, shelter, and information. He did a great job for his division and I enjoyed working with him.

Things just didn't go well for the division. Resistance was light at first as various units pushed their way into Zigzag, but as the infantry reached the first enemy strongpoints the morning of January 1, knowing where the units were became a problem. Commanders could not find their locations on maps which were not up-to-date, and none to accurate to begin with.

To make matters worse, unit radios often refused to work in the thick vegetation. Direct communication with individual units became very difficult, often impossible. Coordination of fire power, and movement of troops, became unattainable.

As a result, battalion and regimental headquarters commanders did not always know where their units were. This complicated use of artillery and, in a few instances, resulted in Americans firing at other Americans. Meanwhile advance patrols had run into a hornet's nest of Japanese. They had a rough time all day trying to find and isolate Japanese positions.

During the night, the Japanese launched counterattacks and harassed the units with mortar and artillery, inflicting casualties. The battle thus went into a phase where scattered companies of infantry battled against an enemy they could not often see, and not knowing for sure which side of the highway they were on, due to the violent twists of the highway and the unimaginable jungle growth.

Little progress was being made. I and two of the reporters found our way back to division headquarters while John Cashman elected to join one of the infantry units. There was concern at headquarters because frontline units were losing some key company officers and NCO's, causing serious reorganization problems.

Major General Henry L.C. Jones, division commander, was not in a good mood. He would feel even worse later on.

There was staff disagreement on where certain infantry companies and platoons were located. The commanders up front were often confused and disoriented as far as consulting the maps was concerned. It was obvious that the division was not functioning as it should. To be honest, it was a real command mess.

About noon, General Hall came up front and saw first-hand the confusion and lack of effective command function. The division was bogged down. Dissatisfied with the situation, Hall told Jones in front of everybody that "the exhibition of your division is the worst I have ever seen."

I had not seen General Hall display publicly such vocal displeasure with a subordinate commander. This was a side of him I hadn't known before. It was his West Point side: duty, honor, country. General Jones was a National Guard officer.

The face of General Jones drained white; he was seething, greatly embarrassed by this dressing-down in front of his staff and reporters. No question about it, it was a severe indictment of a division that had seen very limited action to this point, and apparently had lost some of its confidence and morale. Jones had already relieved one of his regimental commanders in an effort to shake-up the division.

I wasn't close enough to the two generals to hear every word, but it went something like this:

General Hall: "Even your headquarters security seems weak. Where are all your people?"

General Jones: "They've been sent up to the front, sir, because we are short of riflemen. We haven't had a single replacement for over a week."

General Hall: "It seems you've lost your momentum. Why did you not follow the suggestions from my command?"

General Jones: "The Japanese are not in a fire and maneuver mode, sir. They're entrenched in these hills and well trained. I'm concerned that to attempt anything other than digging them out as we go will be very hazardous to any force I might use to envelop their flank."

General Hall: "I am disappointed to hear you say that, General Jones. I want you to move out as I have directed. Are you presuming to take it upon yourself to tell me how to run this Corps?"

General Jones: "Sir, I respect you and your Corps. I am only trying to offer my advice as the commander who must live with the results."

Hall concluded the exchange. "General Jones, if you cannot concur with my recommendations I think you understand that I must relieve you of command, and replace you with someone who will get this division moving."

General Jones, ashen-faced in anger, replied: "Sir, that is your privilege," saluted and walked slowly away with members of his staff who were also boiling mad.

In my opinion, General Hall was under great pressure himself from GHQ because, according to scuttlebutt, General MacArthur wanted certain victories accomplished so they could be reported on his birthday. I do not know this was true, but I do know it could have been ordered, not by MacArthur, but by his doting staff who were constantly "buttering up" the chief.

Meanwhile, in Zigzag Pass, the division by February 4 appeared to be gaining some momentum. At several spots, advance units overcame strongpoints. Over on the north side of Highway 7, forward units were about to capture one of the biggest Japanese strongpoints, along a ridgeline above the road.

Just when it seemed victory was at hand, a vicious Japanese mortar and artillery barrage drove the units back across highway 7. This was the fourth time in three days the enemy had thwarted American attempts to clear these vital positions. The Japanese still controlled the pass, but it was not because our soldiers had not fought hard.

Jim Hutcheson wrote in a dispatch:

"The nights are hell for the men. They're dead tired, but keeping their spirits up. The advance in the narrow defiles is tortuous and slow because a few Japs can turn loose withering fire from hidden positions overlooking the road. The bamboo forests are so thick we have to get within a few feet of the Japs to see them. It is the kind of fighting where we have to go in and root them out."

I can identify with that story because I was with Jim most of the time he was with division infantry units. You cannot imagine the stress of such situations. Every sound is a potential threat and you crouch down with a prayer for your safety with every crack of a rifle, or any unusual noise.

A few feet away is an enemy who will kill you on sight. Off to your left a GI pulls the pin on a grenade and tosses it into the jungle mass. There is an explosion. Someone cries out in pain and you hope it's a Japanese.

The battlefield offers no explanations except those that explain other battles, other wars. There is courage, fear, discipline of varying degrees, insanity, foolhardiness, resignation and a realization that someone, somewhere, contrived a reason for requiring men to die alone and far from home.

Bravery was common in the ranks. Staff Sergeant Joseph Odyniec was involved in an attack on a fortified hill when his platoon received heavy machine gun fire. Without hesitation or orders, he picked up a BAR (Browning Automatic Rifle) from a wounded comrade, picked up some grenades, and started into the thick undergrowth, cutting his way through with a knife.

With enemy fire concentrated on him, he managed to reach the Japanese position — six foxholes with connecting trenches. Odyniec threw several grenades into one of the holes, then assaulted the position with his Browning. He killed 15 Japanese who were heavily armed. Miraculously, he didn't get a scratch.

On the 5th, there was a fire-fight that left only one officer able to function out of two infantry companies. INS Correspondent John Cashman wrote the story which resulted in a decoration for Captain

William Todd, who led his men on a wild charge against a fortified hill. Wounded, he refused to be evacuated until the mission was accomplished. Despite painful leg wounds, he hobbled up the hill waving his men on and firing his Browning automatic rifle into the most intricate system of tunnels and caves any unit of the division had encountered thus far.

Inspired by his conduct, his men rushed from their positions and, in the face of deadly enemy fire, seized the hill. Captain Todd received the Distinguished Service Cross for his valorous action.

Now and then there was something to laugh at. Private Adolph Albers, a 38th Division infantryman, was engaged in a night attack when a enemy soldier rolled a grenade into his foxhole. Albers jumped out and the grenade exploded harmlessly. "Hey, you missed me, you little bastard."

"OK, Joe, I see you later," the Jap soldier replied.

Minutes later Albers heard him returning and quickly shot him. Another GI nearby, hearing the noise, tossed another grenade.

"Hey," came a voice with an injured tone: "Watch that stuff, Joe!"

The Cyclone Division kept pushing along Highway 7, but far slower than anyone had anticipated. In another command conflict, General Hall visited some forward areas and was incensed to find the infantry not moving. He was told they were not moving because of a delayed airstrike.

By this time the San Marcelino airstrip, one of the early objectives, had been made serviceable and fighter planes had begun helping the infantry by dropping bombs and napalm on pinpointed Japanese positions.

Hall asked Jones when he was going to use his artillery. Jones indicated he planned to take all day to insure the guns were registered on precise and identified targets. General Hall told Jones to "cut out the precise stuff" and get the attack underway. Jones reluctantly agreed and gave orders for the infantry to move forward.

The record shows that in three days in Zigzag, the 38th division had lost half as many men as it had during the 78 days in combat on Leyte. Clearly something was amiss.

On February 6, Hall came to the conclusion the division would function better under a new commander. He relieved Jones, who was replaced by General William Chase. Chase was a blood and guts general who had just led one of the 1st Cavalry Division's "flying columns" into Manila. He was a fine officer who was due for a promotion anyway.

General Hall explained his decision: "Lack of aggressiveness on the part of his (Jones) division, unsatisfactory tactical planning and execution, and inadequate reconnaissance measures. He failed to produce the results with his division which might be reasonably expected."

Jones wasn't the only National Guard officer sacked during the war. It was the "West Point Protective Association" in action. In fairness, however, there was no question some National Guard units were not ready for combat. In a few cases, however, it was not entirely the unit's fault, because. they had not been given sufficient time to train properly.

The battle for the pass didn't change much after Chase took over. Complicated maneuvering through dense jungle and over rough terrain characterized each day's action. It was just a foot-by-foot advance with the Japanese continuing their dogged resistance. It was not until the 13th that units of the 38th Division could actually make contact with each other from both sides of the highway.

The battle ended February 15. In retrospect, it appears the 11th Corps intelligence staff had initially underestimated Japanese strength in the pass, and the infantry units were committed piecemeal to the battle in insufficient numbers. Not every operation can go according to plan and completely fulfill expectations — there are too many imponderables involved.

There were those commanders who became obsessed with maps, and who liked to draw lines on the map board, and set timetables for advancing troops. In my opinion they never anticipated a place like Zigzag Pass existed, and refused to accept reality.

I still respected and admired General Hall, but at Zigzag I had seen what pressure can do to a man, even when he has stars on his shoulders.

Incidentally, the United States gave our Navy base at Olongapo to the Philippine government in 1992. When I remember Bataan, and think of the blood spilled in the battles to get it back from the Japanese, I get a little sick.

When the last American left the base, the Philippines were free of foreign military forces for the first time since 1543 when Spanish explorers landed on Mindanao and named the archipelago for Spain's crown prince and later King Philip II.

I suppose it *was* time to clear all foreigners from Philippine soil.

Adventure on Corregidor

Chapter 11

"Many veterans who are honest with themselves will admit, I believe, that the experience of communal effort in battle, even under the altered conditions of modern war, has been a high point in their lives."

— J. Glenn Gray, *The Warriors*

WHILE THE 38TH DIVISION was battling on Bataan, the fight for Manila was taking place with U.S. troops meeting stiff resistance all the way south from Lingayen Gulf. The battle was officially declared over March 3 when General MacArthur was notified by his commanders that all organized resistance in the city had ceased.

I would not see the devastated city until after MacArthur returned to Corregidor March 2, for a flag-raising ceremony, but we could see Manila burning across the bay from the top of Malinta Hill. At night, we could see the flames but during daylight, just heavy smoke.

With Zigzag Pass officially secured, General Walter Krueger, Sixth Army Commander, ordered General Hall to proceed with the mop-up of Bataan. D-Day was set for February 15 involving elements of the 38th Division with some help from 36th Division units. Hall divided his troops into two groups, East Force and South Force.

East Force would push south along the east coast road starting February 14, in order to divert Japanese attention from the Marivales landing set for the 25th. South Force would make an assault landing at Marivales to establish control over southern Bataan and then strike up the east coast to contact the East Force, thus sealing off remaining enemy forces.

Marivales, at the tip of the peninsula, was once a U.S. Army base located a few miles across the bay from Corregidor. The "death march" began at Marivales early in 1942. Sixth Army and XI Corps estimated 6,000 Japanese were still on Bataan south of Zig-Zag but this proved to be another exaggeration by intelligence staffs.

I remained with General Hall for this operation. The naval task force under Admiral Struble would deliver the assault force. His destroyers would sweep mines from the waters across the entrance to Manila Bay, paying special attention to the area between Corregidor and Mariveles, and the channel between Corregidor and Caballo Island. Fifth Air Force planes would provide pre-invasion bombardment and support ground operations.

The task force swept 140 mines from the bay including 28 left over from the U.S. defense effort in '42. Mines damaged two destroyers, however, and the ships also received some fire from artillery batteries on Corregidor. The landings began at 10 a.m., with little resistance, but with plenty of noise from the naval bombardment, plus bombing runs from the air.

A near-miss from a gun on Corregidor wounded several infantrymen as they left their transport ship to climb into a landing craft. That worried me a bit because I and a couple of reporters were slated to get into the next boat. The stuff that flew in our direction wasn't even close. Reporters along for this relatively minor assault included John Cashman, INS, and Russell Brines, AP. Both these reporters were battle-wise and thus relieved me of considerable worry.

As our troops poured ashore, they scrambled over the stony pile of ruins of Marivales. Devastation was everywhere, the rubble full of reminders of the 1942 battle. Old-style helmets, some with bullet holes, rotted gas masks, even old field desks and kitchen equipment were scattered among the tall weeds.

Carefully laid out graveyards told a tragic story. Some gravesites were unfilled, others with whitened remains beside open pits. The enemy had not even permitted their prisoners to bury all their dead.

While viewing the remains of Marivales, I couldn't help but recall the situation on Bataan in those dark days after MacArthur left Corregidor for Australia, and the defenders on the peninsula felt abandoned. While the Filipino troops never lost faith in the general, many American GIs were bitter over the fact that promised equipment and reinforcements never arrived which, history now shows, was not the fault of "Dugout Doug."

Maybe some will recall a stanza from the song they composed:

"We're the battling bastards of Bataan, No mama, no papa, no Uncle Sam, No aunts, No uncles, no nephews, no nieces, No rifles, no planes, or artillery pieces, And nobody gives a damn"

Japanese soldiers haul down the American flag from the parade ground pole on Corregidor early in 1942. This photograph came from a Japanese war book that I found on Corregidor.

The fast-moving infantry units found no enemy before sunset, but during the night about 100 Japanese attacked the perimeter of a battalion east of the town. The attack was repulsed and 60 Japanese died, with our casualties very light.

There was only one other battle of consequence when, during the night of February 15, an estimated 300 Japanese attacked a dug-in unit north of Marivales. The infantry beat them off in fierce hand-to-hand combat. The wild, confused melee cost the enemy at least 80 dead, and we had a few dead as well.

That incident marked the end of organized resistance in southern Bataan. A major tragedy was narrowly averted, however. MacArthur decided to fly over from Manila to see how things were going. He and his party flew to an airstrip near San Fernando and then boarded Jeeps for a trip along the coastal road. They reached a point five miles beyond the South Force's front line, which was a bit risky.

His group did not directly encounter any Japanese forces, although some were in that area. Fifth Air Force P-38s, observing the general's caravan, assumed they had spotted an enemy motor column and requested permission to bomb and strafe. Before granting permission, General Chase, who was commanding the South Force, ordered further investigation, which disclosed that the small convoy was friendly and, indeed, included the theater commander.

You can imagine the uproar that would have occurred had MacArthur been killed by our own Air Force. The general, despite the near-disaster, remained calm and appeared deeply moved by his return to Bataan. When he was forced to turn back after reaching a blown-up bridge, he said: "This day has done me a lot of good."

Chase, a brigadier general at the time, was quickly given another star. He deserved the command anyway. He had been very successful in his missions, he was well-liked and respected by his officers and men, and he was aggressive in the Patton image without the bravado and glamour.

In another interesting sidelight, our troops came upon a cave near Marivales. The entrance had been sealed, but it was blown open. Inside was a former emergency hospital for U.S. soldiers from the terrible days of 1942. There were cots lined up in two rows and on nearly every cot was a skeleton, mostly in rotted uniforms or gowns.

Some of the remains still had dogtags around the neck.

We assumed retreating American soldiers left the wounded in the cave, hoping the Japanese would quickly find them and provide treatment. Apparently the enemy savagely and quickly bayoneted them in their beds and closed the entrance.

With Bataan taken care of, General Hall turned his attention to Corregidor, which had been under attack by Allied planes since January 22. These attacks were gradually stepped up and by D-Day, February 16, 3,150 tons of bombs had been dropped on the island. On the morning of the 16th, bombers struck known and suspected gun positions and the Navy's pre-invasion bombardment began at sun-up in full fury.

Let me tell you, those of us engaged in this relatively small and unsung battle recall with pride the significance of the victory there. Every soldier involved knew the tiny fortress-island had become a beacon of humiliation as well as supreme valor, sacrifice and commitment.

Corregidor was the scene of a rare U.S. surrender involving Americans who had escaped the infamous Bataan "death march" to make their way to the island for a final, heroic stand. Those of us going to Corregidor felt the Japanese had to pay for this blot on our national pride.

After MacArthur was ordered to leave the beleaguered island, transferring command to General Wainwright, Corregidor fell to the Japanese on May 6, 1942. The surrender came after weeks of bombardment and with ammunition, food and medical supplies near depletion. Wainwright had no other choice but to surrender, but the defeat stung the American people to a degree only a bit less than the attack on Pearl Harbor.

We wanted that island back! Each of us felt a special responsibility in getting the job done. We wanted to avenge the sadness of '42.

Due to the isolation of Corregidor, located at the entrance to Manila Harbor from the South China Sea, I set up a rather unique system to transport news dispatches and photos prepared by the correspondents to the United States. I was able to line up a PT boat to carry their copy and film from the island back to Marivales at least once every 12 to 15 hours.

I personally carried the dispatches to Marivales each day, but occasionally, tied up with something else, I would deliver them to an army courier who carried them via Jeep to a small airstrip nearby. There he or I boarded an artillery observation aircraft (like a Piper Cub) which flew us to a radio transmission station located a hundred miles north, where the material was censored and then transmitted back to U.S. newspapers.

This rather-involved system covered a daily route of about 300 miles. I should remind you that every bit of material written by reporters assigned to MacArthur's headquarters had to submit to censorship. Many correspondents believed the reason for this was to protect the image of MacArthur.

I never chose to believe that, but there was reason to suspect the general's inner circle thought they ought to make sure that news reports matched MacArthur's communiques. When viewed in that light, it made some sense since they did not always reflect the true situation.

Unfortunately, the battle for Corregidor never received the publicity it deserved. On the same day we went ashore, the pre-invasion bombardment of Iwo Jima began and within a few days the Marines had suffered so many dead and wounded, their battle plan became suspect. Wholesale deaths on Iwo Jima took over the headlines.

No one, however, could ever question the courage and heroism of the Marine Corps. The Corps has borne the brunt of battle in all our wars and I for one have always understood the *esprit de corps* of that service.

I can only point out that it was MacArthur's policy in every Southwest Pacific campaign to save as many lives as possible. I am not critical of the Marine Corps at all, but emphasize there is a great difference between their frontal assaults and the fire-and-maneuver philosophy of the Army.

The invasion of Corregidor was at hand. I and my band of reporters were on board the flagship of Admiral Russell Berkey's Task Force 77. The correspondents were: Howard Handleman, *International News Service*; Homer Bigart, New *York Herald-Tribune*; Stan Troutman, *Acme News Service* and Richard Harris, *United Press*. I loved these guys, and you'll find out why later on.

The island, shaped like a tadpole, is less than two miles wide at its widest point, and three and a half miles long. Its large, high head, pointed toward the China Sea, was called Topside. It was on this high, flat hill that the old garrison headquarters buildings stood. These included officers' quarters and barracks for the enlisted men, theater, gun emplacements, golf course and the parade ground with the old flagpole still standing.

As a result of the fighting there in 1942, and our pre-invasion bombings, there was little but rubble left on Topside. Even that was entangled

This is the beach area where elements of the 24th infantry division landed. In the background can be seen Caballo Island being bombed and, in between, the dock where Jim Hutchison and I came under fire while debarking from a PT boat.

in undergrowth and splintered trees, amidst bomb and shell craters, crumbled buildings and abandoned armament and supplies.

From Topside, the ground sloped steeply into the "waist" of Corregidor where the tiny barrio of San Jose once stood, with two nearby docks, one on either side of the island. Before World War II, there was a streetcar line running from San Jose, curving up the hill to Topside. All that was left of the trolley line were a few shattered steel poles, and mangled track.

East of Bottomside was famous Malinta Hill, 350 feet above the bay and full of tunnels and storage caves. It was in Malinta tunnel that our men held out in '42 and MacArthur and his family took shelter there until he left for Australia. From Malinta Hill east was the tail of the tadpole which contained a tiny airstrip and the best beaches on the island.

The battle plan for Corregidor was a daring one considering the terrain. The assault force was made up of the 503rd Parachute Battalion, plus a battalion from the 24th Infantry Division, and support units of artillery, engineers and medical. Commanding "Rock" force was Colonel George M. Jones, CO of the 503rd, who would take command of the assault from General Hall once he landed with his paratroopers.

That was easier said than done, because the planners decided the 503rd would drop on the parade ground and golf course on Topside, in spaces measuring only about 50 yards long and 200 yards wide. Both areas dropped off sharply in steep cliffs on the west and south. Col. Jones didn't like it, but being a professional he bowed to his superiors, agreeing that landing on Topside would provide the element of surprise.

In other words, it was a crazy idea and the Japanese would never believe we'd try it.

It was decided to have the paratroopers land from two columns of C-47's, and each plane would have only six seconds over the drop zone. With each man taking half a second to get out, and another 25 seconds to reach the ground from an altitude of 400 feet, the amount of drift would leave no more than 100 yards of ground distance for human error or changes in wind direction.

Each plane would have time to drop but one "stick" of six to eight soldiers each time they passed over Topside. It would take an hour to get 1,000 paratroopers on the ground and then the planes had to return to Mindoro, reload, and bring a second lift forward. This second group would not land until five hours after the first man hit the ground.

Exciting? You bet! Dangerous, uh huh! If the enemy didn't pick 'em off coming down, they faced the prospect of missing the landing zone to splash into the sea or get hung up on the side of the cliffs, where they would become easy targets for Japanese snipers.

The Navy bombardment began just after dawn February 15. Now and then, the Navy would lift its guns to permit fighters and bombers to unload their death and destruction. It wasn't long until the Japanese must have thought they were in hell. The island fairly shook and the air was filled with smoke and flame and the incessant roar of big guns and bombs exploding.

I don't know if you are aware of it or not, but when a battleship or a cruiser fires a broadside from its 14 or 16-inch guns, the ship sometimes jumps sideways. Naval bombardment is terrible punishment if you are on the receiving end.

From our position on Berkey's command ship, we saw the first transport planes head in over the island. It seemed they moved ever so slowly. Then we saw the men falling from the doors and their chutes opening, some of them frighteningly close to the ground. On two occasions I saw what the paratroopers call a "streamer." That's when the chute doesn't open and the soldier smashes into the ground.

Japanese resistance to early elements of the 503rd were remarkably light. The element of surprise theory had worked. Succeeding "sticks" of troopers, however, would meet much greater resistance. Casualties mounted, not just from enemy fire but also from soldiers landing on wrecked buildings, in shell holes and other debris.

One paratrooper floated down to become impaled on the tip of a shattered trolley pole, which entered his lower back and came out his shoulder. He threshed around in agony for what seemed a long time until his body was jolted by bullets to put him out of his misery. The bullets could have come from the Japanese or a paratrooper buddy.

After about an hour, we saw approaching landing craft that had been loaded with the 34th Infantry at Marivales. They circled the west end of the island and then headed in for the Bottomside beach. Although heavy resistance was not evident, the air was soon filled with the smoke, noise, fire and the confusion that is combat. As the men went in, two or three landing craft hit mines, and as the troops headed inland several other mines detonated on or near the beaches.

From the ship, we could not really tell how things were going. The admiral was obviously getting some information from the beach

Soldiers of the 503rd Parachute Battalion begin landing on Corregidor. Many were injured in the drop, and the Japanese put up stiff resistance, but enemy soldiers were no match for our trained paratroops.

but chose not to share it with reporters just yet. All of us were very anxious to get onto the island.

After two waves of infantry splashed ashore, it was time for us to hit the boats. We made it to the beach and I told the correspondents to head for a temporary command post that had been set up about 50 yards from the water. There was regular spasmodic firing from the hills overlooking the beach, so we ran and crawled to try and stay beneath, and out of the line of fire.

I will always remember those moments, for as I ran across the beach to the CP, I almost stepped on the body of an army sergeant who had been hit by something. He was just lying there, with his dog tags around his neck, but his head was missing. Terrible way for a mother's son to die.

By this time the paratroopers on Topside were engaged in deadly combat, the element of surprise having worn off. In addition to providing medical care to those injured in the jump, the 503rd Aid Station began to receive a steady stream of wounded, more than they would have liked to see at this early stage of the battle.

The Japanese commander, Captain Akira Itagaki, did a fine job organizing a defense, but he had not expected the air drop and his forces were caught by surprise. He had gathered a small force at an observation point where he could watch the beach. All of a sudden, his attention was diverted by about 25 paratroopers who had been blown near the cliffs near Itagaki's observation point.

Fired on by the defenders, the paratroopers quickly assembled and attacked. In the ensuing skirmish eight Japanese were killed, including Captain Itagaki. Having lost their leader, the Japanese garrison was no longer capable of coordinated effort. Each group would fight on from isolated and widely scattered defensive strongpoints.

That was the only break the invasion force would get.

It had been hoped the 503rd and the 34th Infantry could make contact with each other by the end of the first day. Because of the doggedness of the brave enemy troops, contact was not made for nearly two days. Instead of there being an estimated 1,500 enemy on Corregidor, over 6,000 Japanese were killed and counted. Intelligence, this time, had underestimated.

Corregidor was hardly the beauty spot recalled by those who had been stationed there before the war. Not one building, not a single installation, was left untouched by the fighting. It wasn't long until that awful smell of death was everywhere, and the flies became so thick they showed up in aerial photographs.

On the second or third day, I needed to return to the command ship to correct a problem in my courier system. I left the reporters in the now-fortified CP area. Sniper fire was still too heavy for them to roam around or spend time with forward units who were busy uprooting the enemy from caves and fortified positions.

As I ran from the CP to the dock and then toward the PT boat, I came under fire but managed to reach the boat unscathed. The minute I jumped into the boat, the skipper gave it full throttle and we fairly zoomed away from the island, the speed of the craft pressing me back in my seat hard.

Aboard the command ship I found AP Correspondent Jim Hutcheson, who had arrived late but wanted in on the action. We boarded the PT boat and headed for the San Jose dock that jutted out from and over the beach. We pulled alongside and were halfway off the boat, and onto the concrete floor of the dock when .50 caliber machine gun fire erupted, directed at the flimsy plywood sides of the PT boat.

Jim and I bellied the rest of the way onto the dock, hoping we could dig a hole in it with our bare hands. By this time, the PT boat crew was returning fire but pulling out of range as fast as the boat would go. With this outbreak of firing, unloading on the beach ceased and anybody with any sense had taken cover, and small landing craft backed away from shore.

For all practical purposes, Jim and I were alone and fully exposed on San Jose dock — which wasn't the way I had planned it!

"Hey, Hutch," I yelled from my prone position, sucking in everything I could to make a smaller target, "let's get off this dock before the boat's out of range and we're the only targets left."

He grunted agreement and we took off down that dock like big-assed birds. It seemed like a mile, but actually I doubt it was over a 50 yards. Jim was puffing by my side when I heard him gasp and stumble. I thought he had been hit. His typewriter case had been struck by a chip of concrete thrown up by one of the bullets. Another chip cut through my fatigues and scratched my leg.

I kept hearing the staccato sound of the machine guns and the occasional "twing" of a rifle. I suddenly thought of Kathy and wondered how she'd spend the insurance money. Funny how quickly you can review your life when you think you're going to die. We finally reached the shore end of the dock and jumped down to the sandy beach.

"For Christ's sake, Snyder, watch out," a voice screamed, "there're mines all over this damn beach!"

The voice belonged to Stan Troutman, who was huddled against some pilings with Howard Handleman and Homer Bigart. Sure enough I had straddled a mine in my jump. I looked down between my feet and saw the black snout of a land mine sticking out of the sand. I moved my feet one at a time, very, very carefully. That done, I felt extremely weak.

From the command ship the admiral had seen the action and dispatched a couple of destroyers which moved in close and began bombarding the Japanese positions on the hillsides. There was intense firing for half an hour and it must have been highly effective for we were then able to begin moving about the beach without attracting immediate enemy fire. There was always a risk from snipers until the very end of the battle.

I will note here I received the Bronze Star for Valor for running the beaches under fire several times, the recommendation coming from the war correspondents who wrote a letter to General Hall and Colonel Diller. I was proud to have been cited by kindred newspapermen and proud that when the official citation was handed to me it had a note pinned to one corner which read:

We found enemy suicide boats in caves along the cliffs. The boats were filled with explosives for the purpose of sinking small boats and landing craft. As far as I know, none were used against our landing craft at Corregidor.

"I would like to give this personally to Snyder." It was signed by General Hall, who pinned the medal with "V" device on my uniform in the Corps headquarters tent.

On Feb. 17, the 1st Battalion of the 503rd and other reinforcements reached Bottomside by landing craft. Their counterparts on Topside had consolidated their positions, systematically reducing enemy bunkers, pillboxes and underground defenses. Our troops developed a pattern for reducing such strongpoints.

First, aircraft and Navy support ships — the air arm using napalm exclusively — destroyed what they could. Then the infantry would attack as the last bomb fell. If this failed, pack howitzers were brought in for direct fire. Next, men with submachine guns and rifles covered other infantry squads who moved forward behind white phosphorus hand grenades and flame-thrower teams.

Sometimes, to avoid flashback and assure deep penetration of cave defenses, flame-thrower operators would project their fuel unignited and then use phosphorus grenades to fire it. If the Japanese still refused to give up, engineer demolition teams closed the entrances with explosive charges. Sometimes the enemy would use underground tunnels and caves to reoccupy positions previously cleared.

There were all sorts of banzai attacks and unorganized charges during the day and at night, particularly on Malinta Hill. All were harrowing, but I will not detail all of them. A few are definitely worth mention.

In the predawn hours of Feb. 19, about 40 Japanese committed suicide by blowing up an ammunition dump, killing or wounding about 20 of our soldiers. These men, unaware of the danger, were in a building directly over the ammo site. Other Japanese, nearly 400 strong, launched a ground attack at the same time which proved difficult to stop, but by 11 o'clock, the 503rd had hunted down all the stragglers.

During the night of Feb. 21-22, what some had feared might happen, did happen. Everyone had been concerned since the landing the enemy might blow up tons of ammunition and explosives known to be stored in the caves and tunnels of Malinta Hill. Earlier that evening we could hear Japanese soldiers singing or chanting inside the main tunnel. We assumed they were high on saki which, along with canned crab meat, was in abundant supply on Corregidor.

At about ten o'clock, a deafening explosion rocked the island. Flames shot out of tunnel entrances; rocks and other debris flew in all directions. Fissures opened along the slopes and six men of the 34th

MacArthur stands erect and salutes as our flag is hoisted once again on the old parade ground.

Infantry were buried alive by a landslide on the south side. Apparently the Japanese planned a controlled explosion for a counterattack. If so, it had gotten completely out of hand, killing an unknown number of their own people within the tunnels.

Some Japanese, attempting to escape to the "tail" of Corregidor during the confusion, were quickly dispatched. Additional explosions continued during the night of February 23-24, believed caused by enemy soldiers committing suicide.

I previously mentioned Japanese suicide boats in an earlier chapter. We discovered a host of them in caves along the cliffs of Topside. As far as I know, none was actually used against any of our vessels at Corregidor.

Shortly after dark on February 26, the Japanese launched their final suicidal tour de force, blowing up an underground arsenal at Monkey Point, creating havoc on both sides. As the dust settled, a huge depression appeared where the arsenal had been. Debris flew as far as Topside, where one man was hit and wounded. Other debris hit a destroyer 2,000 yards offshore.

One of our medium tanks was blown airborne for 50 yards, most of its crew killed. Bits and pieces of U.S. and enemy bodies littered the area; rock slides entombed others and 200 Japanese were killed outright. It took medics an hour and a half to care for the casualties, and at that time a medical officer, an eyewitness to the horror, could only say to reporters:

"As soon as I got all the casualties off, I sat down on a rock and cried. I couldn't stop myself and didn't even want to. I had seen more than a man can stand and stay normal. As long as I had cases to care for, that kept me going, but after that it was just too much."

That explosion marked the end of major resistance on Corregidor. By March 2, General Hall concluded that GHQ could set an official date for termination of the battle. MacArthur decided to return to the island just nine days short of his departure three years before. Col. Jones asked if I cared to go along with him to survey the route the general would take on his arrival. I jumped at the chance.

We got in his Jeep and headed up toward Topside, paralleling the old trolley line. The road was rough and we dodged a few shell craters en route and had a detour or two before reaching the top. All of a sudden, Col. Jones abruptly put on the brakes and he exclaimed: "There's one we missed." All I saw was something like a coconut lying in the road ahead.

General MacArthur completes a visit to Malinta tunnel with members of his staff. It was a somber time for him as old memories began coming alive once more.

The colonel walked to the object and bent down to examine it - and I did the same. What we saw was the top of a Japanese soldier's head. He had been buried up to his chin in his defensive position protecting the road. Colonel Jones lifted his big-booted foot and stomped the soldier's head until it was crushed and pushed into the road.

He then scuffed some dirt over the spot and said:

"We can't have the chief thinking we don't take care of our battlefield dead."

On March 2, 1945, General MacArthur re-

This view of the island was taken from "Topside," where the paratroopers landed. The entrance to Malinta tunnel is just left of the white-textured debris, center foreground. San Jose dock is right center with Monkey Point in the background.

turned to Corregidor with members of the old Bataan staff aboard four PT boats, despite the fact there was still isolated sniper fire. He was in a much happier mood than during those dark days when he was forced to leave. A staff member commented that the island was "pounded almost beyond recognition" to which the general responded:

"Yes, Corregidor is living proof that the era of fortresses is over."

He was driven to the old parade ground, taking the route approved by Colonel Jones a few days earlier. There were U.S. and Filipino soldiers present, along with the key members of his staff who had shared the terrible days of '42. I was able to shake hands with my "boss," Colonel Diller, whom I hadn't seen for weeks, and who would shortly become a one-star general.

Following a brief ceremony, during which Colonel Jones received the Distinguished Service Cross from MacArthur, Jones saluted in a brisk manner, and concluded his remarks with:

"Sir, I present to you Fortress Corregidor."

The general made brief remarks, paused a moment, then said:

"I see the old flagpole still stands. Have your troops hoist the colors to the peak, and let no enemy ever haul them down."

In closing remarks he paid tribute to the original defenders of the island: "Our triumphs today belong equally to that dead army."

Then a bugle sounded and our flag was slowly hoisted up the old flagpole, amid the rubble of two wars and terrible memories. I felt a big lump in my throat and wiped my eyes. The "Battling Bastards of Bataan" had been avenged and Corregidor was no longer a military ghost.

A soldier working in a graves registration company on Corregidor on New Year's Day of 1946, nearly ten months after the assault force had left, happened to look up and was shocked to see a file of Japanese soldiers coming toward him, waving a white flag. They appeared well fed.

The GI nervously accepted their surrender and learned that the eighteen to twenty Japanese soldiers had been living underground in Corregidor's numerous caves and tunnels. When one of them ventured out one night to obtain drinking water, he discovered an old newspaper, and for the first time the hold-outs learned Japan had surrendered and the war was over.

Today, Corregidor is a memorial of sorts for all those men, living and dead, who took part in its dramatic past. For me it is a special place of remembrance, a fitting witness to valiant heroism as well as the frightful horrors of war. The eternal splashing of the ocean dampers the silence, and the lush greenery has healed most of the scars.

The frightful and painful memories, however, will linger forever in the shattered ruins of this hallowed island fortress.

Manila Aftermath

Chapter 12

"Once upon a time our traditional goal in war was victory. Once upon a time we were proud of our strength, our military power. Now we seem ashamed of it. Once upon a time the rest of the world looked to us for leadership. Now they look to us for a quick handout and a fence-straddling posture."

— **Senator Barry M. Goldwater**

I WAS DISAPPOINTED to have missed the battle for Manila, although from high ground on Corregidor we could see the city aflame as American forces moved in from three sides to uproot the Japanese defenders. That was truly a historic event, yet I would not have wanted to miss seeing the American flag raised over Corregidor once again.

Following MacArthur's visit to Corregidor, I was ordered to leave that ravaged island and get over to Manila, where GHQ had set up its new and truly "advanced" headquarters. Most of the major fighting, of course, was officially over except in outlying regions of Luzon, and on a few of the other islands.

Following their landings, and a wild dash south Lingayan Gulf, the 37th Infantry, First Cavalry, and the 11th Airborne Divisions, had raced south to see which unit would get credit for entering Manila first. The record shows that a "flying column" of the First Cavalry entered the city limits February 3. In my heart I felt it was appropriate that a squadron of cavalry achieved this distinction.

The First Cavalry's problems in Manila were shared by the 37th Infantry Division, which entered the city immediately behind the armored column. Their supply lines were kept open by the 112th Cavalry Regiment. The next day the 11th Airborne Division landed from the sea 50 miles south of the city. The encirclement of Manila was assured, but the fighting was block-by-block, building-by-building, in basements and on rooftops.

The cavalry had a little help and some luck in getting there first.

There was a key bridge over a deep gorge near Novaliches, about eight miles north of the city. There was concern that this span, over a stream that had banks too high and too steep to permit fording, might be blown up by the Japanese.

General Chase, who commanded the flying column (this was a few days before he was sent to Bataan to relieve the commanding general of the 38th division in Zigzag Pass) in the drive south, was very pleased to be informed via radio that the bridge was still intact.

He radioed: "By God, grab the damn bridge!"

Just as the leading tanks neared the span, the column was raked by fire from both sides of the approach. Tank hatches clanged shut, brakes squealed, and the armored troops, joined by accompanying infantry, tangled with the enemy defenders in a fire-fight. The tankers began firing their 75-mm guns into suspected enemy strongpoints.

A Navy bomb-disposal officer, James Sutton, had been attached to the cavalry unit for just such a happening. He was informed by an army major that the bridge was mined and that he could see a fuse burning.

The Navy man ran to the bridge, and with Japanese bullets buzzing past his head, he cut the fuse just before it reached the explosives tied to supporting girders. The U.S. Navy thus preserved a major gateway into Manila for the division. Lieutenant Sutton received the Army's Distinguished Service Medal.

There was only light resistance encountered in the areas north, and into the outskirts of the city. The reason for this was that our troops had moved so rapidly down the central plain from Lingayan, the Japanese had been caught by surprise and their defenses were woefully inadequate.

MacArthur later said that he had no fixed timetable for the drive southward, only that it was his intent to get there as rapidly as possible in order to get U.S. prisoners released from various prisons.

Guided by guerrillas, the troops traveled into city streets past hidden Japanese riflemen who sniped away at the invaders. The column finally stopped at the gates of Santo Tomas University which had been utilized as a prison. Inside were almost 4,000 U.S. and Allied internees who were running extremely low on food and medical supplies due to the fighting.

When the cavalry's tanks crashed through the gates, they ignited what was one of the most exciting and moving experiences of the war.

There wasn't much left of Manila by the time fighting subsided. Loss of life was heavy, mainly because the enemy chose to defend the city building by building and block by block. The river shown divides Manila.

Soldiers and internees alternately laughed and cried with joy. People jumped up and down in the streets. It was one of the few times in World War II in the Pacific that American soldiers could share the feeling of their comrades in Europe as true "liberators." There was extreme joy and exhilaration all around.

I was told of the general's quick trip to the prison camp. His Jeep raced through the gate, battered down by the tanks, where he received a tumultuous welcome from a crowd of sick and gaunt survivors in the courtyard. He strode through the corridors inside, jammed with teary-eyed humanity, talking emotionally to Theodore Stevenson, who had served as the camp doctor.

Stevenson had been jailed by the Japanese because he would not change death certificates on which he had plainly scrawled: "Cause of death, malnutrition."

As the general started down a long line to greet the half-starved prisoners, many attempted to stand at attention in front of their cots, but could not do so because of their weakened condition. Most of the conversations were emotional and brief. MacArthur told reporters as

he passed by the scrawny, suffering POWs, each one acknowledged him, sometimes just above a whisper, with "You're back," or "You made it," or "God bless you." He said he could only reply:
"I'm a little late, but we're finally here."
The general placed special emphasis on reaching and liberating other prisoner of war camps. These included Bilibid, Cabanatuand and Los Banos. He had received reports that the Japanese guards in those prisons had become increasingly savage and more sadistic as our troops came closer and closer to them. He felt many would die if they could not be rescued swiftly. Many who greeted him in the camps were little more than skeletons.

Between February 5 and March 10, terrible fighting erupted in the city. The Japanese defenders had placed gasoline and various explosive materials in nearly all the large buildings. These were set ablaze upon the arrival of our troops, and much of the once-beautiful, cosmopolitan city was devastated and turned into burned and shattered rubble. The "Pearl of the Orient" had been severely tarnished.

Thousands of Filipinos were murdered by the Japanese. Hospitals were set afire with patients still inside; corpses were mutilated, and many females were savagely raped before being killed. The Japanese command system fell completely apart; officers could no longer control their units and the Nippon soldiers went wild. It was the last thing MacArthur wanted to happen.

This was a real blow to the morale of everybody. Since the fighting had begun in the South Pacific islands after Pearl Harbor, about all our troops had seen were coconut groves, jungle, sand beaches and thatched huts. They had looked forward to getting into a real city for a change. All they got in Manila was a devil's smorgasbord of death, misery and destruction.

General MacArthur had declared Manila an open city to prevent its destruction by the Japanese. He had also ordered that Allied planes must not drop bombs on the city to spare the population. Japanese commanders decided they would battle the Americans to the last man — and they almost achieved their goal.

The Japanese spared nothing; the enemy spread destruction and carnage deliberately and indiscriminately, and the destruction of Manila and 100,000 of its citizens was one of the great tragedies of the war. Only Stalingrad, Warsaw and Berlin were worse. As a matter of record, the battle for Manila was the only battle in which Japanese and

U.S. forces fought each other in a major city.

In addition to the civilian casualties, our military losses were 6,500. The Japanese lost about 20,000 troops. A few military "experts" have since declared that losses in the battle for Manila were extreme because MacArthur left the Japanese with no escape route. I can tell you that there was never any plan considered in GHQ that would have permitted the enemy to escape encirclement in Manila, only to rise up to fight us again in another place. Most military students considered it a major success.

The general entered the main area of the city February 6, in his Jeep, accompanied by bodyguards armed only with submachine guns. Surveying the areas already taken by U.S. troops, the general quickly realized Manila had suffered and would suffer much more. He was greatly disheartened.

It was unfortunate that GHQ issued a communique later that day declaring that our forces were rapidly clearing the enemy from Manila, that the defenders were surrounded, and that their destruction was eminent. The next issue of *Newsweek* contained the headline: "Prize of the Pacific War Falls to MacArthur Like Ripened Plum."

The problem with that was; it wasn't true. Worst of all, our press censors were told to give explicit instructions to the correspondents that they couldn't expose this victory lie. Manila would not fall for another month. A talked about victory parade through the city was called off simply because the streets of Manila were clogged with rubble and bloody street fighting was at its peak.

This was one of the worst examples of GHQ's manipulation of news during the Pacific war. There was no excuse for it, and all the reporters were extremely angry because of it. I was never able to find out whose decision it was, and it was embarrassing to the press officers to say the least.

By banning air strikes over the city, MacArthur had at least made an earnest effort to spare the residents undue suffering, even if his intent could not be carried out. Once the city was secured, he continued to display concern for the Filipinos and their situation. It was his order that humanitarian needs would take a higher priority over those of the military, the exception being counterattacks or some other emergency combat situation.

He refused to place the city off-limits to the GIs, however, declaring their patronage of stores and service establishments would be a

It isn't pretty, but it is typical. U.S. soldiers often searched the bodies of the dead for Japanese flags, prayer cloths worn about the waist — even gold teeth.

great boost to the city's economy. He also acknowledged that prostitution might be a problem but told a staff member:

"They've got a good treatment for those diseases now, haven't they? I don't want to put this city off-limits to my men; they've been waiting a long time for this."

His statement appeared to minimize the threat of venereal disease, which can take soldiers out of action sometimes more frequently than a bullet. The venereal disease rate in Manila soared, but it was less a problem in the provinces. It is sad that in many countries around the world, American men are remembered most for what they carried in their pants, rather than what they carried in their skulls.

MacArthur's repeated calls to the Japanese commander to surrender were never answered and he knew it would be a fight to the death. House-by-house street fighting ensued for weeks, turning the once beautiful city into shambles. It pained the general to know that his victory proved exceptionally costly to the people he loved.

In the meantime, MacArthur's old penthouse suite in the Manila Hotel had been badly damaged and looted by the enemy. He found a few books from his library and discovered the family's silver relatively undamaged in a container, ready to be shipped to Japan. Eventually he moved into a mansion called "Casa Blanca," and his family arrived not long after from Brisbane, ending months of separation.

I was happy the general could be with his wife, Jean. I envied him as I thought of Kathy who, for some time, had been working at Pratt & Whitney in Kansas City, doing her bit for the war effort.

GHQ headquarters set up in the former city hall, remarkably undamaged except for one corner. The bulk of the press staff, and a number of correspondents, took rooms in a little damaged seven-story apartment building a few blocks south of the Pasig River which curled through the main part of the business district. By this time the engineers were constructing Bailey bridges across the Pasig river to replace the pontoon spans thrown across it during the height of the battle for the city.

Our quarters weren't all that bad. In fact, they were quite comfortable. We had beds to sleep in and in my shared room there was a working radio. I tuned in once power had been restored to the city, and the first music I heard was a new and popular song from the U.S. on the Armed Forces Radio network: "Don't Fence Me In."

As we established ourselves in Manila early in February the summit meeting of Roosevelt, Stalin and Churchill was taking place at Yalta. Germany was about to go down in defeat, although its armies were still fighting hard for what was left of the Fatherland.

I first heard of the plans for the invasion of Japan toward the last of February. Presumably, I would again be attached to General Hall's XI Corps whose yet-to-be-assigned units were slated to make a major assault on the island of Kyushu. What a challenge that was going to be.

The war had been interesting and exciting so far, and I had been very lucky. I recalled, however, how tough it had been to capture all those remote little islands that really didn't mean all that much to the average Japanese soldier. I shuddered to think how difficult it was going to be to take their homeland, having to battle not only their military but the entire civilian population as well.

I did not have a heavy work load during my time in Manila. I assisted with routine desk work including some censorship which I hated. I also accompanied reporters on little jaunts inside and outside the city, to places where they thought there might be some feature material for stories. I recall going to one small barrio south of city to a cathedral where there was a unique bamboo organ, from which came some of the most beautiful music I had ever heard.

While in Manila I discovered that an old friend, Larry Bauer from the Kansas City Bureau of the Associated Press, was a member of the GHQ press staff. He had been pressed into service because of the expected influx of reporters that would migrate to the Far East once the war in Europe was concluded. Quite obviously, there was great interest in the pending invasion of Japan, and our section was taking care of more reporters all the time.

Major Bauer, a transplant from the National Guard, was not a young man. He appeared old to me when I worked at *The Star and Times*. Bauer liked his booze and every time he got loosened up, he would tell me, again, about his post-war ambition. His big dream was to buy *The Knob Noster Gem*, a weekly newspaper located in a community east of Kansas City.

Following Corregidor, and once in uniform in Manila, I noticed I had matured some. War can do that to a soldier.

"I'm gonna buy that little ole' paper and let my arteries harden."

I'm not certain he survived the Manila experience because I don't recall seeing him again, or hearing of him again, even after setting up our headquarters in Japan. Perhaps I just missed him. All I know is he never purchased his favorite newspaper. Perhaps his arteries didn't harden after all.

I also ran into another Star-staffer, Cruise Palmer, who was in the Navy. I don't remember on what island it occurred, but something had happened to his ship, as I recall, and he had lost everything except what he was wearing. I took him to our supply officer who outfitted him with everything he needed, and he then hitched a ride back to where he hoped a Naval shore detachment could help him get in touch with his unit.

Ira McCarty was a tough, Irish reporter for *The Star*. I had admired his work before the war. The paper had sent him to GHQ Pacific to replace another correspondent, Alvin McCoy, who had been in the area for a year or so. McCoy had been aboard the aircraft carrier USS Franklin when it was put out of action during a Kamikaze attack.

His vivid and exclusive stories from the stricken carrier made headlines the world-over. Not long after the war he retired to Ouray, a mountain village in southwest Colorado, perhaps to let his arteries harden.

I kept track of McCarty for some time, but I do not recall if he went with us into Japan or not. I do know he sent back some good copy while with the GHQ staff, because I kept him informed of interesting and timely bits of information that came to my attention.

McCarty retired from his staff job at *The Star* and a few years later I recall seeing his obituary in the paper. Palmer went back to *The Star* and became wealthy as a shareholder when the employee-owned paper was sold to Capital Cities, a news-oriented conglomerate. As of a year ago he was still alive and apparently well.

From April through August, MacArthur's forces continued to rout the Japanese from several other islands in the Philippine chain. He was severely criticized for pursuing these operations which were costly in men and materiel. Capturing this territory had little to do with the outcome of the war. In fact, many thought the effort might well have been better spent mopping up enemy soldiers still running at-large on Leyte and Luzon.

But the general had said, "I shall return," and he made sure his promise was applied to every nook and cranny of the archipelago. In a communique July 5, he proudly announced the end of operations in the Philippines:

"The entire Philippine Islands are now liberated and the campaign is virtually closed. Some guerilla action of a minor nature in the practically uninhabited mountain ranges may occasionally persist, but this great land mass of 115,600 square miles with a population of 17 million is now free of the invader."

That wasn't really true, but the general had a lot of credibility and remained popular in the United States. If he had only shown a little bit of humility along the way.

One of the interesting things I did in Manila was to visit the plants of the major newspapers that existed prior to the Japanese occupation. I discovered none of the larger papers was able to publish as before because the Japanese had largely destroyed the machinery.

All of the pre-war typesetting machines and rotary presses had been sabotaged by explosive charges and incendiary bombs. Almost without exception, the printing machinery had been prepared for demolition and was detonated upon the arrival of U.S. troops. The plants avoiding that fate were later destroyed in the burning of the city.

Even so, as our forces pitched in to assist clearing away rubble and restoring what measure of normalcy could be achieved, several hand-set, single-sheet daily and weekly publications began appearing to satisfy the liberated population, starved for news after three years of Japanese propaganda.

In some offices, workers were trying feverishly to assemble one operating typesetting machine from the wreckage of three or four others. The same was true for the rotary presses, workmen "cannibalizing" several to get one unit in production.

At that time, there was only one high-speed rotary printing unit usable and it was in the DeRoces plant, which had printed a popular magazine before the war. The only reason this press was saved was because a Japanese military policeman lost his enthusiasm for the war.

He revealed to employees the location of the explosives wired to the press, just as American troops were entering the outskirts of the city. This plant had already lost 27 Linotypes in the devastation, and the day I was there, only two were in operable condition.

One large plant, Carmelo-Baurmann, used by the enemy to print propaganda, was largely spared since our soldiers got there so fast the explosives could not be placed in time. Since the plant was west of Manila, it escaped the terrible fires that raged through the city. Some of their machinery was damaged by the Japanese, however, who rammed steel bars into gears and motors while the machines were running!

Just looking at it made me sick.

None the less, this plant had begun printing local editions of *Time, Newsweek* and the overseas edition of *The New York Times*. This plant was also used by the U.S. Office of War Information to publish the Free *Philippines*. This publication was distributed to civilians and army troops and carried no advertising.

It was difficult, however, for the staff to resist the normal impulse of newsmen to be first with the news. The entry of the Russians into Berlin, Hitler's acknowledgment that his armies were defeated, and the death of President Roosevelt all resulted in "extras" topped with scarlet banner headlines.

The large printing plants of Manila's large dailies, *Bulletin, Tribune, Free Press* and the *Chinese Commercial News*, were gutted. I talked with Roy Bennett, editor of the American-owned *Bulletin*, who told me the paper had been awarded a newsprint allocation by the War Production Board in Washington and they hoped to be publishing soon.

Typical of Manila newspapers at the time was the two-month-old *Post*. It appeared six days a week as a four-page, two-column tabloid, served by the Associated Press. It was being printed two pages at a time, on a 14 by 20-inch job-printing press, one thousand copies an hour, with a total circulation of 4,500 copies. Newsprint was obtained on the black market.

Having once printed a community newspaper myself and on the same size press, I could appreciate the *Post's* effort to print the news. The publisher, Abelardo Subido, told me "we are doing our best to serve the public interest." His commitment really pumped me up.

Newspapers in Manila were not only printed in English and Filipino, but also in Togalog, a regional dialect, Chinese and Spanish. I suppose it's pretty much the same there today. It was so good to see the spirit of a free press arise from the ashes of Manila. I felt better than ever about being there.

For the next couple of weeks, I viewed what was left of Manila. Even amid utter ruin, it was obvious it had once been a lovely city. I became fascinated with visits to the old walled city of Intramuros, near the center of the city, where Japanese defenders held out to the very last in some of the most desperate defensive actions of the war.

Intramuros covered about 150 acres and was built by the Spanish in the 16th Century. The fortress itself was enclosed behind high stone walls 40 feet thick and 16 feet high. Near the last of February, following several days of heavy artillery shelling, elements of the 37th Infantry Division crossed the Pasig river in assault boats and began fighting their way into and through the fortress walls.

Other units on the east side of Intramuros breached a gate in the wall and found the enemy holed up in hundreds of underground bunkers. They even fought from sewers, basements, tunnels and old dungeons. The battle ended on the tenth day, when our Infantry demolition teams destroyed the last pocket of resistance. It was a real test for the 37th's valiant troops.

It was about this time the staff was told of MacArthur's displeasure at the decision made by Roosevelt and Churchill at the Yalta Conference. He was furious that the two leaders had pledged generous territorial concessions in the Far East to the Soviets in return for Stalin's promise to unleash the Red Army against Japan two or three months after Germany surrendered.

When informed of the "deal," the general displayed shock and charged the concessions were fantastic and unnecessary since Japan was near defeat. However, the top brass in Washington were probably aware that nearly every senior commander in the Pacific, at one time or another, including MacArthur, favored letting the Russians in on the spoils because they felt it might end the war sooner and save lives.

It was felt around GHQ that "the old man" was miffed because they had not solicited his opinion beforehand. The general was very sensitive about such things, and I think I can understand that because I have grown old with similar tendencies which, if not becoming to MacArthur, have certainly detracted from my own personality.

What was next for me? Instead of sitting on my hands in GHQ Manila, I found myself heading back to the Boondocks.

Borneo Excitement

Chapter 13

"Battles are won by slaughter and maneuver. The greater the general, the more he contributes in maneuver, the less he demands in slaughter."

— **Winston Churchhill**

SEVERAL DAYS INTO MAY, 1945, I was told to report to Colonel Diller's office. This was unusual and I quickly reviewed my recent activity, trying to recall something I might have done that could be labeled a foul-up. I couldn't think of anything, so I presented myself at his office door, squared my shoulders, knocked, walked in and saluted.

Happily, our conversation was a positive one. Diller wanted to compliment me on my performance at Corregidor, having received a letter from the reporters relative to "running the dock" under fire. After discussing with me my novel experience there, he quickly turned to another subject:

"How'd you like to go to Borneo?"

"That sounds fine to me, sir," I quickly responded.

That was the first I had heard of a Borneo assault, assuming the Australians would take care of that little bit of business, which they did but under MacArthur's direction. Actually the Aussies didn't want any part of an invasion to reclaim Borneo. General Thomas Blamey and his commanders had serious doubts about the value or even the necessity of the operation.

MacArthur, however, had already ordered the southern islands of the Philippines taken, to insure that the Borneo invasion would be fully supported by air and naval units from those islands. In a swift series of amphibious landings, the enemy was quickly taken by surprise and overwhelmed on Cebu, Panay, Mindanao and the remainder of the Visayan and southern groups of islands.

As quickly as these islands were captured, they were restored to civilian rule. Little wonder MacArthur was held in such esteem by the Filipino people. He was a conquering hero in every sense of the word.

It was the general's opinion the Borneo invasion would further reduce Japan's oil resources, but by 1945 Japan had already been cut off from its badly-needed oil by the destruction of its navy and our submarine encirclement of shipping lanes. Enemy troops there were completely cut off from needed supplies and were suffering great hardship.

MacArthur utilized Australian troops only in the Borneo encounters whose commanders were not all that keen about more jungle warfare in the tropics, even as the Japanese were being driven back toward their home islands. The Aussies had never organized an amphibious landing before and many felt this one should be scrapped.

Australian government officials suggested it be cancelled, but MacArthur pointed out it had been ordered by the Combined Chiefs of Staff and that was that. The fact he had defied his superiors in the past was not brought up. He would later expose himself to unnecessary dangers at the landing sites as if to prove to Aussie troops that he was willing to do what he had asked them to do.

So in the minds of many, the invasion of Borneo was of dubious value except to return real estate to the British and the Dutch. MacArthur was in complete charge, however, and he got his way. Using elements of the Australia's I Corps under General Sir Leslie Morshead, including the 7th and 9th Australian divisions, the plan was set.

I'll admit I was fascinated with the idea of going to another island I had only read about in books. As a boy I had gone to the old Ashland Theater on Kansas City's east side to see the adventurer and explorer, Frank Buck, in his series of "Bring 'em Back Alive" movies.

I still recalled him slashing his way through the jungle, natives paddling his boats on wilderness rivers with banks that were a tangle of vines and crocodiles. These ominous critters would slide silently into the water as his expedition floated by, with Buck's rifle cocked and ready, the native bearers chanting an ancient hunting song.

As I sat in the theater spellbound, nearly choking from stuffing my mouth with 5-cents-per-sack popcorn, relishing the excitement of it all, I felt this great yearning to one day be an explorer and go to Borneo. Little did I know that 16 years later I would be floating down that same river, with those scary crocodiles sliding off the banks into the treacherous, snake-invested waters. It was no longer just a book or movie. It was reality.

Before my assignment to Borneo, there had already been one landing at the new oil port island of Tarakan, off the island's northeast coast. This occurred May 1, 1945, and involved mostly Aussie troops. The amphibious group was commanded by Admiral Forrest B. Royal, with Admiral Barbey directing the U.S. naval covering group. The Royal Australian Air Force and our 13th Air Force provided air strikes before and during the invasion effort.

The Japanese had not expected an attack there and their defenses were not well prepared, nor were they adequate.

General Morshead chose Brigadier David Whitehead's 26th Brigade to seize Tarakan, and a Dutch battalion was attached to give the Netherlands army some identity with its capture. I never understood why GHQ had not provided a press officer for the initial landing in Borneo, but it quickly became apparent to "the brass" there was more interest in Borneo than had been anticipated.

The Tarakan operation quickly resulted in friction between the Australians and the U.S. military when Admiral Barbey charged the Aussies were "behind the times" in their landing techniques and were "unskilled and knew little about their equipment." He charged the Japanese would not have had time to consolidate their defenses had the Aussies been faster in off-loading supplies and equipment.

I'm sure the admiral regretted his words the minute they came out of his mouth, but the damage had been done.

In reply, Australian officers charged the Americans had not provided them with their best landing craft, suggesting they had been given inferior and outdated equipment. The furor soon reached diplomatic channels, and it was General MacArthur who finally eased the situation in a letter to the Australian War Cabinet and Parliament. He said:

"I am at a loss to account for criticism of the Tarakan operation. It has been completely successful and accomplished without the slightest hitch. The equipment and methods were essentially the same as those used in nearly 40 amphibious landings in all."

He praised the "splendid efficiency" of Whitehead's men and noted that casualties had been light in view of the great objectives achieved. The general's soothing words eased the situation, but Australian criticism over the Borneo operations did not immediately subside.

I flew from Manila to Borneo aboard a Navy PBY aircraft which landed and took off from the water. It was a beautiful trip, flying over parts of Luzon, Mindoro and Palawan before reaching the waters off

Brunei at the northeast tip of the island. We landed in choppy seas and the plane bounced hard several times before we settled into the South China Sea.

We taxied to a spot near Admiral Barbey's command ship, where I was picked up by a small launch and taken to the ship where I had to climb up a rope ladder to reach an opening in the side of the cruiser. I must have been in good shape then because I had my duffle bag slung over my shoulder. I wouldn't be able to do it today.

Several U.S. and Aussie correspondents plus two photographers were already on board. Australian General George Wooten commanded the Brunei Bay assault force while Barbey and Royal again provided U.S. naval support. The June 10 landings along the coast were unopposed. The City of Brunei, at the south end of the bay, was captured with moderate resistance June 15, but a stiff battle developed in a town called Labuan, north of the bay.

MacArthur went ashore a minute or two behind the first assault wave, walking along a road not far from the beach with the threat of snipers all around, plus machine gun fire from both sides. The general walked to a spot where a few Japanese soldiers lay dead. "They look like well trained soldiers," he commented.

About that time Sir Leslie Moorehead, the corps commander, came along to warn MacArthur that he was dangerously close to the front lines. The general replied impatiently that he could see some Aussie troops "just ahead" and wanted to see what was going on.

"That is a forward patrol," Moorehead replied, "and it is under heavy attack. If you go any further, you will likely face enemy fire. I'd prefer, sir, that you wait a bit."

MacArthur retorted: "Let's get up there." At that point General George Kinney, who commanded the Southwest Pacific Air Force and a close friend and advisor to MacArthur, intervened and suggested that the general's presence so far forward might impede the infantry from doing their job.

At this point MacArthur smiled and said: "Oh, all right, George."

Correspondents I recall in Borneo included Pat Robinson, Russel Brines, Don Bell, Frank Kelly, Walter Simmons and Lee Van Atta, plus Carl Mydans, a *Life* magazine photographer. There may have been one or two others. Once on land, several of us headed inland to see what we could see. All of sudden, at the edge of a small lake was a most impressive structure. Someone said it had once been the palace of the

Soldiers move forward in column toward suspected enemy in ruins of oil fields.

Sultan of Brunei.

The magnificent white-latticed building appeared unoccupied. I was curious so I opened a veranda door and before me was the largest and most elaborate pool table I have ever seen. It was inlaid with mother of pearl, made of a variety of exotic woods in fantastic marquetry floral designs, with jewels inserted into the surface of the frame. One of the photographers took a picture of it.

We barely had time to see one upper floor, which obviously had been looted either by the Japanese or by natives. One could visualize, however, how beautiful it must have been. We wondered how the pool table had survived. Before leaving I did see a primitive, three-inch-long metal statue of a dog, lying in some debris in a corner. I suppose it was looting, but I still have my souvenir of the old sultan's palace.

While in Borneo I also acquired a wooden carving of an Indonesian-appearing princess, on the shoulders of a human-like figure with a animal's head and wings. Our group was under fire at the time, running through a house when I nearly turned my ankle on an object beneath a bed sheet. I looked to see what it was and found the carving, somewhat damaged. I picked it up and strung it through a belt loop, carrying it several days until I could find a box and mail it home.

Not far from the palace, I saw a few native women standing beside a path and every one of them had ear lobes that were weighted down with jewelry. I was told this process begins when they are children. Their ears are pierced and the lobes gradually expand and lengthen. It appeared to me that their hallowed out ear lobes hung down at least four or five inches — a thing of beauty to them.

I hope this fad never catches on in America, but since we already see earrings in male ears, and similar pieces piercing the navels of our young ladies, I make no guarantees.

Not too distant was a native village, a cluster of small shacks on stilts in an inlet off the bay, about ten feet above the water. Before I left Borneo I had seen hundreds of such villages built out over the water.

The Aussie troops had made good headway in their drive inland. In fact, the 24th Brigade advanced 20 miles up the coast and seized Beaufort. The 20th Brigade, in a sudden amphibious maneuver, took Lutong, 70 miles south of Brunei, and on June 20 to 25, captured the sabotaged Mira-Seria oil fields. There were bothersome encounters with the enemy from time to time, but the "diggers" were tough, brave jungle fighters.

You had to be tough. A couple of reporters and I observed an embarrassing situation at a forward CP. A unit had been held up and a unit commander came forward to see what was going on. The brigadier said to an lieutenant colonel at the situation map board:

"Where is our front line?"

The officer replied: "It's right about here, sir," pointing to a blue line on the acetate-covered map.

"What's holding them back?" The reply he received indicated there were extensive enemy fortifications along the front, delaying the advance.

The brigadier was impatient: "What do you mean extensive?"

"Well, there are a number of bunkers reinforced by ..."

"Have you observed them?"

"Me? No, I haven't, sir. I only have the reports sent to me from up there."

The brigadier, irritated, was closing in, knowing the officer hadn't been forward personally to check. He gruffly told him to go forward to the point of the trouble and lead a patrol out to determine the situation.

"A patrol?", the officer questioned.

"Yes, you heard me. Do you think you're better than they are? They're up there pinned down, waiting to hear from somebody."

"With all due respect, sir, those are not my duties. My duties ..."

The brigadier's face reddened and he bellowed out: "You're relieved, colonel, now! Get your gear and clear out."

The beleaguered officer became pale and confused but managed to stammer out:

"Very good, sir."

That incident was one of the few of its kind I witnessed during the war. I must say the Aussie commander was no less blunt than was General Hall on Bataan in relieving General Jones. To tell you the truth, I felt sorry for both officers whose careers were ruined. There's no bigger disgrace in the life of a professional soldier than being relieved of your post or command.

We did not experience a lot of action near Brunei. There were stories filed; in fact, I flew a couple of flights back to Manila with photos and stories because everything had to be censored. Even the Australian correspondents' copy was subject to MacArthur censorship, which they didn't appreciate.

Quite suddenly we received word, via courier, of the approaching landing at Balikpapan. Those wanting to go, and all of them did, were soon en route to the southeast part of Borneo, to a point some distance from Balikpapan, Borneo's main oil-shipping port.

We were greeted aboard a Navy ship somewhere in the Makassa Strait by Australian Major Ian Richardson, the press officer for the Australian invasion force. He was a polished gentleman and a great guy.

It was then we learned that MacArthur, aboard the cruiser Boise following his visit at Brunei Bay, would also be on hand for the landings at Balikpapan. This was certainly a surprise to me and to our group of correspondents. It was downright embarrassing to me, because I was supposed to know about such things so the reporters could make plans. Communications had broken down somewhere.

Waiting, waiting, waiting for another assault landing; "Hurry up and wait," was an old army adage. How true those words are. I became a bit apprehensive and began to wonder if I was suffering from stress. I asked a sailor standing on the deck nearby what he was thinking about. He said:

"Nothing really, sir. Just waiting."

I was glad to know I was not the only one and replied:

"Well, we'll have plenty to think about real soon."

Major General E. J. Milford's 7th Division landed three miles south of Balikpapan July 1. They weren't sure what of a reception they might

Many Americans were involved in the Borneo operation, but a few paid the price. An Australian soldier stands guard over a dead American, wrapped in the flag of his country.

receive, but they were ready for any eventuality.

The enemy's 37th Army, commanded by Japanese General Masao Baba, although weakened by units being transferred to other combat areas, was still believed to have around 30,000 troops near Balikpapan. As it turned out, he had splintered his forces along both coasts and had only about 4,000 men in the immediate area. We were lucky, again.

MacArthur once again showed up on the beach, just a few steps behind the assault wave, even though he had been warned to stay on the command ship a while longer. He wasn't about to miss what would become the last amphibious landing of World War II.

He headed straight for a small hill, less than 200 yards from Japanese positions and, borrowing a map from an Aussie officer, began studying it. All of a sudden, an enemy machine-gun opened up and everyone around dropped to the ground ... except the general. He continued to study the map, displaying little concern for the worry he was causing everyone else.

One of the photographers apologized to MacArthur for hitting the dirt, but the general replied: "You did the right thing, my boy."

Nonetheless, enemy troops had prepared formidable defenses, with artillery and mortars emplaced on the hills overlooking the city and the bay. There were thousands of mines in the bay and at the beaches, as well as elaborate beach hindrances. After all, the enemy knew the second largest oil center in the Southwest Pacific would be considered a top prize by the Allies, and that they would fight hard to regain it.

MacArthur had ordered a full-fledged bombardment to precede the Balikpapan attack, and extensive mine-sweeping was undertaken. This was to be no picnic. Six Allied ships were sunk by enemy fire and mines during this preliminary operation. There were plenty of explosions, flashes of light, the whooshing of shells overhead and combat confusion as the men were climbing into the Higgins boats.

Happily, Milford's force escaped trouble as they rushed the beaches, and encountered light opposition going inland. The reporters, including several Aussie writers, were anxious to get ashore so we climbed down into an LCI (landing craft, infantry) and followed the second wave. Major Richardson pointed us in the direction he felt we should go — and we hardly wet a whisker getting in.

Within two days Milford's troops had seized Balikpapan and one of the two airfields. At this point the situation became nastier and the battle began to gather intensity. Heavy fighting was required to drive the enemy from the fortified hills, but the Aussies advanced steadily not without substantial casualties.

It was really something, watching the Aussies maneuver through the jungle and brush. They were experienced, many had served combat time with the 7th in North Africa against Rommel, and some had fought along the Kokoda trail in New Guinea. They knew what they were doing, and didn't mind the opportunity to kill more Japanese. They had good reason to hate the enemy.

I heard some harrowing tales from the Aussies about Japanese cruelty and treatment of POW's early in the war. Thousands of Australian and British troops had been captured when the Japanese overran the South Pacific and Indonesia during the first weeks of the war.

Nurses were raped and brutalized, all prisoners were tortured, starved and often shot without cause. In fact, there were numerous mass executions, and cannibalism was not uncommon. The brutality of the Japanese was not unexpected since they had already demonstrated their beastiality in China.

Perhaps the worst account of barbaric behavior took place on Borneo following its fall to the enemy early in 1942. The Aussie officer who told me about it shook as he related the horrible details. An Aussie PW was taken to a clearing near the encampment serving as a temporary prison. An officer followed, carrying a stool and a knife with a blade about 6 to 8 inches in length. Another officer carried a hammer.

The prisoner, half-starved and so weak he could not stand alone, was dragged to a large timber cross. The Japanese officer then stood on the stool and raised the prisoner's arm and drove a nail through the palm of his hand into the cross-arm. When the man attempted to resist and scream, the officer pushed the prisoner's body against the upright post and stuffed a wad of cotton into the soldier's mouth.

The officer then nailed the other hand to the cross, and proceeded to complete the crucifixion by nailing the Aussie's feet to the upright, and driving a long nail through the man's forehead into the upright. He then took the knife and cut flesh from the stomach of the PW on both sides, and then put on some gloves.

In the next animalistic move he then reached into the man's stomach and pulled out his intestines and placed them on a board. He completed his inhuman activity by cutting flesh from the man's thighs, both arms and his neck.

After hearing that tale, and other stories of Japanese brutality, including their treatment of U.S. soldiers on Bataan and Corregidor, I can understand why the Aussies questioned why they had to be on Borneo amidst such memories, enduring one the most miserable and most isolated spots on the globe. It was a choice of perfectly insufferable evils, with peat swamp forests and vast coastal mangrove entanglements to deal with now and then. Still, it gave them an opportunity to avenge their "comrade on the cross."

Later, as we trudged through one of the swampy areas toward the front, I saw a turtle that must have weighed 200 pounds, and spotted a crocodile that must have been 20 feet in length. Borneo was a wildlife wonderland and a floral treasure.

In about 20 minutes or so, our press group crouched beside some Aussie GIs huddled behind trees, prone behind bushes and tall grass, in water-filled holes and beneath fallen trees. It rained intermittently, as if to wash the agony of war away. A machine gun opened up a few yards in front of us, its tracers marking an orange path through the leaves and slugs thudding into tree trunks.

"Hell's bells," I said to myself, "we're under fire!"

My mouth went dry. One of the reporters yelled: "Holy S—!" I seconded the motion and began looking for cover. I wasn't supposed to let these guys get themselves into a dangerous situation, and I certainly had no intention of getting them into the middle of a fire fight. For ten minutes we hugged the damp, moss-covered ground with considerable pleasure as the opposing forces exchanged fire, with a few grenades and even some mortar rounds. I even fired my carbine a few times and believe I may have "scored" at least once. It was a sticky situation. If I had owned a cross, I'd have kissed it.

Finally, one by one, the infantrymen ahead of us got up and began moving forward, swerving ahead in calculated formation, each one covering the other. I heard more firing, a few grenades, and then through the tangled foliage we saw the devil's tongue of a flame-thrower. There was a savage exchange of fire off to the right and then silence — if there is such a thing in the jungle.

In a couple of minute, we moved ahead and soon passed a Japanese bunker, an evil place where at least a dozen soldiers died. Several bodies lay in a black, swampy area, rocking gently in the little waves made by our walking through it. One Aussie soldier had cradled another in his arms:

"Those murdering bastards," he cried.

Several wounded came into view. One Aussie soldier, on his stomach on a litter, was swathed in bandages that had slipped to reveal a gaping hole from which blood oozed out like thick soup. Another soldier limped past with a medic holding a bottle of plasma high above the man's head. Others plodded past with obvious wounds to legs, arms and head.

The enemy soldiers hit by the flame-thrower looked as if they had been barbecued over a spit.

Before long we reached the huge oil refineries owned by the Dutch. There had been quite a battle here, with the dead being placed in body bags and the wounded on litters for transfer to surgical tents or to a hospital ship. There were a sizeable number of enemy dead lying around. At least seven had committed hara-kiri with knives or grenades held close to the stomach.

It was at the refinery area I caught my first glimpse of the Dayaks, a pygmy tribe of natives, who battled the Japanese during the occupation of Borneo. These diminutive warriors used blowguns and spears. I noticed all of them had some sort of a belt around their waists. A close look confirmed what I had already heard, they cut the ears off dead Japanese and made an ornamental belt of them. The more ears, the more courageous the warrior.

Lunchtime at hand, some of us joined a squad or two of Aussie soldiers who were eating their rations in a small clearing inside the refinery grounds. An Aussie soldier had brewed some tea and was just pouring some for me when, all of a sudden, there was a burst of fire. It came from the mouth of a small bunker nearby.

All of us hunkered down and saw a Japanese soldier holding a rapid-fire weapon of some sort in his arms, firing wildly in all directions. In less time than I can relate it, an Australian soldier with a flame-thrower ran toward the enemy and shot a full load of fiery napalm full force into the mouth of the bunker, which erupted in flames.

Out of this inferno came the Japanese soldier, on fire from head to toe, flames shooting 15 feet into the air. He ran perhaps 10 or 15 steps before his oxygen was depleted and he crumbled to the ground in a flaming heap, like a burning pile of leaves in autumn.

Life magazine photographer Carl Mydans was with us at the time, and he snapped a photo of the Japanese soldier fully engulfed in fire as he ran toward us. It turned out to be one of the most widely distributed pictures of the war, was given full page treatment in *Life,* and won many awards.

MacArthur eventually reached the area, having two or three reporters in tow. By this time most of us looked pretty shabby, particularly since we'd had no chance to change from our sweat-stained and muddied fatigues, or take a bath. We were a sorry-looking band of information people.

One of the reporters who had followed along with MacArthur, told me that the general had earlier stopped near a small stream to talk with Aussie soldiers trying to manhandle a small artillery piece across it. One soldier looked up and saw him, exclaiming: "Kee-rist, it's the f_____ messiah!"

MacArthur, seeking to be friendly, said: "How goes it, gentlemen?"

The soldiers sort of bristled and turned away with disgust. It was explained the soldiers knew they were not exactly gentlemen in that situation and considered MacArthur's remark hypocritical. Had the general used a few cuss words, the Aussies soldiers would have responded, but to be addressed that way seemingly offended them.

After a few seconds of embarrassing silence, MacArthur walked away. I'm sure the general meant well and, quite honestly, felt he had been treated in a shabby, uncouth manner. Sometimes the Aussies could be pretty crude.

One Australian soldier I talked with told me of his close call from a Japanese perched in a tree.

"I was walking along a trail when I heard the `ping' of a rifle and a slug plowed into the dirt by my side. Several more rounds came in as I clung to the ground. I noticed the slugs were hitting the ground on a slant. By God, they had to came from a damn Jap in a tree.

"I got on one knee and fired a burst with my Tommy gun to a spot where I thought I saw a movement in the canopy of leaves. I rested a minute and crawled forward. All of a sudden I saw a drip of blood right before my bloomin' face, then another and another. I got that bastard good and proper."

That night the Boise hauled anchor and headed back to Manila. Once again MacArthur had pulled off a front-line visit under fire and escaped without a scratch. He had done this repeatedly throughout the war. Whether it was bravado or a secret wish to die in battle, we'll never know. Perhaps he did it to show the troops he knew how tough their job was.

Before I left Borneo, the correspondents anxious to return to Manila, I talked Major Richardson out of a pair of Aussie boots, which were far superior to our GI combat boots. I gave him a paratrooper jacket I had acquired on Corregidor. Secret diplomatic negotiation between nations has its advantages.

Just before leaving, I was fortunate to see a Borneo orangutan in a line of trees not far from where we were camped. They have orange-tinted hair and often weigh over 200 pounds. I was told these creatures rule the jungle and can even kill crocodiles by jumping on their backs, opening up their jaws, then ripping out their throats.

Oh yes, I also saw a Borneo "barking" deer. They look much like our white-tailed deer, except they make a unique sound which natives interpret as a dog's bark. Their antlers do not have points but are more like simple horns. I found Borneo a scenic country, full of wild flowers, lovely mountains, seaside vistas, waterfalls, spectacular wildlife and valuable natural resources.

No wonder the English and Dutch wanted us to retain their interests there. Borneo with its oil and numerous natural resources was well worth owning.

"Downfall" for Japan

Chapter 14

"I love the infantry because they are the underdogs. They are the mud-rain-and-wind boys. They have no comforts, they learn to live without necessities. And in the end they are the guys that wars can't be won without."

— Ernie Pyle

IT WAS RATHER A PLEASANT FEELING to get back with friends in GHQ in Manila after a few weeks in Borneo, although I must admit to a fondness for the Australians. I developed admiration for their conduct in battle, their ruggedness, and their desire to make a "Yank" comfortable in their midst. They taught me more about how to make and drink tea than I ever wanted to know. Battle in progress or not, they stopped to have a tea break.

I was very pleased to visit with old friends in XI Corps, who had just completed some tough combat assignments outside Manila. They had set up headquarters in an area known as Grace Park in a former shoe factory. The Japanese converted it into an aircraft engine repair facility. It looked good from the outside, but inside it was a mess and provided enough leaks to run a river.

I was told General Hall had been awarded the Distinguished Service Medal and also promoted to Lieutenant General, three stars. I was pleased to learn about this recognition, because I greatly admired him and believed him to be a fine example of what a professional soldier ought to be. Now and then he had a bad day, but didn't we all?

It wasn't long until word passed around the press section that solid planning for the invasion of Japan was well underway. After all, MacArthur's forces in the Southwest Pacific, and those battling across the Central Pacific under Admiral Nimitz, had virtually closed in on the outer defenses of Japan itself.

The operation was labeled "Downfall," and the primary phases of planning were done in Washington by Joint Chiefs of Staff planners with full input, of course, from MacArthur, Nimitz, and their staffs. It seemed to me, along with the excitement and anticipation of our biggest challenge ever, there was a cloud of dread and uneasiness over the assault on Japan, because most of us were thinking to ourselves:

"If the Japanese fought so hard to defend islands thousands of miles from home that in reality meant little to them personally, how difficult will an assault be on their homeland, where every man, woman and child will be defending their homes, their emperor and country, to the death?"

In Japan, the generals were preparing for the invasion. Even though they had lost the Philippines, and other islands, the bulk of their vast army in the homeland and on mainland China, was intact. Indeed, they could not believe any nation would have the nerve to attempt landings on their homeland. They bragged that Allied troops would face the fiercest defense in history. It was called "Ketsu-Go, Operation Decision."

The objective was to "annihilate the enemy landing force by fierce and bold offensive attacks." Therefore, all soldiers should pray for the eternal existence of Japan and give their all in accomplishing the objectives. "Every soldier should fight to the last moment," an order declared.

Subsequent instructions directed that "the wounded and sick will not be evacuated to the rear. There will be no retreat. Men will stand and die. Soldiers without weapons will take them from dead enemy soldiers. There will be no dropping out."

As for Japanese civilians, they also were ordered to fight unto death. People were given a song to sing: "One hundred million souls for the Emperor." Each person was supposed to kill at least ten Americans before dying.

Our intelligence people were aware Japan had stockpiled suicide weapons including 10,000 kamikazi aircraft, and several hundred rocket-powered piloted bombs called "Baka's." The Japanese Navy's contribution was a manned torpedo. These cylinders were cut in half, with a special section inserted for the pilot, and his controls. They were also producing tiny submarines to attack our invasion fleet.

Their navy was also training men to become human mines. These men were supposed to swim beneath our ships and blow them up with explosive charges pressed against the hulls.

Indeed, our invasion fleet would have been large, a 1,400 ship armada, the largest in history, with a capacity to carry a half-million troops with equipment and supplies. For this invasion, I would once more be serving with General Hall's XI Corps who would land the First Cavalry, the 43rd Infantry and American Divisions, on the southern reaches of Kyushu. This operation was called "Olympic."

U.S. casualties for taking the Japanese homeland were estimated to be as high as 600,000 — and it was anybody's guess — considering their coastal defenses of caves, tunnels and fortifications, plus the fanatical philosophy of their soldiers and citizenry. The people would be equipped with weapons ranging from ancient bronze cannon, to spears, bows and arrows, guns and other weapons. Our soldiers would have been opposed by about two and a -half million defenders.

It was said in headquarters that MacArthur was, as usual, optimistic about the invasion. In early August, 1945, however, he was told by his intelligence staff that it would be an "extremely costly operation." Planners were aware of Japanese fanaticism and conceded an invasion of Japan would be more difficult than the Normandy invasion.

We had a troop morale problem as well. Most GIs who had been in combat, unless wounded or assigned to less hazardous duty, had not been home since the war began. A regular rotation policy had not even begun until 1944, and few GIs knew anyone who had actually gone home. More and more men were beginning to feel a hopelessness or despair about combat. One infantryman said:

"We're being drowned in battle. As long as we can keep going they're going to send us in again and again. We all pray for a wound that will get us home without suffering permanent disability. We'll be kept here until we're out of our head or blown to bits. We've done our bit and we've earned our right to go home."

I couldn't argue with that. I shared their feelings.

Indeed, an army opinion poll conducted by *Army Times* revealed that 66 percent of army personnel polled believed that 18 months in combat should be the limit. This was solid thinking but the problem was, there was a similar feeling with the men that served in Europe, who were now being ordered into the Pacific to help defeat Japan.

Some higher-ups believed that "war weariness" in the U.S. might possibly force a too-rapid return of soldiers to the U.S. and thus endanger the assault on Japan.

While the tours of duty in World War II were long, the rotation system was far better than that employed in the Vietnam War. One can't imagine a more messed-up situation for soldiers than existed in

Vietnam. In World War II we all realized we would keep fighting until the war was won.

In Vietnam, the military sent a soldier over for one year. He probably spent the first six months learning his job, and perhaps for three months, he was a good soldier. The last three months he likely spent trying to make sure he stayed alive. It was not an efficient use of manpower, and we all know that Vietnam was not one of America's greatest and most admirable undertakings.

It wasn't long until we received more information about Downfall, both officially and unofficially. Rumors flew around headquarters like sea gulls over ships. Olympic, the assault on Kyushu, was now scheduled for October, 1945. Coronet, the invasion of the main island of Honshu, was set for March of 1946.

The plan called for a Coronet invasion force of 650,000 ground troops. The battle would involve landings at three different localities, with one corps of two divisions making a divisionary move elsewhere to divert attention from the main assault. The campaign would be directed toward securing the southern third of Honshu, where the Allies could establish air bases and staging areas for the final assault on Honshu.

No one I ever talked with about the invasion doubted that casualties would be extremely high. For Kyushu alone, it was estimated we might suffer at least 280,000 dead and wounded. By the time we had overcome all of Japan, it was said our losses could approach a million. Such estimates, of course, did little to boost morale.

By this time, the influx of correspondents into Manila had grown considerably. It seemed every newspaper and radio network wanted their man on the spot. We already had so many reporters in the theater that, during the Philippines fighting, we often had to limit the number of reporters on major landings or key engagements simply because we could not take care of so many in a combat situation.

This was called "pooling," which meant that two or three reporters would accompany troops or airmen on critical missions and then would share their stories and photographs with their fellow newsmen. This was not always popular, but experienced correspondents realized the logistical problems involved with too many reporters trying to cover the same story.

I was eating lunch when I first heard the scuttlebutt that the U.S. had tested a new and deadly bomb in the New Mexico desert. None of us at that time was aware of the potential of this new weapon, but as the rumors grew we all came to realize this was something really big. That proved to be an understatement.

The "super" bomb turned out to be an atomic weapon of unsurpassed power and magnitude. President Harry S. Truman, replacing Franklin D. Roosevelt who had died April 12, mentioned the bomb to Stalin at Yalta, and the Russian dictator had replied: "I am glad to hear it."

He could be afford to be casual about it. The Russians already knew of the bomb's development because U.S. citizens and British spies had supplied helpful information to them about its technology. Actually, we had heard rumors that the Japanese had a "super bomb" under development, but lacked a certain key ingredient to complete it. We assumed it had to be uranium.

As a matter of fact our government knew that Japan was experimenting with atomic weapons. In May, 1945, a German submarine surrendered to some U.S. ships off the Atlantic Coast. Navy personnel, boarding the submarine, found several Japanese officers and over a half-ton of uranium ordered by Japan. After Germany surrendered to the Allies, all submarines were ordered to surface and head for an Allied port.

Truman, at age 60, fit and feisty, took over the presidency and the responsibility for the war as if he had been born to it. Those of us from Missouri, who knew something of his background, had a feeling Harry would not dilly-dally around with Japan this far into the struggle with victory within grasp.

Every effort had been made to draw Russia into the war at the Yalta conference because of the advantage it would give the U.S. A Russian drive into Manchuria, at the same time we invaded Japan, would prevent the movement of forces south into Korea and North China and keep Japanese troops tied down in Asia. With the atomic bomb a reality, Truman sort of "backed away" from Soviet participation in the war, considering it unnecessary.

A *New York Times* correspondent told me one day that special crews were training in B-29 bombers to deliver the A-bomb on Japan. This was supposed to be secret. I was astounded to hear this from a civilian newsman. The Japanese had become accustomed to B-29 raids, so test runs with simulated atomic bombs had been in progress for some time without unusual notice, but we had no idea such momentous news would be bandied about so casually.

Truman insisted to his dying day, he suffered no sense of guilt or regret over his decision to use the bombs. Actually there was never any doubt atomic weapons would be used. Proponents advanced the argument that the Japanese were "savage fanatics" who cared nothing about human life. The sneak attack on Pearl Harbor, their abuse of POWs, the Kamikazes and the tenacity of their troops in battle, had hardened American public opinion against them.

Had Truman decided against using the atomic bombs, America would have faced at least 16 more months of war and the terrible cost of an invasion of the Japanese homeland. That was the basis for his decision.

Those of us on the scene had no regrets about use of the A-bombs. Some sources today argue the U.S. should have dropped a "demonstration" bomb somewhere to let the Japanese see what a powerful weapon it was. Others say we should not have dropped the second bomb on Nagasaki so soon, etc.

The atomic bomb saved millions of American and Japanese lives. My argument for use of the bomb has always been that if Japan had developed the A-bomb first, they would have most certainly used it against us. No question about it.

On August 6, 1945, three B-29s took off from the huge air base at Tinian, in the Marianas, arriving over Hiroshima just after eight in the morning. Leading the way was the bomber Enola Gay, piloted by Colonel Paul Tibbets. This plane carried the bomb which was a dull black cylinder just over ten feet in length, twenty-nine inches in diameter, and weighing ninety-seven hundred pounds.

The other two B-29s carried cameras and scientific equipment. Hiroshima, eighth largest city in Japan, was clearly visible from 31,000 feet.

At 8:15 p.m., the Enola Gay's bomb bay doors opened and the so-called "little boy" bomb was released as Tibbets banked sharply to get away from the target area. The bomb took forty-three seconds to reach its point of detonation, about nineteen hundred feet above the ground. Most of Hiroshima disappeared in a blast of heat and light. Around 100,000 people died instantly; thousands more died later of burns, shock or radiation sickness.

Truman issued a statement shortly thereafter, announcing the existence of this terrible new weapon. He urged the Japanese to surren-

"DOWNFALL" FOR JAPAN

American servicemen at the American Red Cross center in Manila crowd around Daily Pacifican *newspapers reporting Russia's entry into the war. They were far more enthusiastic about it than was MacArthur and the GHQ staff.*

der or "face a rain of ruin from the air, the like of which has never been seen on this earth." He meant every word of it.

Two days later Russia declared war on Japan. Some said it was another diplomatic error. Just as we had held back General Patton from taking Berlin, allowing the Russians to get into the city to claim a share, the Allies had once again permitted Russia to come in late to share the spoils of war. How foolish these decisions were.

Red Army troops and aircraft wasted little time in launching an attack into Manchuria. Since it was not preceded by air attacks or artillery bombardment, the famed Kwantung Army was caught flat-footed and quickly subdued. Those of us in the press section were told that the attack involved over a million Russian men and at least 5,000 tanks and self-propelled guns.

In the meantime, a second atomic weapon had been loaded aboard another B-29, Bock's Car, named for Captain Fred Bock, which was piloted by Major Charles Sweeney, pilot of the monitoring plane during the Hiroshima mission two days earlier. The primary target, Kokura, was obscured by smoke from fire bombings the night before, and also heavy cloud cover, so the plane was diverted to Nagasaki.

Bock's Car carried the "fat man" bomb which was larger in size than the "little boy" bomb dropped on Hiroshima. Two minutes after the bomb exploded, the plane was buffeted by five distinct shock waves which had bounced off the mountains overlooking the city. In an instant the city was devastated and 40,000 or more people had died instantly from incineration.

A press conference was quickly convened in Manila for our contingent of correspondents, now numbered in the hundreds. Dr. Robert Compton, one of the so-called "fathers" of the atomic bomb, had been flown in from the States to brief reporters, and he answered as many questions as he could.

He was surprisingly frank, admitting no one really knew how much devastation the bombs might create, and even less on the immediate and long-range health risk to those exposed to the radiation. Some people in our headquarters had thought that perhaps the atomic reaction, once activated, might not stop with just one explosion — but keep splitting atoms in a world-wide destructive conflagration.

Thank goodness, they were wrong.

Doctor Compton displayed aerial photographs of both cities and it was obvious that just one bomb had delivered death and destruction on a scale seen only after raids involving hundreds and hundreds of bombers, and thousands and thousands of bombs. Quite naturally, the reporters wanted to see for themselves, but it would be awhile before they could visit both cities.

MacArthur kept Hiroshima and Nagasaki off-limits far longer than most everyone thought he should, but I believe he was concerned about the health of those visiting the highly irradiated cities too soon. Who really knows?

Japan was in turmoil. The emperor stepped in to oppose those militarists who did not want to surrender. It was touch and go for hours, and on August 14, a group of fanatical army officers took control of the Central Guards in Tokyo, killed the commander, and broke into the palace grounds. They were trying to find the tape Hirohito would use to address the Japanese people, bearing his surrender message.

Fortunately for us, they did not succeed and the rebellion was repulsed by troops loyal to the emperor.

Meantime, U.S. planes showered Tokyo with leaflets detailing the

Riotous jubilation filled the streets of Manila when word came Japan had surrendered. The celebration lasted for hours.

text of the Japanese government's surrender offer, and our acceptance of the terms. General Anami Korechicka, the war minister who had opposed surrender to the bitter end, committed suicide on the 14th so he would not hear the emperor read the surrender proclamation, and also to show he had taken responsibility for Japan's defeat.

In a Radio Tokyo broadcast August 14, the long-awaited news was flashed around the world that the Japanese government had decided to accept the Allied terms of surrender. When Truman received the news officially, he declared a two-day national holiday. The Japanese war machine, which had begun its mischief in China eight years earlier, had been derailed and wrecked.

In Manila there was great jubilation. Outside MacArthur's headquarters, several hundred GI's gathered just below the general's offices and began to yell for his appearance. After a few minutes he appeared at a window and in a subdued, emotional manner he said:

"I hope from the bottom of my heart that this is the end of the war. If it is, it is largely due to your efforts. Very soon, I hope, we will all be going home."

The general quickly turned around and disappeared from view amidst wild cheering from those assembled, including some of us inside the building. Just a few days before, MacArthur had been named

Supreme Commander of Allied Powers by President Truman. It was MacArthur the president chose to preside at the surrender ceremony. Neither of these appointments pleased the hierarchy of the U. S. Navy. Old wounds between the services take a long time to heal, if ever.

Communications between Manila and Tokyo reached a high level over the next two weeks as MacArthur and officials of the Japanese government worked out the complicated details regarding surrender arrangements. The general ordered a delegation of Japanese officials headed by General Toroshiro Kawabe, vice chief of the Imperial General Staff, to Manila for face-to-face discussions. They made the trip in a specially marked aircraft to avoid possible tragedy.

This delegation reached Manila August 19 to receive direction from GHQ and to provide the data needed for the first phase of the occupation. MacArthur watched them arrive but at no time did he personally intervene in the discussions. He left the details to members of his "inner" staff, those who had been with him since the war began and mainly those who had departed Corregidor with him.

The Japanese brought with them various reports, maps and charts showing the location of prison camps, military installations, airfields, defense installations and minefields. The talks went on for hours. Kawabe informed GHQ staff of the unrest of some military units in Japan, and as a result, the landing of U.S. units at the Atsugi airfield west of Yokohama August 23 was moved to the 26th. It seemed some Kamikaze pilots in the area continued to remain in a rebellious state.

We were told later that the propellers had been removed from several hundred Kamikaze aircraft around Tokyo to eliminate the threat of a pre-surrender coup or uprising, or possible attacks on the surrender ceremony.

Reams of paperwork were completed, including the wording of the surrender document as well as billeting arrangements of the advance units. An unintentional affront to the emperor of Japan, due to an innocent misuse of language in the surrender document which alarmed Japanese delegates, was quickly settled by MacArthur, who said:

"I have no desire whatever to debase him in the eyes of his own people, as through him it will be possible to maintain a completely orderly government." How wise he was on this issue.

Meanwhile, Emperor Hirohito had ordered his armed forces to halt hostile actions; members of the imperial family were dispatched to far-flung regions to expedite compliance with the surrender, and units in the Yokohama-Tokyo area prepared to receive the victors. It was a sad and demeaning time for them, to be sure.

Because of a severe typhoon that swept southern Japan, the arrival of the advance U.S. units at Atsugi was postponed until August 28 and the surrender ceremony confirmed for September 2 in Tokyo Bay. These two weeks were some of the busiest in MacArthur's long career. There was still fighting in progress in several areas of the Pacific and Japan and the Chinese were still battling the Japanese in northern China.

Russian troops were pushing southward in Korea, reaching the 38th parallel which a few years later became, unfortunately, the demarcation line for Russian and American forces. It was a bad decision and one that came to haunt us in a few years when the 38th parallel became a household word during the so-called Korean "police action."

At GHQ things were now moving very fast. The surrender ceremony planning was completed and I was told I was to be a participant. My job, along with several other junior officers, was to make sure all the accredited correspondents and photographers had suitable places to observe and photograph the proceedings. It was then I learned for the first time that the battleship USS Missouri was steaming into Tokyo Bay and the ceremony would be held on its deck.

Our press staff had a floor plan of the deck and from that we drew in reserved sections for the dignitaries, the press and radio reporters, as well as Allied officers who managed to secure permission to attend. It wasn't as simple as it sounds, for it seemed every officer in the Pacific wanted to witness this historic event — and who could blame them?

By August 28 detachment of engineers and communications experts had landed at Atsugi airfield and were received without incident by the Japanese. In fact, the Japanese "welcoming" committee had fresh orange juice waiting for our forces and a delicious lunch was served on white tablecloths, followed by wine — and no "Banzai" for dessert.

Later in the day, 36 C-54's landed, bearing advance troops of the 11th Airborne Division. Within a few hours a C-54 was landing every three minutes, bringing in the remainder of the division. About the same time, the 4th Marines were going ashore to secure the Yokosuka/Yokohama region. One Marine officer was quoted as saying:

"Our first wave was made up entirely of admirals trying to beat

MacArthur ashore."

By this time the general and his personal staff, plus as many reporters as we could pack in, headed for Japan. There was an overnight stopover on Okinawa which gave me an opportunity to meet one of my brothers-in-law, whose outfit was on that island. Kathy had written me her brother, Donald Weide, was stationed there, but I never dreamed I would be lucky enough to find him.

Once on the ground, I asked around and discovered his unit was camped just a few miles away. I requisitioned a Jeep and within minutes we had introduced ourselves and were "talking family." Our conversation lasted an hour or so and began a friendship that lasted until his death December 29, 1991, after a long career in retailing. Don was a good and gentle man who was loved by many.

I went to bed that night knowing tomorrow I would be in Japan and, like everyone else, not knowing what the future might hold. It was an especially risky move for MacArthur. After the war, Sir Winston Churchill called the general's early entry into Japan, "an amazing deed of bravery."

That's true; the appearance of the Supreme Commander in the Japanese homeland on the afternoon of August 30 was a real gamble at a time when he could have become a victim of Japanese trickery, or a surprise attack from a fanatical element of the Army.

Tomorrow we would get up early, board our three C-54's, and discover what was in store for us. This was rare excitement! The Japanese homeland at last!

USS Missouri Spectacle

Chapter 15

"Victory has a thousand fathers but defeat is an orphan."
— **President John F. Kennedy**

THE PRESS PLANE, carrying a host of reporters and members of the GHQ press staff to Japan landed at Atsugi airfield right behind General MacArthur's "Bataan," which was the first to hit the landing strip. There was a rousing cheer aboard our C-54 as its wheels crunched and squealed as they made contact with the runway for a rubbery landing. It was about 2p.m., August 27th, 1945.

Most of us were off our plane in time to see the general climb down the steps from his plane, assisted by one or two of his personal staff. He seemed jovial and confident, with his shirt open at the neck and his corncob pipe in his mouth. His staffers were a happy bunch of campers because this was one of the most "gentle" military invasions in all history. The general was quickly surrounded by reporters and photographers.

The 11th Airborne Division band members had collected themselves and their instruments together and played brisk military music as MacArthur and his trusted inner staff congratulated one another on setting foot on Japanese soil without a shot being fired. I could not distinquish what he said word for word, but the reporters who clustered around him indicated it was something like: "Yes, this the pay day we've been waiting for."

As we flew in over the coastline, I had noticed miles of narrow beaches which might have been the same stretches of rock and sand we would have had to assault. Today, however, they were nearly colorless and empty. Inland from the beaches were cultivated fields and scenic hills, deeply etched in green, the color spreading finger-like from the base of ancient gullied mountains.

The fields had been planted with rice and the shoots were several inches high, but from the air the landscape appeared like a soft, flat carpet. Here and there were clumps of trees of various kinds and the rice paddies were lined with hedges. The Japanese might well be the world's best farmers and gardeners; there was a planned orderliness to the landscape and nothing seemed out of place except in areas that obviously had not escaped our bombing.

As our plane glided in for its landing, I noticed hundreds of houses with thatched roofs lining the dirt roads. Most of the people I saw on the roads, even paths, were carrying good-sized bundles or else were pulling heavy carts. Some of the quaint carts were pulled by oxen, its owner plodding patiently alongside.

Could these be the same people who nearly dominated the South Pacific and fought with such ferocity? None of them this memorable day were even looking up at our line of descending aircraft.

Atsugi Airfield was hardly a model of construction. There were two long runways, not hard-surfaced, surrounded by some camouflaged hangars and rickety-looking barracks. At one end of the field I could see what was obviously a large graveyard of Japanese aircraft, some glinting silver in the sun where their green paint had worn off. They looked like the broken toys of children, some aircraft on their noses, others crumpled over on a wing.

The airfield had been put in as good a condition as any of us could have hoped for. The work was accomplished by advance elements of the 63rd Airdrome squad and the 21st Air Freight Transport unit who had arrived in Japan two days before. That same afternoon an armada of 36 C-54's had landed advance troops of the 11th Airborne Division, along with petroleum and supplies. The balance of the division arrived the same day as the GHQ advance group and reporters.

These men did not know what to expect on their arrival at Atsugi; some fully expected to be massacred. Within three miles of the airfield, behind barbed wire, there were 50,000 Kamikaze pilots, and within 50 miles were an estimated million regular troops. One could forgive the nervousness of the moment.

However, they were greeted by very pleasant, courteous Japanese officers and officials, plus a few Russian diplomats who apparently had been stationed in Tokyo, but who had been placed under restriction since the Mother Country barged into the war.

As we stood near our plane, a company of Japanese soldiers marched down the runway, but one could not tell where they were going. Very soon all of us on the three C-54's were instructed to move

Two Japanese newspapermen, surrounded by military personnel, appeared confused and bewildered by all the attention — and who could blame them. A Japanese interpreter has his back to the camera.

toward a ramshackle control shed where U.S. officers were busily arranging for our transportation into Yokohama.

With the help of the docile Japanese, the advance party had assembled a vast motor pool of assorted cars and trucks. It looked like a parking lot at a country fair or sporting event.

Our baggage had been taken from the planes (there wasn't much, we were traveling light) and as other planes landed, loaded with battle-ready troops, the terminal area was jam-packed. Almost as soon as they arrived, the soldiers climbed into trucks and were whisked away, perhaps to pre-arranged locations along MacArthur's route into Yokohama or to billeting areas. I'm sure they were apprehensive about what they might encounter.

There were Japanese interpreters all over the place, dressed in uniforms or civilian garb, standing in small groups gesturing nervously, standing on one foot and then the other. They wore yellow bands around their arm to signify their purpose there. They did their best to remain impassive which I know had to be extremly difficult.

On the far side of the field, near what appeared to be the administration building, was a contingent of Japanese soldiers who saluted every American who came within a hundred yards. Black uniformed police carrying small swords in silver scabbards were guarding the roads, looking sinister in this situation. The squad's lieutenant was lying on his back, his feet against his backside, making waving movements with his knees, obviously some sort of oriental exercise.

The GIs who arrived early were housed in large barracks. The Japanese government, anxious to please, had supplied them with waiters from a hotel. The atmosphere, what with the almost comic selflessness that characterizes good waiters, was unreal. For example, one GI yelled "Over here, James," as he snapped his fingers for a glass of ice-water.

I was told that beneath this part of the airfield, the Japanese had constructed tunnels and spaces sufficient for a complete machine shop. This area, too, was clogged with broken-down trucks and automobiles. The airfield was like a huge salvage yard.

The Japanese had somehow found General MacArthur an American automobile to ride in. It appeared to be an aging Lincoln sedan in poor condition of undetermined vintage. GHQ had wanted the Japanese to supply at least 40 or 50 automoblles, but because of the bombings, there weren't that many serviceable automobiles left. Due to the shortage of gasoline, the comical and dilapidated fleet of cars and trucks they assembled had to be fueled with charcoal.

Believe it or not, they used a fire truck as the lead vehicle in the motorcade. The motors revved up and no sooner had the column begun to move than a car loaded with Japanese officials broke down. Others in the column lurched, bucked and stalled, as the procession moved toward the city. As the truck I occupied moved by, I saw one Japanese official sitting on its fender, with his Samurai sword dangling between his legs, with a dozen other Japanese running around in confusion.

Believe it or not, it took over an hour to go the 20 miles to Yokohama, but it was not the slowness of the journey, nor the breakdown of vehicles along the way, that made this trip memorable. It was the hundreds of enemy soldiers lining both sides of the roadway. They stood facing the road as we approached, but as we came alongside they abruptly turned their backs on us as if in defiance of our presence.

This seemed very ominous at the time, but it was explained to us later this wall of soldiers was placed along the route to Yokohama to protect the general, and others of us who were with him, against the possibility of attack by dissidents. This "turning of faces," which we first considered an insult, was in their culture an honor previously accorded only to the Emperor and his family!

One could only contemplate the true feelings of the Japanese people at this point. After all, Japan to that time was the only major nation in the world whose soil had not been walked on by an enemy soldier. I'm sure the events of the past month had created great indignation, grief and disbelief. Surrender was unthinkable but what citizen, born a Japanese, could not obey the Emperor's command, which had been given with a broken heart?

Yokohama was in shambles from our B-29 raids. I found it hard to believe the devastation spread out before my eyes. Most of the damage was from fire bombing, but the big demolition bombs had destroyed what the flames had missed. There was no question the people there had faced misery and deprivation for some time. In fact, food was in such short supply that MacArthur issued an order forbidding the commandeering of civilian food supplies by our troops.

A hotel suite had been prepared for MacArthur in the New Grand Hotel. It was nothing short of miraculous that the hotel was still standing amidst all the destruction. He went to bed that night with 500 paratroopers guarding the building, but there were no problems. The press section and reporters were divided between the New Grand and another hotel nearby. These were exciting times, with the surrender ceremony now just a few days away. Our exuberance overcame whatever concerns we had held.

Tokyo, 15 miles away, had been declared off limits by the general, which was not popular with many correspondents. They were anxious, of course, to interview important officials and, if possible, secure an audience with the emperor. No way could that happen with the situation so precarious and insecure.

Japanese officials were greatly impressed by the "civilized" conduct and positive attitudes displayed by the occupation commanders and their troops. Actually it was a surprise to me, that American troops did not display more hostility toward the enemy than they did. They had every right to be vengeful, but with few exceptions, they conducted themselves with remarkable restraint and kindness.

Perhaps it was because, once the fighting ended, their thoughts were mainly concentrated on going home and putting their lives back together. That's how I felt, too. There was little use in punishing innocent citizens. The war was over, I was alive, and nothing was more important now than to be with my family.

Some Japanese had expected "unbearable horrors" from Americans. One officer explained he was surprised at the understanding and friendly manners of the conquerors. He said he had not felt a sense of defeat even during the worst fire raids, but when he saw a child begging for scraps of food from American GIs, he realized it was the Japanese who had lost the war.

By this time General Wainwright had been located in a Manchurian prison camp, as well as General Arthur Percival, who had been forced to surrender at Singapore early in the war. General MacArthur wanted both present for the surrender ceremony. On August 28, the two generals and several other high-ranking officers arrived in Yokohama.

MacArthur was in the hotel dining room when someone told him Wainwright had just entered the lobby. I did not see their meeting, but I was told the general rushed to the lobby to see the scrawny Wainwright, who was walking with a cane. He managed a smile but quickly choked up as MacArthur embraced him. It was an emotional high for MacArthur, too, and all he could manage was "Jim ... Jim."

At dinner MacArthur quickly and earnestly offered Wainwright "any command he wanted" after Wainwright confided to him that, since he had surrendered U.S. forces on Corregidor, he thought he would never again be permitted to command troops. The general immediately reassured him that he was a hero, not a scapegoat. Unfortunately, Wainwright's health had deteriorated in the POW camp to the extent he was never able to serve under MacArthur or any other commander again.

There was tremendous support for General Wainwright among army personnel because he had always been considered the "fall guy" since those early days on Corregidor. MacArthur's words to him in the hotel helped sooth those feelings, but there was something he did not know.

Right after Wainwright had been taken prisoner, General George C. Marshall, Army Chief of Staff, sent MacArthur a radiogram recommending Wainwright for the Congressional Medal of Honor. Marshall had appreciated the splendid effort of Wainwright and his troops on Luzon, and wanted to recognize him with the nation's highest honor.

Wainwright needed MacArthur's endorsement since "Mac" was his commanding officer. Surprisingly, MacArthur refused to approve the request because he blamed Wainwright for the heavy losses on Bataan and Corregidor. His reply to Marshall reflected great hostility to Wainwright, and did not offer any support for his opinions. This despite the fact MacArthur had publicly praised Wainwright's withdrawal into Bataan " as fine as anything in history."

Who can explain the ego of MacArthur. General Wainwright received the Medal of Honor once he arrived back in the U.S. He was no longer under MacArthur's command. It was presented to him September 10, 1945 in the White House by President Harry Truman who assured him he was a true leader and hero to the American people.

Truman had written in his dairy some months before: "I don't see why in hell Roosevelt didn't order Wainwright home and let MacArthur be a martyr. We'd have had a real general and a fighting man if we had Wainwright, and not a play actor like MacArthur and a bunco man as we have now."

In the early light of September 2, 1945, over 250 warships were at anchor in Tokyo Bay, its surface smooth as glass. It was a gray day, with low-hanging clouds floating lazily over the great armada of ships, as officers and dignitaries of the nations involved in the war against Japan began gathering aboard the USS Missouri, anchored about five miles off Yokohama.

The five-starred flags of the Pacific Fleet and MacArthur's command, and also the American flag that was flying over our nation's capitol on December 7, 1941, were raised over the great battleship at daybreak.

It seems like only yesterday, but as I write this it has been 52 years ago that I watched General Douglas MacArthur, officials of the Japanese government, and representatives of the Allied powers, sign the documents that brought World War II to an end. It has always remained to me one of those "unforgettable moments."

The privilege and significance of being a part of such a historic event has grown on me as the years roll by. I am astounded that as a mere captain in the U.S. Army, I was to play a rather minor role in the proceedings and thus given the rare opportunity to be present for the end of history's greatest and most costly war.

Many people believe President Harry Truman was responsible for selecting the USS Missouri for the ceremony. Actually, Admiral Nimitz chose the battleship because it was named for Truman's home state, and Margaret was chosen as its sponsor. When the battleship was re-commissioned in San Francisco in May 1986, she was one of the honored guests.

MacArthur let the Navy choose the site for the surrender since the Army had the honor of landing on Japanese soil a few days ear-

PARA(GRAPH) TROOPER FOR MacARTHUR

An overall view of the small deck where the ceremony took place. MacArthur stands on the near side of the table while awaiting Japanese officials to step forward. Photographers and reporters are behind the railing at the right side of the photo. Army, Navy, Air Force and Marine dignitaries, along with Allied delegates, border the site on the left and bottom of photo.

lier. It was a matter of interservice diplomacy and tact, attributes that unfortunately had been rarely displayed during the conduct and strategy of the war.

It seemed like everybody wanted in on "the greatest show on earth." GHQ had news media people to deal with from all points of the compass. There would be no shortage of news coverage for this event. It was my job to help insure that all the accredited newsmen and photographers had space to do their jobs.

In order to make room for everyone on the Veranda Deck, the Navy had to build a plywood platform for photographers over a battery of 40 mm guns. We worked from a floor plan of the deck supplied by the Navy which set aside sufficient space for all approved personnel.

There were 194 war correspondents and photographers authorized to go aboard the battleship, with Lt. Colonel Richard Powell in charge of our GHQ press section. We all boarded the destroyer USS Taylor for the short voyage from the Yokohama dock, and the hull of the Missouri loomed high as we pulled alongside at 7:07 a.m.

A short time later, the destroyer USS Buchanan arrived and dis-

Allied war correspondents and photographers, plus the GHQ press staff, head for the USS Missouri aboard the destroyer USS Taylor which saw early action in the war at Guadalcanal.

embarked an assortment of generals, admirals and foreign dignitaries. At 8:05, Admiral Chester W. Nimitz, who headed all Naval forces in the Pacific, came aboard from his personal launch. He had been on the USS South Dakota, some distance away.

General MacArthur came aboard at 8:38 from the USS Nicholas. The general appeared apprehensive, looking a bit tired and worn, but lean-faced and bronzed. His step was firm and confident as he crossed the deck wearing his old battered cap that had become his trademark, his shirt open at the neck as was his custom.

He wore no ribbons or decorations, but he was a magnificent presence and I will never forget being near him for a brief moment or two on this most historic occasion.

Shortly thereafter, the Japanese contingent came aboard from the destroyer Lansdowne. From it came one of the saddest faces I will ever see. Foreign Minister Mamoru Shigemitsu was a melancholy little man, wearing a tall silk hat, cutaway coat, and ascot vest. He experienced great difficulty climbing the 40 or 50 narrow steps up the side of the ship from the destroyer to the surrender deck.

Many of those present were not aware that his left leg had been blown off by an assassin's bomb in China years before. Apparently his artificial limb had a stiff knee joint. The completely silent Allied assembly watched his laborious journey up the ladder and across the deck to his assigned spot. The Japanese received no honors; they looked like relatives gathering for a funeral, only this was much worse for them.

One of the Japanese officials, Toshikazu Kase, an Amherst-Harvard graduate and secretary to the foreign minister, was in a business suit. He spoke good English and later told reporters that the delegation was "subjected to the torture of the pillory. A million eyes seemed to beat on us with a million shafts of a rattling storm of arrows barbed with fire."

There was little question they were under close scrutiny.

The sun quickly replaced the clouds and the ceremony began at 9:02 a.m. with 50 official representatives from 10 nations: U.S., China, England, Russia, Australia, Canada, France, New Zealand, Holland and, of course, Japan. It had been 1,365 days and nearly a million casualties since Pearl Harbor. It was six years to the day Hitler began the war by marching into Poland, and 98 days since Germany had capitulated.

Just prior to the start of the ceremony, I discovered three places reserved for two reporters and myself had been taken by three Russian reporters who had never been on anybody's list. How they got aboard we'll never know. They were boisterous undisciplined men, running around sticking their cameras in people's faces, flashing photo bulbs, yelling and gesturing like wild men. Their boorish behavior was inexcusable.

I was instructed by Col. Powell to "put them somewhere," which was not one of the memorable commands given during the Pacific war, nor was it applicable, because there was no place for them except in my spot, and two spaces reserved for designated reporters.

It was obvious Powell had no idea where they could be placed. I told them "where to go" but they didn't understand my English. They just grinned and took over our assigned spots, yelling "USA, USA ... good!"

I do not recall the second reporter, but the first was Boyd Stutler, a correspondent for *The American Legion Magazine*. It was his suggestion we go up a deck and try to find a place to stand. We went up one deck and it was jam-packed. We took another ladder and found ourselves in a crowded gun turret. It was from this point we watched the proceedings.

I was able to get some good pictures by aiming my camera over MacArthur's left shoulder. Our original reserved spaces would have been much better but, what the heck, we were lucky to be anywhere on the ship — and we were in easy earshot of all that was said. In retrospect I now wish I had put one of them in Col. Powell's spot.

I should tell you the Navy had held a rehearsal of the ceremony the day before, utilizing 300 of the ship's personnel. Nobody wanted to play the part of the Japanese. Several men would be selected only to disappear. Finally a Marine guard was brought up to keep the "actors" in place.

To play the part of Admiral Nimitz the Navy selected a burly bosun's mate, a veteran of many years at sea and in the bars. He had to ascend the gangway, then come aboard like a swaggering admiral. When he reached his proper place he faced a large assembly of men at attention, the ship's band, and a full Marine guard of 90 men.

Suddenly the band broke into the "Admiral's March," preceded by traditional ruffles and flourishes. It proved too much for the bosun's mate. The grizzled vet stood stockstill, pushed his cap back on his head, and exclaimed: "Well, I'll be God-damned," and turned and ran away.

The surrender ceremony was something to see. There was a cluster of microphones at a long table, covered with a green cloth. On top of the table were the large ledger-size documents of surrender bound in brown covers, two copies for us in English, and one copy for them in Japanese.

Aside from the table and two chairs, there was a case containing the American flag raised over Japanese soil by Admiral Perry. The USS Missouri was anchored over the same spot as was Perry's USS Mississippi in 1853.

The assembly of "brass and braid" was spectacular — a mass of gold and silver sparkling with rainbows of decorations and ribbons. British and Australian Army officers had scarlet stripes on their caps and on their collars. The French were more conservative except for the acres of vivid decorations and ribbons on their chests. The Russian officers wore gold shoulder boards and red-striped trousers.

The British wore snow-white uniforms with shorts and knee-length socks. The olive drab of the Chinese was rather plain except for their ribbons. The most modestly dressed officers there were the Americans. The army was in traditional khaki with few adornments, but gold-braided caps. Navy personnel were in their plain suntan uniforms, with no medals or ribbons, since Navy regulations prohibit decorations or medals on shirts.

Admiral Nimitz, one of the outstanding military figures of my generation, stood out a bit because of his go-to-hell cap which reflected

General MacArthur (behind microphone) looks on as a member of the Japanese delegation signs the official surrender documents. An aide stands by to be sure the Japanese sign on the proper line.

his aggressive, determined personality.

As soon as the Japanese were comfortably seated, at 9:05 a.m., MacArthur, Nimitz and Admiral William F. Halsey emerged from the latter's cabin and walked to their positions across the table from the Japanese. MacArthur took his place at the microphone, presenting a commanding appearance.

There was a deafening silence, with only the shriek of a few sea gulls and the lapping of waves against the ship to be heard. As MacArthur reached the table the sun broke through the clouds and in the distance one could see the snow-capped peak of Mount Fujiyama. I thought the general spoke quite forcibly, but his emphasis could hardly be classed as vindictive. His hands trembled slightly:

"We are gathered here, representatives of the major warring powers, to conclude a solemn agreement whereby peace may be restored."

His words came sonorously as he emphasized the necessity that both victors and vanquished rise to a greater dignity in order that the world might emerge forever from blood and carnage. He declared his firm intention as Supreme Commander to "discharge my responsibility with justice and tolerance while taking all the necessary dispositions to insure that the terms of surrender are fully, promptly and faithfully complied with."

The Japanese stood at attenion as the general spoke, their faces grave but otherwise showing little emotion. When the representatives of the Emperor were invited to sign, Shigemitsu hobbled forward, laid aside his hat and cane, and lowered himself slowly into a chair. He had worked hard as he dared to opt for peace and been chosen by Emperor Hirohito as foreign minister of a hastily organized peace government, even as he eyed Russia with open hostility.

He was followed by General Yoshijiro Umesu, chief of general staff, whom the Allies determined should sign because the die-hards he commanded had tried to prevent the broadcast of the surrender to the Japanese homeland. It was the army that had masterminded the Pacific war, and Umesu had opposed surrender and threatened suicide until the emperor personally ordered him to cooperate by remaining alive to face the music.

Umesu wore an olive-green uniform, knee-high boots and appeared insolent and even angry. His unforgiving expression was definitely not one of defeat and acceptance. He was there only because his emperor had ordered it. He let everyone know it.

You cannot imagine with what agony these men affixed their names to the capitulation papers. It was a deserved, but most humiliating moment, for them and Japan. A Japanese reporter said the experience was "pure torture," but that MacArthur's speech about "the emergence of a better world" helped transform the deck "into an altar of peace."

As the Japanese signed the document, the two Chinese delegates took out their handkerchiefs and began to spit in them with considerable sound effects. I later learned this was a sign of disrespect to the Japanese because of Japan's military excursions into their country.

MacArthur used six pens in signing the documents. One was given to General Wainwright and one to General Percival. For three years these officers had drank the bitter brew of defeat and suffered countless indignities while prisoners of the enemy. MacArthur saved one pen for West Point, one for the War College, and one for the MacArthurs. The sixth pen was not assigned as far as I know.

The general left two on the table and they were slyly picked up by British Admiral Bruce Frazier. Gen. C. A. Willoughby, a member of the GHQ staff, quickly got them back. When Frazier took the pens somebody in the gathering exclaimed:

"Well, I see the British are still lend-leasing our equipment."

The only hitch in the ceremony came near the end when Colonel L. Moore Cosgrove of Canada signed on the wrong line. General Richard K. Sutherland, MacArthur's Chief of Staff, quickly straightened it out. He simply initialed the signature in the traditional rule of Army paper work.

After everyone had placed their signatures on the documents, MacArthur said slowly:

"Let us pray that peace be now restored in the world and that God will preserve it always. These proceedings are now closed."

As the document covers were closed, a sailor close by added a postscript that must have been inspired by the ghost of Ernie Pyle. He was heard to exclaim: "Brother, I hope my discharge papers are in there."

At that moment World War II ended, just off the coast of the nation that began it December 7, 1941. Germany had declared war on us three days later and World War II had gone into high gear. Millions of lives had been affected.

The ceremony over, the skies over Tokyo Bay were filled with formations of B-29 bombers, carrier and fighter planes, flashing over the Missouri and the Naval armada in one final, powerful, roar of engines in an impressive salute. A salute to victory! The reality of the war finally coming to an end hit me all at once.

The killing would stop! The stream of body bags would now cease. I thought of all those fine young men who had not made it this far. I found it hard to keep the tears back; there was a big lump in my throat. Stutler began wiping his eyes. We weren't the only ones. I could visualize my mom and dad in Kansas City heaving a big sigh of relief. Their son was coming home! Now Kathy and I could start our family.

Within two hours the battleship was devoid of visitors. In the interval MacArthur had made a radio address to the American people, saying:

"Today the guns are silent. A great tragedy has ended. A great victory has been won."

He concluded: "And so my fellow countrymen, today I report to you that your sons and daughters have served you well and faithfully."

Later that day, all GHQ staff members aboard were given a card signifying their presence at the surrender ceremony. It was signed by MacArthur and Nimitz.

Nagasaki Inferno

Chapter 16

"You think of the lives which would have been lost in an invasion of Japan's home islands — a staggering number of Americans but millions more of Japanese — and you thank God for the atomic bomb.

— Author William Manchester

WITH THE OFFICIAL SURRENDER of Imperial Japan now concluded, those of us who had been drafted or volunteered for service in the war began to think about going home. I was hoping my orders for release would come fairly soon but, realistically, the GHQ press section still had a host of correspondents to deal with. I had a feeling I would not be going home next week or next month.

Reporters were pressing us for permission to visit the atomic-bombed cities of Hiroshima and Nagasaki. This was understandable and some of us wanted to view the destruction as well, but General MacArthur had forbidden any reporter under his jurisdiction to enter either city until he gave the word.

I considered this rather restrictive, not that my opinion mattered, but I didn't understand why such a decision had been made unless the general was concerned about the radiation factor and the health of the reporters. If that was the reason, why not let us inform them? As a result, I and other press officers took a lot of gaff from correspondents who could not reach the general to complain.

As I expected, the general's order was soon violated. Wilfred Burchett of the *London Daily Express* left our press headquarters, now located in the Radio Tokyo building, and simply boarded a train bound for Hiroshima and got off when it reached that city. It was that simple.

His graphic report from Hiroshima was widely distributed a month following the bombing and his account was the first to describe radiation sickness. The GHQ press section "bosses" foolishly refuted his story, which was not only petty but very quickly disproved by scien-

This was once the City of Nagasaki. A single bomb erased most of it from the earth. The devastation was unbelievable.

tists who were already there sifting through the radiation-scarred city and examining the dead and surviving victims.

Burchett's ingenuity thus broke the "blockade" on news from the two ravaged cities, and all of a sudden I found myself boarding a transport plane packed with reporters headed for Nagasaki. Other officers and correspondents headed for Hiroshima about the same time, so the world would soon know more than it was prepared to digest about the horrors of the atomic bomb.

Flying time to Nagasaki was relatively short, but was made even shorter by the anticipation reflected in the comments of correspondents who had been chomping at the bit to get there. In about an hour we were over the city. Looking down on the red-tinged brown, scarred landscape, it was difficult to imagine that the area we were looking at was once the smoky and busy industrial section of this once great steel-producing city.

It wasn't hard to imagine why Japan's emperor and loon militant military leaders decided, a few hours after the second atomic bomb was dropped, they must end the war. Even for a nation that considered suicide as an honorable transport route to eternity, its leaders realized the futility of continuing the war.

From the air, it was easy to visualize why parts of this city were spared complete destruction. It was because Nagasaki is divided in half by a bay and a river and much of the city lies in a valley between two hills. While the fiery blast completely erased the heart of Nagasaki, the searing, blast effect was somewhat diminished where the sides of the valley offered limited protection.

Unlike Nagasaki, Hiroshima was located on a flat plain and the devastation extended over a much wider area. It is also understandable Hiroshima is remembered by more people than Nagasaki simply because the first bomb was dropped there. Nagasaki has become more or less the "forgotten" Ground Zero, but there was actually more destruction there than in Hiroshima.

Like Hiroshima, Nagasaki had a high percentage of wooden buildings, few of which exceeded two stories. Residential streets twisted and turned up into the terraced hills, so steep in places that steps had been cut into them. Nagasaki escaped the hideous "firestorm" that hit Hiroshima. The damage here was mostly from the blast itself, although the blast did start many large fires.

Being a fan of the composer, Puccini, and his wistful *Madame Butterfly*, it came to me there that this once lovely city was the setting for that superb opera.

As our plane flew over the city, skimming over this man-made wasteland, sometimes barely 75 feet above the ground, one got the impression the hearts of the residents of the city had been burned out as well. As we throttled back, few of the people on the streets even bothered to look up.

They kept walking, seemingly paying no attention. Perhaps they were to the point that even if 5,000 planes had flown over in formation, they were past really caring. What further punishment could be inflicted upon these despairing people?

They must have been filled with a bitter longing for revenge. As we completed our circling of the city, we wondered what the limits of their tolerance and patience would be when we began to walk around their city. Ours was one of the first unarmed planes to fly over this area of Japan, and we had been flying low enough that even small arms fire could reach us. Still we saw little but indifference, silent, subtle hostility.

A few miles down the bay from Nagasaki was a Prisoner of War camp on a small island called Koyagi Shima. As we flew over, we could see some American, British, Chinese and Dutch flags the POWs had somehow constructed. It appeared the prisoners were unguarded. If the people of Nagasaki had wanted to exercise their hatred of America over the bomb, they surely could have stormed the camp and killed its occupants. Ah, those imperturbable Orientals.

After a final swoop over the city, to pacify the photo guys who never seem to run out of film and who always have to take "just one more," we sought out our airfield which was just a few miles outside the city. From ground level we obtained a far different view of the destruction — and we were able to actually view people who had been injured and who were suffering from the effects of the bombing.

The destruction here was nothing like what we had witnessed in Manila. There was very little rubble to be seen. All you could see was a two or three mile square area of a once busy city that had been reduced to mere outlines of homes and buildings. I toured the city with the AP's Jim Hutcheson, among others. He and I had become good friends since our narrow escape on Corregidor.

It was strange to see most of the streets completely clean, knowing it was far too soon after the blast for the people there to have cleaned them so well. You could not see a single brick, or pile of lumber, or plaster anywhere in the stricken areas. It was just like the scientists had told us to expect. In most areas of the city the bomb blast had not only demolished the buildings, but swept up the wreckage as well.

Out of the corner of my eye, I saw a young woman with a child at her side. She had on a loose-fitting blouse and I could see she bore ugly burns on her arms. I walked over to her and smiled to indicate she was in no danger. I then held up my camera as a signal I wanted to take a picture of her and her baby.

She did not quite understand. I only intended to show the burns on her arms, but she quickly shed her blouse which was all she had on above the waist. It was then I saw the extent of her burns, which covered most of her body. I could not prevent myself from an exclamation of anguish and sorrow.

She began to sob, and the baby grasped her mother by the leg and became excited and began to cry loudly. I patted the innocent little fellow on his head and quickly bowed from the waist like Orientals do. I'll have to admit I walked away rather ashamedly as Hutch wrote down some notes.

We passed a streetcar still sitting on the rails, but everything had been burned away except its steel skeleton. I noticed most of the bridges across the river were still standing. The huge network of tracks in the rail yards were still in place, but little left on the tracks but skeletal steel framework here and there. The city appeared as if a giant broom had swept nearly everything away under a rug of nothingness. I had seen bombed cities before, but I couldn't believe that a single bomb could cause so much destruction. Everything was scorched, blackened or charred. The fiery core of the bomb, that consumed birds in flight, had turned the city into a killing blast furnace.

One must remember, however, that Nagasaki was selected, actually a second choice for the bomb that day, because of its many war plants. Kokura was the intended target but clouds obscured the city and its huge army arsenal, so the flight was diverted to Nagasaki.

Jim Hutchison, AP correspondent, is shown on a street in Nagasaki. He and I were close friends, perhaps because of our experience on the dock at Corregidor. He was an excellent reporter and risked his own life to "get the story."

We walked farther into the valley, approaching what had once been the Mitsubishi Steel and Arms factory. Its production at the time was making torpedoes. It was nothing now but a tangle of steel girders, some of them melted by the intense heat. I looked over to the left, up the side of the hill, where the city's hospital stood. One could clearly visualize the dimensions of the bomb's incinerating blast.

You could follow its path of ferocious destruction from the valley floor, up the side of the hill, where it had neatly removed one corner of the hospital as if a giant Samurai warrior had sliced it off with his sword. The rest of the hospital was a blackened ruin.

In outlying sections of the city there was the distinct smell of the dead. The Japanese were still cremating bodies in piles at intersections. In the center of the city, where the bomb detonated 1,600 feet above street level, there was not sufficient debris to hide a corpse.

We then saw several men carrying bundles of straw. Jim wanted to talk to some of them, so I began looking for the Japanese naval officer who had been assigned to us at the airport as an interpreter. He was with another group of reporters not far away, but I was able to obtain his services for our group for awhile and this enabled Hutcheson and others to obtain some firsthand information.

We learned the men hadn't been in the city when the bomb actually exploded. It was hard to find anyone who was. I assumed all the people who had experienced the blast were either dead or in a hospital, or like the woman with her child wandering in the street. The fact there were no healthy survivors to be found proved this was by far one of the two most devastating man-made disasters in history.

We were in luck, however. Our interpreter took us to an abandoned structure some distance from the ground zero area where we were introduced to Shinji Owada, a man with a bandaged arm and head. He had held a minor government position and had come from another city to his home about an hour before the blast.

Owada said he did not remember seeing or hearing anything out of the ordinary until he witnessed a "flash of light" which quickly turned into a bright orange color, a massive fireball. Millions of degrees at its core, it roared in boiling waves down into the city, finally sucking the life from Nagasaki, turning it into a pillar of dust and debris that the bomber crew said reached 80,000 feet into the sky.

Owada was knocked to the ground by a wave of heat and concussion. He said his house shook and began to fall down, some of the debris falling on him. He said that was how he got the cut on his head. Owada said his wife and son, who were inside the house, emerged from the wreckage virtually unscathed, although his wife was momentarily stunned and felt like she was "in an oven, roasting."

"Our house did not catch fire immediately," he said, "but I saw huge balls of orange smoke coming toward us from across the city. I knew something terrible had happened, so I took my family to the home of a relative about two miles away, battling hysterical citizens who were milling around in shock with many horribly burned and threshing around on the ground."

He said he saw many people running toward the river with their arms and legs in charred shreds of flesh, hanging from the bones.

He said he tried to return to his office but it wasn't there any more; the entire building was missing.

"Besides," he added, "the heat was so unbearable, and the view so violent and depressing, I quickly left so I wouldn't have to see the wreckage and the bodies lying in the streets. I knew it was a terrible thing, there was such suffering."

He said the city burned for two days. Relief work was impossible because all the fire stations had been destroyed, along with the hospital. It was quite a few hours before the government began moving food and medical supplies into the area. Later, he said, trains began arriving with supplies and rescue workers:

"But they were too late for most of my friends," he said, but quickly added: "I have aged and I am wiser now. I do not hate Americans. I only hate war."

One of the correspondents asked him how many bombs he thought were dropped on Nagasaki. He said his family first thought that it was hundreds of planes dropping thousands of bombs. He said at first he could not believe such damage could be inflicted with just one plane and one bomb.

Owada said one thing that surprised him, and others he had talked with, was that he heard no noise before and after the blast. Owada and some others we talked with said they were deaf for a week following the bombing, but at the time they heard no sounds.

This was not true away from the city. Japanese who lived 10 miles from the impact zone said they heard a terrible, ear-splitting roar. One said it was like a tornado or a "great wind," and the trees bent to the ground from the force.

There were thousands of stories in Nagasaki and our group saw many pitiful sights of people with radiation burns who, in dreadful agony, were slowly dying. The first thing Japanese doctors asked was if American doctors had a cure for the bomb's effect on the human body.

At that time they were having little success treating the ill, whose white corpuscles had been drained from their bloodstream. Those affected reacted like those exposed to powerful X-ray treatments. They developed a temperature, their hair began falling out and they vomited blood.

At that time, doctors were trying to restore white corpuscles with transfusions, but nothing seemed to prevent repeated loss of white corpuscles. We received a report from GHQ that American doctors were coming to Nagasaki soon to study the radioactive effect on humans. It is obvious, however, in view of the modern-era Chernobyl nuclear

This is a display casing of the "Fat Boy" bomb that was dropped on Nagasaki. The case was somewhat larger than the one that wiped out Hiroshima, and is on display at the Admiral Nimitz museum in Fredericksburg, Texas.

power plant accident in Russia, no satisfactory treatment has thus far emerged.

Japanese doctors, who were manning a temporary treatment center at the outskirts of the city, told us that clothing did offer some protection from radiation. Those wearing heavier clothing were not as badly burned as those wearing, say, just a kimono or a T-shirt. They said two men were playing catch in a park when the explosion came. The man facing the bomb died quickly but the other, burned only on the back of his neck, lived about a week.

Many rumors were circulating at the time we entered the city. Some believed those entering the city within two weeks of the blast would become sterile and lose their hair. Some doctors suggested the residue of radiation in the soil might prevent people from having children. They were not sure how safe the city was, or how long it would take to become livable. This was a worry for a time.

One doctor said he had already tested the soil and found no radiation. As it turned out, seasonal rainfall and strong tides cleansed the land and harbor far more quickly than anyone expected. Within two months after the bomb fell, seedlings began to push up through the barren soil.

Those in our press group had been warned of possible dangers, but apparently none of us suffered ill effect. As for me, I have lost much of my hair and I haven't had any children for nearly 50 years. I suspect that wasn't caused by the bomb, but Mother Nature penalizing me for 79 years of wear and tear.

Today, near the center of Nagasaki is a small plot of open space called Hypocenter Park, located beside one of the main thoroughfares of the city. Lovely shade trees form a green cathedral above neatly-trimmed hedges, providing a hospitable haven for rest, prayer and meditation. At the north edge of this memorial park is a boulder of stark black stone, commemorating a momentous event of terrible significance, not only for Japan but for the world.

The people of Nagasaki paid a high price for this park. In a blink of an eye, two-thirds of the 245,000 residents within the city were killed outright or hideously injured; three square miles of their city were virtually wiped off the map. There is a famous church bell, salvaged from the ruins, that is rung twice each day as a reminder of this city's "holocaust."

Before leaving Nagasaki, with memories I will never forget, we walked around what had been residential areas. We saw people looking for missing relatives or visiting shrines to offer prayers, and police trying to restore order out of chaos. Some people were just sitting, dazed, looking silently at what had once been their home and their city.

I heard that a report from the Japanese Prefecture read: "Our city is like a graveyard without a tombstone standing."

If there was any resentment in the hearts or minds of the people, we did not see it or sense it. Our interpreter, however, said many Japanese people considered use of the atomic bomb as something 'way beyond the normal contingencies of war. He stared at us through his horn-rimmed glasses and said: "There is surely some hate here. How would you like to have such a horror dropped on your city?"

No one managed a reply. What could we say?

As if a visit to an atomic-bombed city wasn't enough excitement for one trip out of Tokyo, we boarded our plane for the trip home and had flown for what seemed a short distance, when we flew into the gales of a developing typhoon. Pretty soon our C-46 transport was bouncing around in an alarming manner, sufficiently rough to disturb not only me, but a number of reporters as well.

At one point I heard some strange popping sounds and made my

An unexpected storm enroute to Tokyo from Nagasaki created this wreckage. Our transport plane was twisted in two, and the Japanese truck we had used for an anchor was thrown atop the pile.

way to the front of the plane where I asked the pilot to identify the noises I had been hearing.

"It's nothing really, Cap'n," he yelled back as he battled the controls, "it's just some rivets popping out."

I didn't know whether he was joking or not, but that was the last thing I wanted to hear. I soon realized, however, that we were indeed in trouble when I heard the pilot radio for help in locating an airstrip we could land on. Back came a voice over the crackling radio which advised him to put down on a nearby abandoned Japanese airfield, which we did.

By this time the winds had really picked up. We evacuated the aircraft, but before taking shelter in a nearby bomb shelter some of us assisted the pilot and co-pilot in anchoring the plane to the ground. There was a Japanese truck parked nearby so we used some cable and rope to tie the plane's wings to the truck, making sure we headed it into the wind which by now was making it difficult to even stand upright without holding on to something.

None of us at the time were aware, or else too worried to think clearly, that a typhoon blows from all points of the compass during its cycle of destruction. Our sturdy old plane withstood the high wind as long as it was headed directly into it, but once the wind direction changed, and began blowing from the side and back of the plane, the aircraft began jumping up and down on its landing gear, which finally collapsed.

I cannot describe how heavy the rain squalls were. It was awesome.

The wind eventually became so fierce that the truck was violently jerked up on top of the fuselage which by this time had been twisted nearly in half. The horrific wind began peeling large sections of corrugated metal from the sides and roofs of hangars and buildings, which were flying through the air like jack-straws.

During the storm I peeked through an opening in the shelter and saw a Japanese man riding a bicycle down a sloping street with his back to the wind. I'll bet the rider was going at least 90 miles an hour, and I presume he didn't stop until he reached the sea in one big heap.

We spent the rest of the day and all night in the shelter but as the wind began to subside, and being anxious to get help and get back to Tokyo, we returned to the plane where the crew was able to get a radio working and signal our predicament. The pilot informed us his superiors had been worried about us, but I was never given a logical explanation on why we were permitted to leave Nagasaki and fly into such a terrible storm.

It could have been a public relations disaster with so many war correspondents on board. As the old saying goes, "All's well that ends well," I was happy to be back in Tokyo, hopefully with all my valuable body parts atomically unaltered.

Despite the storm, I was thrilled to have had such a memorable experience. It remains vivid in my memory even today.

Tokyo Duty, Then Home

Chapter 17

"Once war is forced upon us, there is no alternative than to apply every available means to bring it to a swift end. War's very object is victory, not prolonged indecision. In war there is no substitute for victory."

— **General Douglas MacArthur**

UPON MY RETURN from Nagasaki, I resumed my normal duties, and was housed in the Dai Itchi Hotel near the center of downtown Tokyo. It was not far from Emperor Hirohito's moated and beautifully landscaped palace and grounds.

At last I had an opportunity, during my spare time, to visit areas of the city including the suburbs. Before Air Force General Curtis LeMay and his airmen began their devastating series of low-level incendiary bombing raids in March, these areas were heavily saturated not only with large factories but hundreds of thousands of homes. What was left to visit wasn't pretty.

It didn't take long to see the extent of devastation in Tokyo. Some of the streets appeared not to have been repaired, even on a temporary basis since the bombing raids began. In the interval between the end of the war and the arrival of Allied forces in the city, thousands of Japanese families had returned to the ruins of their neighborhoods and their homes.

Once there, they began scavenging materials to rebuild: pieces of lumber, sections of corrugated metal, a few blackened stones — anything they could scrounge to provide a bit of shelter. The area reminded me of the poor Mexican villages on the U.S. border.

Here and there, a family would wave. One little boy I saw saluted and gave me a big grin. Most were just too busy to pay any attention to visitors.

People who had visited Japan before the war would barely recognize Tokyo's Fifth Avenue — the Ginza. Sixty percent of the buildings

Everywhere we went in the Pacific we met the innocent victims of the war — the children. I can tell you without hesitation that children of all nations are sweet, loving and deserving of our assistance. This little guy got a candy bar for letting me take his picture, and I got a hug in return.

were either burned down or wrecked inside. Many of the famous department stores had English and French signs over their doors. Of the few large retailers relatively undamaged, mainly those serving upper-income families, several boasted indirect lighting and arty color schemes. Most of the display windows were covered with corrugated metal for protection against bombs and, possibly, looting.

A few movie theaters were still running on indeterminate schedules. A former drug store was a mess and a pipe still dribbled water over what was once a tile floor. I was pleased to note that the longest lines downtown were at a newspaper office, waiting for the latest editions. The press runs were small because of a shortage of paper and getting a copy was on a first-come, first-served basis.

The area of the city I thought the most heavily damaged from the B-29 raids was the suburb of Asakusa Ku, a residential area with a population of about 150,000 people per square mile. There was hardly anything left of this particular neighborhood. Most of the wooden structures were burned to the ground.

It was graphic proof of the success of this new strategy of mass fire bombing, conceived in Europe. The idea was to destroy whole areas of cities, rather than major individual targets. This was particularly effective in Japan because most of their production came, not from giant factories, but small installations and dwellings which were actually well-organized, unified satellite factories.

One could see evidence of the people's fear of the Superforts everywhere. There were many bomb shelters, some streets were lined with them. The shelters were not very deep, boasting cement walls and entrances at each end. One can only imagine what it was like to experience such horrible incendiary firestorms, huddled in darkness, not knowing if your home would be destroyed or so badly damaged you could not live in it or, for that matter, if you would survive the firestorms.

When we first arrived in Tokyo from Yokohama, even before going to Nagasaki, there wasn't much traffic on the streets except U.S. army trucks, some buses and overloaded streetcars and, of course, streams of bicycles. The people I saw then appeared truly downcast, crushed, despondent and shabbily dressed. Their clothing was not clean and their shoes, mostly sandals, were well worn. The wooden sandals made quite a clatter on the pavement.

No one, however, appeared malnourished. I guessed the food supply had been maintained, since the Japanese might well be the world's most successful gardeners. I did not see one obese person on the streets. Most of the women appeared shapeless, but that was because of the baggy clothing they wore. Not very sexy but very practical!

As in Nagasaki, the people accepted us with impeccable Japanese calm. Seldom did anyone display any emotion. They went about their business just like ants in a mound when you kick it with your foot. Busy, busy, busy, but, just like ants, they knew what they had to do and where they were going. I had a feeling they hadn't lost their pride and still felt a bit superior. They might have lost the war, but they weren't about to go to their knees in front of us.

Their attitude was understandable as far as I was concerned. It was not in me to play the role of an invader because, once the fighting ceased and I came to Japan, I only felt sorrow and pain for the Japanese people. I greatly appreciated MacArthur's keen instincts and intellect in handling the surrender and the rebuilding of Japan through their emperor.

Had U.S. Forces attempted to imprison him, or impose any sort of sanction upon him or the royal family, Japan would have been in chaos from one end to the other, and American losses would have horrendous. As it was, the transition from an aggressor nation into a modern, democratic society, was accomplished flawlessly.

Even more surprising, Hirohito's new style of ruling permitted him to move among his people, much like European royalty once did. Newspapers pictured him kissing babies, appearing at flower shows, at the beach with his striped pants rolled up to permit his wading in the surf. Unless one is a student of Japanese history, one cannot appreciate what a shift in Japanese culture this represented. The people were surprised and pleased.

They had discovered their emperor was only a special man by tradition, his presence no longer blinded them. All of a sudden, he found himself more popular and revered than ever.

There were Japanese army personnel on the streets, complete with polished boots and Samurai swords. They would look at us without expression, but would usually cross the street to avoid meeting you face to face. I guess I couldn't blame them. Often I wished I could greet them with a "Howdy," but feared that the word to a Japanese might mean something I hadn't intended.

Almost every Japanese person carries an umbrella because it rains and drizzles a lot. The women would manage to maneuver their umbrellas so, when we passed on the street, we could not see their faces. The women always walked a few paces behind their men, but when directly confronted they would bow and step aside.

It was impossible to communicate with people on the street because I did not learn any Japanese phrases for awhile, and most Japanese knew no English. Nonetheless, I felt they wanted to be helpful. I never actually saw an unpleasant expression on anyone's face. I suppose they really didn't know what to expect of "the conquerors." Sometimes a smile and a pleasant facial expression is a form of communication.

I was able to talk with a Japanese reporter who had been given accreditation to our headquarters. He spoke English quite well and told me that most educated Japanese had known for a year that Japan was going to lose the war. He said, however, the abruptness with which it ended came as a complete surprise. When the news came he said people cried, were very agitated, but after a day or two they recovered their composure.

He seemed most anxious to remind me in a rather bragging tone: "Our submarines lobbed shells on the California coast early in the war, didn't they?"

The journalist asked me how much censorship we had in the United States during the war. I was ashamed to tell him of the weird decisions often made at GHQ, but I did let him know that anyone was free to criticize the government or the military without fear of retaliation. He was astounded but admitted he had heard that before. He said he hoped he would soon be given more freedom to write and speak out as he pleased.

A few days after arriving in Tokyo, we lost another war correspondent. Robert Bellaire, who wrote for *Collier's* magazine, suffered fatal injuries in a Jeep accident in downtown Tokyo. Bob was press bureau manager for United Press in Japan when war broke out. He was interned by the Japanese and tortured to obtain military information.

He was later repatriated, he just couldn't stay away from the action. Bob once told me that he just couldn't help admiring the Japanese people. Fate deals strange hands.

Transportation was a mess in Tokyo. The streetcar system was in disarray and most of the buses had been destroyed. The quality of the transportation still running was deplorable. There were some good American automobiles left, but they had been damaged by the use of inferior fuels and lack of proper maintenance. Many vehicles were running on charcoal burners.

Americans who had looked forward to having a good time were somewhat disappointed as far as wine, women and song were concerned. There was not much fraternization with women at first; most of the established night clubs and burlesque houses had either been burned down or flattened by explosive bombs. Japan has always been strong on sex shops, and a few of those had reopened and doubtless their business flourished once our soldiers discovered them.

Then, too, Tokyo citizens had been through quite an ordeal, their lives disrupted almost beyond description for months, and most just weren't in the mood to get on a stage and play happy or sexy.

This large and impressive building, located across the street from the imperial palace, was taken over by the occupation forces for GHQ offices. MacArthur's suite was on an upper floor.

There seemed to be plenty of beer. At our dining room in the Dai Itchi, we were served beer twice a day with meals, and the waiters would keep bringing it as long as you drank it. Saki, the famous rice wine, was rationed to Japanese citizens, but as occupation guests we could have all we could consume just by asking. I did not care for the flavor of saki too much but tried it several times.

I loved the hotel in which I was billeted because it had been designed and built to fit the average Japanese — which for my five-foot, seven-and-a- half-inch frame was just great. The doorways were undersized and the hallways narrow. The elevator in our hotel would only carry about six people at a time. It made a lot of noise and jumped unevenly when running, which caused you to think perhaps a Kamikaze pilot was in charge.

My room was quite small but adequate, and my bathtub was barely five feet long. Oh, what a luxury it was after months in the jungle. The supply of water was not dependable and, at best, little more than a trickle. I guess I was lucky, because some of our guys were quartered in a less expensive hotel where bathing was done in four stone tubs.

In that hotel, you first stepped into a tub with hot water where you lathered and washed off. Next, you stepped into a cold water tub and shivered. Then you dipped into the third tub, which contained warm water. You finished your bath in the fourth tub, which was ice cold, after which you vigorously rubbed your body with a towel to get your blood circulating again.

The Japanese often beat themselves with sticks following a cold bath to restore circulation. This was a custom few Americans adopted.

There was no toilet and seat to rest one's posterior on when nature called. There was a porcelain hole in the floor with sloped sides. It was a test of one's balance and stamina at times, but it sure beat the slit trenches and pee tubes we had in the islands. By the way, there were no window screens and Tokyo seemed to have more than their share of aggressive mosquitoes.

I never felt lost in my mini-bed, either, but the pillow was like resting your head on a cardboard box filled with rock salt. The linens on the bed were stiff like sailcloth and crackled when one moved around. But, hey, was I complaining? It was far superior to lying down in the boondocks with all those Kamikazi insects ready to attack you.

The food was unique, to say the least. The Japanese consume much of their diet from the sea, so we had lots of salmon, sardines, crab

A typical street scene in a section of Tokyo that escaped heavy damage. Life got back to normal much faster than expected.

meat, usually served with a cold potato salad of sorts, and the seasonings were not familiar to most of us at all. The meal usually began with a barley soup. Often we had boiled cabbage, powdered eggs, and bread that just didn't taste like the bread back home.

Your choice of drinks could include hot tea, which didn't taste like the tea I enjoyed at home or in Borneo. The dining room was rather drab and depressing, but the waiters in the officer's mess were attentive and polite. Our food was served on fancy china any American home would have been proud to display.

The waiters usually served us silently, and so meekly I felt they thought they were under guard. As time went on they loosened up a bit, and smiled at our attempts to be friendly. It was far better than the mess tents and the K and C-rations we lived on while in the field or combat.

I had plenty of time to explore the city, and one of my first stops was at the palace grounds. There was a moat and a high stone wall surrounding the grounds, and there was such abundant and lush greenery one could not see the palace itself, just some auxiliary buildings. I was told there was a second moat within the grounds that surrounded the palace itself.

Vehicles were not permitted anywhere close to the palace. Cars were parked some distance away and people gathered near an entrance, sometimes in family groups or just alone. They stood there looking intently at the direction of the emperor's quarters, and they would bow low in prayer. Then they would put on their hats and steal silently away.

One day I passed by and saw a Buddhist priest there, wearing yellow robes, standing near the moat, beating an ancient drum. I saw several Japanese officers there, too. After standing at rigid attention for a time, they bowed low from the waist, then saluted smartly before leaving. It is hard for Americans to realize the respect and reverence the Japanese people felt for their emperor. Nothing like it has ever existed in America, even for our most popular and beloved public figures.

One of the miracles of the war took place in Tokyo after the surrender. For a city left in charred shambles, it was amazing how quickly the city began its recovery. Hour by hour, and day by day, the businesses of Tokyo arose from the debris. More often than not, the resurrected store did not resemble the old one, but the storekeeper put to-

Several English-speaking Japanese prisoners of war read the news in the infamous Bilibed Prison.

The Radio Tokyo building was used as the GHQ Press center in Tokyo. My work area was on the second floor, and my desk just above the sign over the front entrance. The press center was quite close to the Dai Itchi building where the general's headquarters was located.

gether four walls and a roof and opened for business.

Likewise, the entertainment industry found a way to get movie houses going, along with other types of entertainment. One of the press section officers had reported a burlesque show in operation. I had never been to a burlesque show in my life but, what the heck, I might as well see all I could see because when I got home, I knew I would not be going to girlie shows.

It was quite an eye-opener, watching petite Japanese girls in beautiful kimonos take off their clothing layer by layer until they were, for all practical purposes, "scantily clad" and then some. The straight men, dressed in colorful robes, cavorted about the stage uttering the strangest and shrillest sounds I have ever heard come from the human throat. Hardly like a performance of Madam Butterfly.

There was some bodily contact and speaking on the stage, but I couldn't understand a word they said or sung. Even in Japan, however, body language is easy to interpret and I clearly understood what was taking place.

Since I had been celibate during my time overseas, that show did little to alleviate my longing for Kathy's bed. I knew it would not be long until I would be heading stateside with all the pleasures of marriage and home.

During my time in Tokyo, I was also given a pass to attend the opening session of the Japanese Diet, the governing body equivalent to our Congress. The building was quite impressive, set well back from the traffic, a huge wrought-iron gate controlling access to the well-manicured grounds and exotic plantings. The inside was very ornate and the furnishings made of matched delicately-grained woods, highly polished.

Despite the circumstances, it appeared the delegates had official matters well in hand and they conducted that session with dignity and calm, they were perhaps even a bit subdued. Yet there was no malice or disrespect shown the visitors, despite the pain that surely throbbed in the breasts of Japanese lawmakers and patriots.

I had a chance to visit the park where three of the Doolittle flyers were beheaded following the raid in April 1942. Many people are not aware that these crewmen were not shot down over Japan, but in China over territory controlled by Japan.

They were returned to Tokyo, led through the streets naked in chains, mocked and humiliated by the crowds, and eventually executed in public. These cruel acts greatly inflamed the American public against the Japanese.

I was also present for the arrest of "Tokyo Rose," the well-known propagandist for the Japanese whose specialty was trying to make American soldiers homesick. Her voice was aired all over the South Pacific during the war and she could be heard usually at night. She would say such things as:

"Well, GI, isn't it nice to hear a female voice? Wouldn't it be wonderful if you and your girlfriend could slip under the sheets right now?

"Oh, I know how lonely you are. Your sweetheart or wife is lonely, too. She may not wait for you to come home. She might this very minute be in the arms of another guy while you're stuck over here in a war, secretly arranged by your politicians and capitalists. Well, here's a goodnight kiss and try not to miss too much what you're not getting."

Well, that sounds pretty silly, I know, but for men fighting in the jungle and not knowing if or when they might get back home, hearing this night after night did affect the morale level of some individuals. The only surprise for me was that Tokyo Rose was much older and less attractive than she sounded on the airwaves.

One day as I was walking along one of the streets, I passed a rebuilt store front window which displayed what I would call antiques. I was examining some of the items through the glass when a man strolled out, bowed, and said to me in rather clumsy English: "How you are, friend? I am happily seeing you."

We conversed as best we could and I could see he was trying his best to be friendly and courteous. He finally let me know that a typewriter he had salvaged from his store needed repair. The part he needed was the cord that caused the carriage to return. You must remember that in 1945 we used typewriters; personal computers hadn't been invented.

It just so happened I was able to help him. We had a typewriter repair crew attached to our unit. I assured him I could get it fixed, and within three days, I was able to take it back to him. His smile was as broad as any I'd ever seen since the surrender, and he bowed and bowed in thanks, saying "I am great thankful for you."

He went to a table and presented me with what I learned later was an Emperor Meiji shrine. It was in a black oval case, about six inches high, with two folding hinged doors on the front. Inside was a small wood-carved statue of the emperor, complete with ceremonial spear. The interior of the shrine was gilded a gold color.

This type of shrine was used during travel. If it was not convenient to go to a temple, the traveler could set the shrine on a table or dresser, open the doors, and say their daily prayers before it.

I protested he did not owe me anything; that my gesture was one of friendship. He insisted I take the little shrine and so I did. It has some value today and remains one of my meaningful souvenirs of the war.

It was surprising how rapidly downtown Tokyo recovered. It was not long until signs of rebuilding were everywhere, trains were running, and there were street vendors on every corner, obviously aware of their new market, the American soldier. Tokyo streets began filling up with cars and trucks, and the sidewalks became congested.

I did some shopping before I came home. I purchased some traditional Japanese prints on rice paper, several embroidered pictures, a couple of small ivory carvings, silver salt and pepper shakers shaped like Mt. Fuji, a toothpick holder made from bamboo, and some tiny colored birds carved from whalebone, souvenirs for those back home.

At the time I had no idea I would be back in Tokyo five years later, to find the city westernized. The women were no longer walking behind the men, and while I saw traditional Japanese dress, the younger generation had taken to more westernized garments.

Meanwhile, General MacArthur and his staff were nicely settled in the former Dai Itchi insurance company building, across from the palace grounds. I can't explain it, but it was truly remarkable how quickly the Japanese people came to respect and revere the general. MacArthur, without a doubt, was the most popular man in Japan.

Every morning and evening, huge crowds would gather to see him enter and leave the building. At first there was polite applause, but as time went on, this turned to loud clapping and cheering. His dramatic style, his insistence on loyalty and demands for complete obedience, his jaunty cap and corncob pipe, somehow held great appeal for the Japanese psyche.

As his limousine passed along the streets of Tokyo, traffic would come to a halt. People on the streets would bow in respect as his car with the five-star flag passed by. It has been a long time since even a president of the U.S. received this kind of respect and admiration.

Those who never liked MacArthur can perhaps fault his possible negligence following the bombing of Pearl Harbor, when the Japanese found our air force sitting like ducks on runways at Clark Field. If they are fair, however, they will recognize his skill in conducting the war in the Southwest Pacific, and especially his genius in introducing democracy to Japan.

The key to this was his diplomatic coup in retaining the emperor as the spiritual leader of the nation. Who else could have transformed Hirohito from a virtual "God" to a government figurehead without creating years of revolt, disruption and insurgency? The general greatly admired the emperor's ancient image and took great pains to preserve the people's love and esteem for him.

Think about MacArthur's first moves. He ordered free elections for the first time in Japan's history. Next he abolished centuries of tradition and instituted women's rights. He quickly gave Japanese farmers 90 percent of the land, which was a key move in preventing the spread of communism there.

He also ordered major reforms in Japan's medical system which, some experts claimed, actually saved about two million lives, that total far greater than all the lives lost during the war.

MacArthur provided Japanese citizens with hope and inspired leadership during a critical period in their history, and precisely at the right time, mired as they were in despair and confusion. To the average Japanese citizen, everything they had come to believe about themselves was crumbling, their power and discipline had evaporated, and they appeared to be drifting in aimless chaos amid great suffering.

The general must have seemed to them a "White Knight," who with determination and justice would create a new order and give purpose to their lives. His dramatic bearing, his thundering, flowery oratory, apparently had a strong emotional appeal to the Japanese. He may have appeared omnipotent to some, but he imposed freedom and democracy there with diplomatic and authoritarian skills that amazed the world.

When MacArthur was removed from his post during the Korean War, thousands of people wept openly on the streets of Tokyo. This was not a ceremonial display of grief, but a sign of genuine respect, adoration and sorrow. There is little question he was one of the most memorable figures of the post-war world.

As one writer once put it, "One might imagine him saying, during a rare quiet evening with his shirt open at the collar and his Missouri corncob pipe lit: '`How am I doing, Dad?'" The question would be posed to his late father, General Arthur MacArthur, who also left his mark in the annals of history, both in the Philippines and the U.S. Army.

Just prior to leaving Japan for home, I stumbled across a most unique story, the details given me by a Navy officer. I met him in the officers' lounge in GHQ headquarters; he had been attached to the Office of Strategic Services for the last year of the war.

I knew the army utilized "war dogs" on the battlefield; that pigeons had been used to carry messages, and that the navy once considered using pigeons as a key in the guidance system in the pioneering phase of its missile program. However, I was shocked to learn the OSS had mobilized foxes as part of the invasion plan for Japan.

The story of "Operation Foxes" was one of the best-kept secrets of the war. It concerned 30 of the strangest fighting units ever conceived in the art of warfare.

When V-J Day finally came, these veterans of the plains and forests were being groomed to spearhead the invasion forces. It was fortunate the Japanese surrendered, because Operation Foxes was designed to scare the living daylights out of them.

The prestigious OSS deserves credit for the scheme, but career Army and Navy officers involved in it remain embarrassed when admitting to its existence. The cloak and dagger agency, however, maintains the war might have been shortened by months if they could have gotten their foxes to the beaches.

Actually, it was some researchers, professor types, who conceived the idea. Psychological warfare experts were seeking a way to create panic among the Japanese people ahead of the landing of Allied forces. So they called upon some anthropologists for advice and assistance.

OSS officers were told that the most widely accepted and terrifying superstition in Japan had to do with fox spirits. For a Japanese to see a fox in daylight wasn't all that bad — comparable to a black cat crossing one's path in America — but to see a fox spirit at night, glowing with luminous light, was a sure sign of pending calamity.

Still worse, to see one running around on its hind legs, glowing like a Christmas tree, signaled an early and permanent disaster of major proportions. The professors' claims were borne out by fact. Millions of Japanese share this superstition, and some claim to have seen a "night-blooming fox" just prior to the devastating earthquake of 1923.

The concept intrigued the OSS. They arranged to have 30 foxes taken prisoner and immediately transported to the Central Park Zoo in New York City. Chemists then went to work on a radium paint similar to that once used on clock dials. The chemists were not told how the paint would be used, only that it must cling to hair and remain durable for several weeks.

The initial tests were pleasing enough. The paint glowed as promised, all too briefly though, but long enough to scare the Holy Ned out of the poor foxes. After all, they hadn't seen a luminous fox before, either. The trouble was the foxes had inherent standards of cleanliness, and they promptly licked off the glow. So the chemists went back to work to develop a lick-proof paint.

The problem was soon solved. By this time the OSS had contacted taxidermists who were busily stuffing the front halves of other foxes to strap on the backs of the 30 original foxes. The idea was to create an image of foxes running about on their hind legs. The agency had already tried to teach the foxes to run on their hind legs to no avail.

Classified reports confirmed it was quite a sight! OSS officers could barely stand to enter their own offices after dark with all those luminous, glowing foxes prancing about in a somewhat upright position. They became so enthused with the project, however, they became impatient. They said: "Why wait for the invasion? Let's have a go at it via submarine."

This posed a new problem. Would the paint retain its brilliance in salt water? How close would the submarine have to approach the coastline in order to preserve the paint for shore duty? No one knew for certain just how far a fox could swim with half a fox strapped to his shoulders. So the zoo's hippopotamus pool was cleared and the foxes dumped in to swim until exhausted. Their endurance was carefully timed.

By this time the "brass hats" were calling for action. Operation Foxes by this time had turned into a costly experiment. They wanted results. The foxes were shipped to Washington, D.C., for a live demonstration.

The results proved beyond all doubt the OSS really had something! It was confirmed by the number of hysterical and wide-eyed lovers and drunks who came stampeding out of the bushes and off the benches in the park where the foxes had been released.

Most of them were yelling about ghosts and mysterious green-tinted objects that darted around at incredible speed. A few of those exposed to this phenomenon actually swore off drinking. The OSS toasted their success!

Unfortunately, while the foxes were enroute to the Far East, the atomic bombs were dropped and the war ended. History will never be able to judge the comparative merits of glowing fox spirits against the effects of atomic weapons. The foxes didn't get to blow a single Nippon mind.

It is said the OSS retired the foxes with appropriate military honors. They were first shaved to prevent possible death from radiation, and then sent to zoos where suitable homes were provided.

Luminous foxes? Pigeons pecking away at spots on a screen to direct the flight of rockets? Dolphins carrying out complicated detonation jobs beneath the seas? All fantastic, but true stories nonetheless.

Finally, that great day came when my orders to leave Japan were placed in the "IN" box on my desk. It was November, and I knew I would be home in time for Christmas. It was a day I had looked forward to for many months, and even with the orders in my hands, it was hard to believe. I began gathering up my things, mailing off items I couldn't get in my duffle bag, and discarding things I once had considered important.

The day for departing GHQ arrived, and as I bid all my friends in the press section good-bye, there was a sadness about it. We had been through a lot, but the anticipation of going home, seeing our families again, greatly overshadowed the regret of leaving one's associates.

All of us were proud of the service we had rendered and thankful we weren't going home on a hospital ship or in a shipping container. In my case, I knew whom to thank for that!

The next few days were spent in a factory building in Tokyo. There we would await our ship or aircraft and the journey back to the good old U.S.A. There was some spare time which was spent around Tokyo, seeing all we could before leaving. Tokyo's recovery was miraculous. If there are harder working people than the Japanese, I have yet to see them.

The night before I left, I woke in early morning to find my cot shaking. Tokyo was having an earth tremor. I looked up to see the light fixtures swinging wildly in an arc — and plaster flaking off the wall. I must be honest — I was truly frightened.

"Good Lord," I exclaimed to myself: "You mean I made it through the war with barely a scratch, and now I'm gonna' die in this damned old building just ready to go home?"

The shaking lasted less than a minute, and the hundred or so guys on that floor with me gave out with a big cheer. The Lord is good!

I left for home aboard a large Air Force transport plane which stopped briefly in Hawaii for fuel. We arrived in Los Angeles, where upon hitting the ground, we all cheered again. Another plane carried me to Kansas City, where I greeted Kathy with one of the most rewarding hug and kissing fests in my life. Mother and Dad were there, too, but nearly speechless with the joy of having their son back safe and sound.

A nice surprise at the airport was seeing my brother-in-law, Don Weide, whom I had last seen on Okinawa a few months back. He had beaten me home and was in Kansas City on business, but came along with the family to welcome me home. I really appreciated that.

I got to drive my 1941 Chevy coupe to Leavenworth, where it had all begun four years earlier. I was relieved from active duty but assigned to a reserve unit which, I discovered a few years later, was definitely a binding agreement for service during the Korean War. Home looked mighty good. Everything was just beautiful! I knew my family was proud of me, and there was plenty of love to go around.

It was some homecoming for Kathy and me, with a new beginning and a future ahead of us. God, it was good to be alive!

I believe the speech General MacArthur made at West Point, May 12, 1962, is one of the greatest ever made. I am proud to include it in my book.

—*Joe Snyder*

Duty, Honor, Country (1962)

On May 12, 1962, MacArthur visited West Point to receive the Sylvanus Thayer Award and to participate in the ceremonies of the day. After being presented with the award, MacArthur made this statement to the Corps of Cadets. Delivered extemporaneously, it is an eloquent summary of the code of honor of the professional soldier.

No human being could fail to be deeply moved by such a tribute as this. Coming from a profession I have served so long and a people I have loved so well, it fills me with an emotion I cannot express. But this award is not intended primarily to honor a personality, but to symbolize a great moral code — a code of conduct and chivalry of those who guard this beloved land of culture and ancient descent. For all hours and for all time, it is an expression of the ethics of the American soldier. That I should be integrated in this way with so noble an ideal arouses a sense of pride, and yet of humility, which will be with me always.

Duty, honor, country: Those three hallowed words reverently dictate what you ought to be, what you can be, what you will be. They are your rallying point to build courage when courage seems to fail, to regain faith when there seems to be little cause for faith, to create hope when hope becomes forlorn.

Unhappily, I possess neither that eloquence of diction, that poetry of imagination, nor that brilliance of metaphor to tell you all that they mean.

The unbelievers will say they are but words, but a slogan, but a flamboyant phrase. Every pedant, every demagogue, every cynic every hypocrite, every troublemaker, and, I am sorry to say, some others of an entirely different character, will try to downgrade them even to the extent of mockery and ridicule.

But these are some of the things they do. They build your basic character. They mold you for your future roles as the custodians of the nation's defense. They make you strong enough to know when you are weak, and brave enough to face yourself when you are afraid.

They teach you to be proud and unbending in honest failure, but humble and gentle in success; not to substitute words for actions, not to seek the path of comfort, but to face the stress and spur of difficulty and challenge; to learn to stand up in the storm, but to have compassion on those who fall; to master yourself before you seek to master others; to have a heart that is clean, a goal that is high; to learn to laugh, yet never forget how to weep; to reach into the future, yet never neglect the past; to be serious, yet never to take yourself too seriously; to be modest so that you will remember the simplicity of true greatness, the open mind of true wisdom, the meekness of true strength.

They will give you a temperate will, a quality of the imagination, a vigor of the emotions, a freshness of the deep springs of life, a temperamental predominance of courage over timidity, of an appetite for adventure over love of ease.

They create in your heart the sense of wonder, the unfailing hope of what next, and the joy and inspiration of life. They teach you in this way to be an officer and a gentleman. . . .

The code which those words perpetuate embraces the highest moral law and will stand the test of any ethics or philosophies ever promulgated for the uplift of mankind. Its requirements are for the things that are right and its restraints are from the things that are wrong. The soldier, above all other men, is required to practice the greatest act of religious training — sacrifice. In battle, and in the face of danger and death, he discloses those divine attributes which his Maker gave when He created man in His own image. No physical courage and no greater strength can take the place of the divine help which alone can sustain him. However hard the incidents of war may be, the soldier who is called upon to offer and to give his life for his country is the noblest development of mankind.

You now face a new world, a world of change. The thrust into outer space of the satellite spheres and missiles marks a beginning of another epoch in the long story of mankind. In the five or more billions of years the scientists tell us it has taken to form the earth, in the three or more billion years of development of the human race, there has never been a more abrupt or staggering evolution.

We deal now, not with things of this world alone, but with the illimitable distances and as yet unfathomed mysteries of the universe. We are reaching out for a new and boundless frontier. We speak in strange terms of harnessing the cosmic energy; of making winds and tides work for us; of creating unheard-of synthetic materials to supplement or even replace our old standard basics, to purify sea water for our drink; of mining ocean floors for new fields of wealth and food; of disease preventives to expand life into the hundreds of years; of controlling the weather for a more equitable distribution of heat and cold, of rain and shine; of spaceships to the moon; of the primary target in war no longer limited to the armed forces of an enemy, but instead to include his civil populations; of ultimate conflict between a united human race and the sinister forces of some other planetary galaxy; of such dreams and fantasies as to make life the most exciting of all times.

And through all this welter of change and development your mission remains fixed, determined, inviolable. It is to win our wars. Everything else in your professional career is but corollary to this vital dedication. All other public purposes, all other public projects, all other public needs, great or small, will find others for their accomplishment; but you are the ones who are trained to fight.

Yours is the profession of arms, the will to win, the sure knowledge that in war there is no substitute for victory, that if you lose, the nation will be destroyed, that the very obsession of your public service must be duty, honor, country.

Others will debate the controversial issues, national and international, which divide men's minds. But serene, calm, aloof, you stand as the nation's war guardian, as its lifeguard from the raging tides of international conflict, as its gladiator in the arena of battle. For a century and a half you have defended, guarded, and protected its hallowed traditions of liberty and freedom, of right and justice.

Let civilian voices argue the merits or demerits of our processes of government: Whether our strength is being sapped by deficit financing indulged in too long, by Federal paternalism grown too mighty, by power groups grown too arrogant, by politics grown too corrupt, by crime grown too rampant, by morals grown too low, by taxes grown too high, by extremists grown too violent, whether our personal liberties are as thorough and complete as they should be.

These great national problems are not for your professional participation or military solution. Your guidepost stands out like a tenfold beacon in the night: duty, honor, country.

You are the leaven which binds together the entire fabric of our national system of great captains who hold the nation's destiny in their hands the moment the war tocsin sounds.

The long grey line has never failed us. Were you to do so, a million ghosts in olive drab, in brown khaki, in blue and grey, would rise from their white crosses, thundering those magic words: Duty, honor, country.

This does not mean that you are warmongers. On the contrary, the soldier above all other people prays for peace, for he must suffer and bear the deepest wounds and scars of war. But always in our ears ring the ominous words of Plato, that wisest of all philosophers: "Only the dead have seen the end of war."

The shadows are lengthening for me. The twilight is here. My days of old have vanished — tone and tint. They have gone glimmering through the dreams of things that were. Their memory is one of wondrous beauty, watered by tears and coaxed and caressed by the smiles of yesterday. I listen vainly, but with thirsty ear, for the witching melody of faint bugles blowing reveille, of far drums beating the long roll.

In my dreams I hear again the crash of guns, the rattle of musketry, the strange, mournful mutter of the battlefield. But in the evening of my memory always I come back to West Point. Always there echoes and re-echoes: Duty, honor, country.

Today marks my final rollcall with you. But I want you to know that, when I cross the river, my last conscious thoughts will be of the corps, and the corps, and the corps.

I bid you farewell.